D0919213

THE ENIGMA OF ANNA O.

THE ENIGMA OF ANNA O.

A Biography of Bertha Pappenheim

Melinda Given Guttmann

MOYER BELL
Wickford, Rhode Island & London

Published by Moyer Bell

Joseph Oppenheims, *Drawing of Bertha Pappenheim*, 1934 (photo © Leo Baeck Institute)

First Edition

LIBRARY OF CONGRESS CATALOGING-IN-PUBLICATION DATA

Guttmann, Melinda Given, 1944-
The enigma of Anna O. / by Melinda Given Guttmann—1st edition

p. cm.

Includes stories by Bertha Pappenheim.
Includes index.
1. Pappenheim, Bertha, 1859--1936. 2. Jews—Germany—Biography. 3. Jewish women—Germany—Biography. 4. Women and psychoanalysis. 5. Analysands—Germany—Biography. 6. Feminists—Germany—Biography. 7. Psychoanalysis—Germany—History. 8. Feminism—Germany—History. I Pappenheim, Bertha, 1859--1936. II. Title
DS135.G5 P344 2001
616.85'24'0092—dc21 CIP
[B] 00-044507
ISBN 1-55921-285-3 (cl)

Distributed in North America by Publishers Group West, 1700 Fourth Street, Berkeley CA 94710 800-788-3123 (in California 510-528-1444) and in Europe by Gazelle Book Services Ltd., Falcon House, Queen Square, Lancaster LA1 1RN England 524-68765

With boundless love
for my mentor

MARGARET BRENMAN-GIBSON

and for my Vassar Soul Sisters
and their daughters

CONTENTS

List of Illustrations

THE ENIGMA OF ANNA O.

A Biography of
Bertha Pappenheim

INTRODUCTION

Just as a person cannot sign his name exactly the same way twice so also an artist cannot sing or play a role identically twice. In such variance lies the charm of an original artistic effort as compared to the art recording or film—I would like to write a book about the value and meaning of the unique.

• • •

The greatness of the smallest work of art lies in its unearthliness, its super-earthliness, whose measure, infinitude, the individual carries happily within him.

• • •

With respect to works of art and to people which one can only "truly appreciate" or "understand" when annotated, I am very suspicious, I advise you to be also.

Bertha Pappenheim

In my search for Bertha Pappenheim (1859–1936), I first journeyed to her gravesite in the Old Jewish Cemetery in Frankfurt, Germany. Finding the ornate gate, framed by Doric pillars, locked, I called the office of the Jewish Community. Its secretary informed me that due to recent neo-Nazi desecrations, entry to the cemetery was restricted. On my informing her that I was an American professor researching Bertha Pappenheim, she graciously gave me the number of the grave site. She also told me that the key to the cemetery was across the street at a flower shop called simply *Blumen*—flowers. At Blumen, I received the key and bought a lily. The Jewish cemetery, I discovered, was a wilderness of weeds, overthrown tombstones, and narrow dirt paths. The Christian cemetery abutting it was, by contrast, landscaped with colorful flowers and well-kept lawns. By following the names of her relatives—the Warburgs, the Guggenheims, and the Goldschmidt-Rothschilds—I came upon Bertha's grave. I located her simple headstone inscribed in Hebrew, which stood next to the headstone of her mother, Recha Pappenheim née Goldschmidt. Having been raised a Christian, I placed the lily on her grave, not knowing then that one of Bertha's last requests was that those who remembered her should, following Orthodox Jewish tradition, bring a stone from their homeland to place on it. I knelt down and meditated on the mysterious Hebrew. When I rose, a few tombstones away I saw my own name inscribed: Guttmann.

During the next two years, I visited the houses and sanatoria where Bertha had lived, and the institutions where she had reigned as one of the first Jewish feminists and professional social workers. This in turn led me to follow her travels in Eastern Europe, North Africa, and the Middle East.

Like Søren Kierkegaard on his fruitless search for spiritual truth through the Church, the priests, and the Bible, I discovered that Bertha's presence was not to be found in the architecture of these houses, exotic journeys, psychoanalytic scholarship, or historical archives, but paradoxically, as Kierkegaard discovered, truth is subjectivity. "Only in subjectivity is there decisiveness, to seek objectivity is to be in error," he wrote in *Concluding Unscientific Postscript*. In my contemplation of Bertha, using my introspective and empathic powers, I felt a vibrant consciousness marking itself on my own in the present; an inward experience of her as "being-in-the-world"; apprehended by a "leap of faith" beyond time; beyond the inert object of a historical study. I was seized with Bertha's utter reality. This experience compelled me to construct this biographical portrait.

Bertha's story begins in the "Vienna of Dreams" at the beginning of the nineteenth century's fin de siècle and ends with the Nazi rise to power and campaign against the Jewish people in the 1930s. In Vienna Bertha discovered the "talking cure," which gave birth to psychoanalysis and upon which all modern psychotherapies are based; in Frankfurt, influenced by the European feminist movement, she became a visionary creator and charismatic leader of its Jewish counterpart. Throughout her life Bertha remained a controversial figure; no one was ever neutral about her. Some idealized her as a "Jewish saint"; others referred to her as the "epitome of European culture"; still others contemptuously derided her as a "man hater."

Psychoanalysis and feminism were revolutionary ideas conceived in the nineteenth century. Both attempted to create international languages based on the subjective experience of women. It is remarkable that the origins of both psychoanalysis and Jewish feminism should be unified in the life history of one woman, whose case history has served as a Rosetta stone for feminists, historians, psychiatrists, social workers, and a wide range of social scientists.

Josef Breuer published the case history of Bertha Pappenheim under the pseudonym "Fräulein Anna O." in 1895. Generally considered the first important document in the history of psychoanalysis, it is also the first case in the canon of psychoanalytic literature and opens Breuer and Sigmund Freud's *Studies on Hysteria.*

Although Anna O. is the patient to whom Freud referred most often, he himself never treated her. Freud was a young neurologist of twenty-four, when Breuer, fourteen years his senior, embarked on his two-year pioneering adventure with Anna O.

In his 1909 lectures at Clark University in Massachusetts, Freud acknowledged Breuer and Anna O.'s joint creation of the "talking cure" as the germ and source of psychoanalysis. Freud stated that "if it is a merit to have brought psychoanalysis into being, that merit is not mine. I had no shape in its earliest beginnings. I was a student and working for my final examinations at the time when another Viennese physician, Dr. Josef Breuer, first made use of this procedure on a girl suffering from hysteria." In 1914, in his *History of the Psycho-analytic Movement,* Freud claimed, "psycho-analysis is my creation," discrediting his mentor Breuer after a bitter personal break in their relationship.

In 1953, Freud's biographer, Ernest Jones, broke the code of confidentiality and revealed that Anna O. was Bertha Pappenheim, the famous German-Jewish feminist and social worker. Ever since, the story of Anna O./Bertha Pappenheim has been riddled with mystery and controversy.

In writing about Bertha Pappenheim, the biographer is confronted by portraits of several contradictory personae. The Anna O. presented by Breuer in *Studies on Hysteria* is an enchanting, witty, delicate young woman of twenty-one, nestled in the wealthy protective milieu of the Viennese Orthodox Jewish *haute bourgeoisie* of the 1880s. Her mother called in Josef Breuer, the family doctor, because of Bertha's persistent "cough," fearing that Bertha had contracted her father's tuberculosis. Although Breuer diagnosed the cough as "hysterical," a condition that most medical practitioners of the time treated with disdain, Breuer did not abandon his patient. He was drawn to this young woman, whom he described as bubbling over with a "powerful intellect" and "great poetic and imaginative gifts." Soon, however, her condition deteriorated to the point where she became bedridden with severe hysterical symptoms, including paralysis of three limbs, language disturbances, and terrifying hallucinations, all initially appearing as she nursed her beloved father. Her work with Breuer germinated in Bertha's falling into a self-hypnotic trance during which she recounted "fairy tales" in an astonishingly imaginative outpouring from what she called her "private theatre." After the telling of each of these initial fairy tales, Bertha experienced relief from her anguish and felt calm and cheerful. The die was cast, and for nearly two years Breuer and Bertha immersed themselves in a pioneering method of healing.

Bertha's genius lay in inventing what she called the "talking cure." Breuer's genius was in following her lead and foreseeing its revolutionary significance.

In 1888, after Bertha recovered from her hysterical illness, she and her widowed mother moved from Vienna to Frankfurt. Outraging the sensibilities of her fellow German-Jewish assimilationists, Bertha journeyed alone throughout Eastern Europe, rescuing and researching, and publishing articles on Jewish prostitutes, victims of white slavery, and the plight of abandoned wives and unwed mothers. She fought on all fronts for the political, educational, and economic equality of Jewish women. With the support of kindred spirits, she first envisioned and then cofounded the first national organization of Jewish women, the Jüdischer Frauenbund, in 1904. Soon after, in 1907, she built a Home for Wayward Girls in nearby Neu-Isenburg to protect and educate Jewish girls and women at the margins of society.

Breuer's portrait of Bertha in his case history differs greatly from the feminist portrayals of Bertha almost one hundred years later. In 1968, Dora Edinger published an anthology of Bertha's letters and essays, *Bertha Pappenheim: Freud's Anna O.* In 1979, Marion Kaplan published her classic social history, *The Jewish Feminist Movement in Germany: The Campaigns of the Jüdischer Frauenbund 1904–1938.* In 1984, Ellen Jensen published studious explorations of Bertha's life in Germany, *Streifzüge durch das Leben von Anna O./Bertha Pappenheim.* These works all describe Bertha as a severe, autocratic, zealous woman immersed in the public theatre of social affairs, although each has a distinctive orientation as to the significance of Bertha's life. The most recent monograph on Bertha, *Remembering Anna O.* by Mikkel Borch-Jacobson (1996) focuses on the case history and asserts the unverifiable premise that Bertha faked her hysterical symptoms.

Bertha Pappenheim, a woman of heroic stature, has not been the subject of a comprehensive biographical study until now. This book is both the first biographical portrait and first chronological biographical study.

Having explored her entire archive, I feel I am positioned to overturn the mythical cast, created by psychoanalysts, of Bertha as a pathological, pathetic, fragile hysteric, and by transcending the materialist feminism of social historians, to establish her proper place in history as a fuller Bertha—charismatic leader, artist, mystic, and Jewish revolutionary. During her twenties Bertha was beleaguered by severe hysteric symptoms, which should be interpreted by what Henri Ellenberger termed a "creative illness"; she underwent experiences which transfigured her and infused her life with a passionate, soulful mission. The recurrent thread among her apparent contradictory personae is her enormous creativity manifested in the "private theatre" of her literary texts.

Both the psychoanalytic and historical interpretations of her life essentially ignored Bertha's literary estate. Despite a plethora of plays, poems, stories, essays, and prayers, none of Bertha's exegetes have used her literary output as "the Royal Road" to illuminating her life. The reader will discover here how Bertha, after the end of her relationship with Breuer, continued to self-heal by pursuing her "talking cure" through the act of publishing the contents of her "private theatre."

The most salient aspect of the transformation of her psyche, overlooked by psychoanalysts and historical portrayals alike, is Bertha's intense spirituality. Bertha wrote of the super-earthliness and infinitude that "the individual carries happily within him." Her search for the "holy" in Judaism permeated her prolific writing and social work. Her dictum was the ethical necessity of performing "small holy deeds," her watchword to "love thy neighbor as thyself." The original biblical quotation is "Love thy neighbor as thyself. I am the Lord," which can be interpreted to mean that those who love in this fashion find God and bring God and the World together. Bertha's writing during the Nazi era displays a mystical relationship with God. In Gotthold Lessing's play, *Nathan the Wise,* Nathan establishes that all religions are valid as long as each follower embodies true faith in God. *Nathan the Wise* served as the leitmotif for Bertha's spirituality. In 1912, at the age of fifty-three, Bertha first alluded to this work. She often spoke of it thereafter, and twenty-two years later she wrote her own version of a segment of the play, her last important fairy tale, "The True Ring." Bertha's story was a symbolic response to Nazi terrorism. In this tale she invokes her faith in the transcendent justice of her Jewish God and her messianic belief in God's triumph over evil.

Bertha's life can be re-visioned as a series of transformations, moving from the private theatre of the hysteric to the public theatre of feminism, to the Jewish realm of what the French philosopher Henri Bergson terms "Mystic Activism." In 1933, at the age of seventy-six, she wrote:

> No Jew could have conceived the idea of the Cologne cathedral because we lack the refinement and strength of the visual vocabulary as well as the technical productive patience and perseverance, and because the Jewish conception of God would shatter the vaulting of a cathedral.

The majority of Bertha's interpreters have not only focused on the pathology of her years of hysterical illness, but those aware of her later activities have assumed that her spinsterhood and feminism reveal pathological vestiges of this illness. Bergson questioned why the inner evolution of the great mystics had been identified with the mentally diseased. He found that their supreme good sense revealed a deep-rooted mental health. Opposing the concept of mysticism as insanity, he believed that great mystics undergo altered states of ecstasy, vision, and journey to the darkest depths of the soul to reach a human goal. Mystics, through loving God, love all mankind with a divine love—they "love thy neighbor."

Bertha's place in history should be re-viewed so that she is seen not as a pathetic patient but as an individual of enduring psychic health and enormous creativity. Her story is a spiritual journey of the heroic order.

The dynamic that unifies Bertha's apparently contradictory personae—her political activism with her artistic creations, her inner life with her being-in-the-world—is her continual self-healing through imaginative acts that functioned as extensions and variations of her original "talking cure."

My primary goal is to let Bertha speak for herself for the first time. She was equally suspicious of works of art and of people who could only be truly understood when "annotated." I have chosen to refer to her as "Bertha," not "Pappenheim" or "Miss Pappenheim," as she was formerly called, because I wish to narrow the distance between her and the reader. In addition, I do not want to follow the custom of referring to women by their patrilineage. Here, the French feminists' interpretation of Jacques Lacan is helpful. In feminist Lacanian terms, when a female child separates from her symbiosis with her mother, termed the "Imaginary" or "Mirror Stage," and enters into "Language," the "Symbolic Stage," she takes on the name of the father and thereby enters the patriarchal "Law" of the father.

Feminist scholars who research the construction of gender in culture have created the finest "lenses" for us to use in reconciling what appear to be Bertha's constantly shifting personae, roles, or masks. As she noted, "Just as a person cannot sign his name exactly the same way twice so also an artist cannot sing or play a role identically twice." From this perspective, neither the hyperfeminine hysteric nor the pseudo-masculine feminist activist are fixed pathological states; rather, they were social constructs of the phallocentric "gaze" of her era. She also desired to write a book about "the value of the 'unique'"; the value of the impermanent "self" whose charm is in the original moment compared to the "art recording or film." During the first wave of feminism, which was conservative and bourgeois, her creation of a specifically Jewish feminism retained those attributes.

In the 1960s and 1970s a second wave of feminism emerged that generated a pluralism of feminisms. Bertha's feminism, codified in the fin de siècle era, is now called "biologic," or "essentialist," feminism. Based on the notion of innate sexual difference, biologic feminism accepts the binary split of culture into separate spheres for females and males. The social "role" of women, from this perspective, is organically connected to their biological instincts for reproduction, nurturing, and mothering. Besides Bertha's own brand of feminism, several approaches lightly color my portraiture. French radical feminists like Hélène Cixous in "Le Rire de la Meduse" (1975) negate Lacan's phallocentric psychoanalytic system, imploring women to write themselves into the text through the flowing language of their bodies, "flying in language" against the long history of gynocide, proclaiming that the new history is coming, "it's not a dream . . . woman unthinks the unifying regulating history that homogenizes . . . she is an integral part of all liberations." Similarly, Luce Irigaray, in "Ce sexe qui n'en est pas un" (1977), celebrates the superiority of women's bodies, while simultaneously deconstructing Western philosophical discourse. I also rely to some degree on several American radical feminists who, focusing on race, class, and political power, call for a cross-cultural approach, dislocating women's culture from its inferior position within the dominant patriarchal culture. An approach that corresponds to my own is that of cultural/spiritual feminists like Mary Daly, who in *Gyn/ecology: The Metaethics of Radical Feminism* (1978) posits that the cultural construction of the feminine allows women the transcendent spiritual and visionary wisdom repressed in the cultural construction of the masculine.

Elaine Showalter describes the continuing proliferation of "a wilderness" of feminisms in *Sexual Anarchy: Gender and Culture at the Fin de Siècle* (1990), as well as the crisis in masculinity which "blamed rebellious women for the decline and fall of the Western world." If I were to choose a single analytic mode and impose a feminist superstructure on my biographical portrait of Bertha Pappenheim, the reader, I believe, would be distanced from my narrative. An analytic overlay would also obstruct the experiencing of an affective response to Bertha's fascinating life, with the integrity of the reader's own interpretative "lens" negated.

As we move past the millennium, we may see how Showalter's exposure of myths, metaphors, and images of sexual crises parallels both the late nineteenth century and our own fin de siècle—a brilliant, relevant comparison. Both eras mirror the fears of moral degeneracy in the images of the City—its poverty, madness, homelessness, prostitution, intermarriage, battle of the sexes, and plagues of sexual disease (syphilis then, AIDS now). In both eras, the longing for strict borders defining race, class, gender, and nationality are hauntingly similar, dissolving a comforting sense of stable "identity" and cultural stability.

Obviously, the constructs of male theorists, psychoanalytic historians, and psychologists also help in illuminating Bertha's story. Among them are several concepts that guide humans to self-realization and transcendence—Ken Wilber's Transpersonal psychology and philosophy traces the evolution and transformations of human consciousness on a spectrum of numerous levels of self-identity, from the narrow boundary of the "persona" level to the level of "no boundary" of unified consciousness. Various self-identities can coexist or emerge as fragments. He also postulates that suffering is a kind of grace, through which awareness of false boundaries becomes apparent. The prime self-identity I feel blessed to share with Bertha are her hints of a sublime experience of a momentary sense of union with God or the Divine.

Among other theories are Henri Ellenberger's concept of "creative illness," Erik Erikson's critical stages of the "Life Cycle" during which generative "identities" are forged; and James Hillman's "soul," psyche, or self, conceived as flowing from the "imaginal." Through fantasy we know ourselves most profoundly; this strikes me as pertinent to Bertha's development. The bedrock of the definition of "Imagination" for this book is Coleridge's definition of primary Imagination as "a repetition in the finite mind of the eternal act of creation in the infinite I AM." Fancy, by contrast, is the merely decorative. Bertha appears to be subliminally infused with the Romantic aesthetic.

Erikson's concepts are particularly useful in understanding the importance of focusing on "life history" rather than "case history." They are especially potent in describing the last years of Bertha's life under Nazi oppression. I use both Erikson's and Hillman's concepts to frame Bertha's creative responses to suffering and aging. Bertha's last decades transcend the all-too-prevalent gerontological stereotypes of the paralyzing despair of aging, and inspire us to rage against the overwhelming sense of helplessness in confronting the political evil of our own dark era.

The "conventions" of this biographical portrait are, as much of the previous discussion suggests, strongly allied to feminist postmodernist culture. In postmodernist terms, any search for Bertha's "core" being is an illusion. In writing about a woman's life, the biographer longs to discover a stable, "unified self" that defies time and place. She finds instead an indeterminate constellation of "selves" continually threatened by dissolution and the void.

Bertha was self-consciously her own artistic creation. The image most appropriate for her portrait would not be created by paint on a flat canvas, but would be composed of light: a holographic representation of lace. Bertha was conscious of the connection between her life desire and her fascination with the intricate intertwining and diverse patterns of lace which she obsessively tatted and collected during her travels. In 1912, she wrote, "If I were not an enemy of poetic comparisons, and if such comparisons were not lame, I would say that our lives should be made out of fine, flawless material and be interwoven in a way which is sometimes simple and sometimes complex, sometimes aesthetic and sometimes ethical, but this is the only longing I have: to live such a life. I hate the clumsy fingers which disturb my beautiful planning and tear my threads or destroy them."

Historically, the foremost reason for the absence of a thorough, richly detailed, analytic biography of Bertha Pappenheim similar to those thick tomes that rose to prominence in the Victorian era is that, sadly, hers is an incomplete archive. No childhood material has been discovered and none of her diaries are extant. We do know, however, that Bertha wanted her biography to be written. In 1935, a year before her death from cancer, Bertha entrusted papers she had selected for her biography to her best friend, Hannah Karminski. Fearing the Nazis, Hannah gave the papers to a Swiss friend for safekeeping. But during World War II the friend's house was bombed and the papers were destroyed. Yet all was not lost. In Vienna, Frankfurt, Jerusalem, and New York, devoted followers of Bertha Pappenheim donated letters, belles lettres, rare books, poems, and documents to various archives. Furthermore, several books have established that Bertha was in and out of sanatoria after she was allegedly cured in 1882 by Breuer. These findings help account for the seven missing years of her life, until her reemergence in Frankfurt at the end of 1888. I am referring to the distinguished Canadian psychiatrist Henri Ellenberger's *The History of the Unconscious* (1972) and the German scholar Albrecht Hirschmuller's *The Life and Work of Josef Breuer* (1978).

In addition, I have unearthed letters, photographs, and newspaper articles. I have searched for reminiscences from her friends and solicited testimony from her followers. I gathered these materials during my researches in the archives of the City of Frankfurt, the Frankfurt Jewish Museum, the library of Neu-Isenburg, Sanatoriam Bellevue in Switzerland, the Leo Baeck Institute in New York, and, most recently, in the *Bund Archiv* in the former East Berlin. Jewish Studies scholar Roberta Schwartz has graciously shared previously untranslated or published letters from Bertha to the philosopher Martin Buber from the Buber Archive at the Jewish National and University Library in Jerusalem; letters to Felix Warburg from the American Jewish Archive in Cincinnati; and a collection of videotapes from friends or relations of friends who were acquainted with Bertha.

Bertha's correspondences with Buber and Warburg reveal her willful, imperious manner when she essayed to force powerful men into fulfilling her needs. Although both correspondences appear professional and impersonal, she occasionally lapses into a confessional tone, revealing her loneliness and despair.

Only a few letters to Bertha's American cousin Felix Warburg have been discovered. Her main reason for writing to Warburg was to ask for money for her impoverished projects during and after World War I; however, that was not the sole subject of their correspondence. Bertha also wrote to him of a long, chilling rescue mission through occupied territory in 1923. Arriving exhausted to an unheated home, she writes Felix in despair: "But why need I, an old, lonely woman, wake up in the morning?" Felix's replies are restrained and lofty.

Bertha's relationship with Martin Buber, by contrast (although only her side of the correspondence remains), reveals a complicated negotiation, which underlies their discussions of mutual projects on Jewish social policy, education, religion, and politics. Although they were united in their mystical "spiritual resistance" to the Nazis, Bertha constantly chides him for his Zionism, cerebral writing, and much else. She rebukes him in a letter, dated June 17, 1918, about his *Drei Reden über das Judentum* (Three Speeches About Judaism) with the question, "Does one really need for this, which is obvious, such a large scientific apparatus, so many things and words a woman—and there are among Jewesses thousands like me—does not know?" Their complicated negotiation took other forms as well. In 1935, under Nazi oppression, Bertha wrote poignantly, "I have been away and had a difficult time, alone of course, without love, and with a pinch of hate, when toward the end I came across something of a neighborly love. When one believes in a 'calling' then one also has to believe in one's fate not to meet anyone." Here, as in all Bertha's relations, it is often difficult to distinguish between her straightforwardness and her manipulations.

After considering all aspects of my research, I believe that Bertha's literary work is the element of utmost importance. I discovered that Bertha first established her reputation as an author before she became renowned as a social worker and reformer. The reader will not discover a lost artist of great import; but a talented, fascinating, and profoundly moving writer emerges nonetheless. My portrait of Bertha, therefore, is not a literary biography, but a biography mostly constructed, by necessity, from literary sources.

I have found it crucial to frame Bertha's work within the social-historical milieu of her era. Although the "talking cure" is Bertha's unique invention, the travail of innumerable women in Europe, England, and North America who formed the first wave of feminism paved the way for her internationally celebrated feminist social work. The recent work of many excellent feminist historians has aided me in placing women's history and Jewish history in the foreground and using men's history and Christian history as a backdrop.

My biographical portrait is dedicated to the general and the feminist reader. Because the narrative is supported by a wide range of archival material and texts never before translated or published in English, this portrait will be of interest to a wide range of scholars.

Scholars are still experimenting with the nature of feminist biography. Since my biographical portrait is closely allied with postmodernist culture, the nostalgic desire to reproduce a flesh-and-blood woman like Bertha through "naturalist" conventions is a ghost of paradigms lost. My structure bares the bones of conventional biography by revealing it as artifice, not a "mimesis" of nature.

As my colleague Marion Kaplan suggested, the primary theme of the whole book is the conversion of Bertha's "Private Theatre" into her "Public Theatre." One must, in other words, transform the inner self in order to transform the world.

I have constructed as well as possible a chronologically complete story of Bertha's life that, because of the narrowness of the archive, has salient ellipses, especially in her early years. The slimness of the archive has also led me to devise an original structure, with both complete and edited translations of Bertha's writing as separate chapters of the book. These texts, as previously mentioned, have either never before been translated into English or re-published in German; many are newly discovered. They not only take the place of what Bertha's lost diaries or memoirs might have imparted, but may be in fact more revealing than the conventional diary entries of an *haute-bourgeoisie* Victorian woman, as her writing discloses the ever-shifting, deepening planes of her artistry.

By interrupting the narrative, I am attempting to subvert the false presentation of the linear, unified "self" that emerges from the sole use of chronological order and "realist" conventions. The use of Bertha's texts in this manner was inspired by the "interventions" employed in the texts of French feminists. Whereas French feminists use the interruptions in the manner of a Brechtian alienation effect (*Verfremdung*) to interact with the text as well as subvert it, thereby distancing the reader from the text, my insertions bring the reader closer to Bertha. By allowing her to speak for herself for the first time, I invite the reader to empathize with her voice and create his or her own interpretations.

The photographs throughout are for the most part posed portraits that were the convention of Bertha's time. Photographs are not merely documents. As John Berger shows us, every time we look at a photograph, we are aware, however slightly, "of the photographer selecting that sight from an infinity of other possible sights."

If images were created to conjure appearances of what was absent and can outlast what was represented, my hope is to make Bertha Pappenheim present to the reader from the infinity of their own visions, which will outlast this representation.

I hope that all readers meditate on her widening concern for all she generated through love. This superpersonal love, which expanded in ever-widening circles, marked her transition into old age. In 1928, at the age of sixty-nine, Bertha celebrated the anniversary of the Girl's Club she had formed twenty-five years earlier, reflecting: "Is it a tragedy or a grace to be old and to get old? It is a tragedy when one realizes what things we still want, which are still like frames yet to be filled—but to be old in some moments is grace—grace if one feels one had created something, that one has not passed by great things without taking an interest—at this moment I feel grace."

Until her death on May 28, 1936 at the age of seventy-nine, Bertha continued to reinvent herself, in Erikson's terms, by fighting against despair to achieve wisdom and integrity, and in Hillman's terms, by achieving the continual creation of the "soul" through the imaginal. In March 1933, Adolf Hitler became chancellor of Germany and instituted the first set of racial laws restricting Jewish civil rights. After this point, her writing became increasingly mystical, and despite failing health she stood up to the omnipresent evil with daring public speeches and publications. Holding fast against despair, she retained her faith in her Hebrew God of Justice who would protect the Jews under Nazi persecution and the threat of annihilation until the passage in 1935 of the Nuremberg Laws.

The "talking cure" of her youth became the necessary angel of her last days as she dictated poems, prayers, and fairy tales from her deathbed.

After Bertha's death, most of the women and children whom she spent her life saving were sent to various death camps and murdered during the Holocaust. The Jüdischer Frauenbund was dissolved and most of its leaders were deported to Auschwitz in 1942.

My last journey for this book was to search for Bertha's Home in Neu-Isenburg. Following the musical sounds of a young boy strolling in the front garden while playing the violin, I came upon the Home for the first time. It had become a Rudolf

Steiner school, but a plaque on the main building commemorates Bertha Pappenheim's work.

Allow me to conclude this introduction with a prayer Bertha composed in the last year of her life:

> Only not to become blind—not with the soul, to no longer distinguish the small from the great, the narrow from the wide, the exalted from the burdened, or that which shines in eternal light.

Chapter One

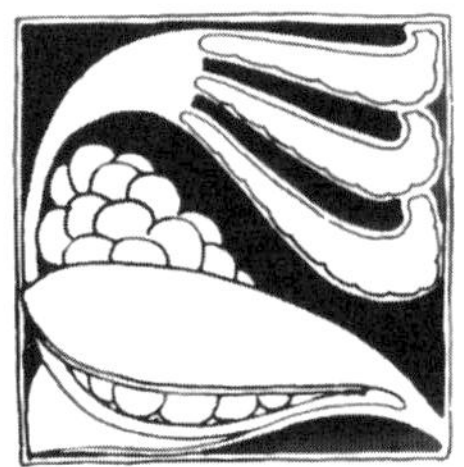

PUBLIC THEATRE/ PRIVATE THEATRE (1880-1881)

> She embellished her life which probably influenced her decisively in the direction of her illness, by indulging in systematic day-dreaming, which she described as her "private theatre."
>
> Josef Breuer, in *Studies on Hysteria*
>
> • • •
>
> A volcano lived in this woman; it erupted when she was angered. . . . Her fight against the abuse of women was almost a physically felt pain for her.
>
> Cora Berliner, vice president, Jüdischer Frauenbund

In July 1880, in the fashionable Austrian resort of Bad Ischl, the summer home of Kaiser Wilhelm and his opulent, decadently sublime Court, an acculturated, *haute-bourgeois* Jewish grain merchant, Sigmund Pappenheim, lay dying in the bedroom of his villa. His daughter, as was customary at the time, kept vigil at his bedside. Her name was Bertha Pappenheim. She was twenty-one years old, beautiful, petite, 4'11", with dark hair and sparkling blue eyes. No one looking at this conventionally beautiful portrait would have suspected that this well-bred, young "European Lady"—the "angel of the house"—was about to experience a defining moment. No one could have imagined that through her journeys intertwining creative madness, revolutionary Jewish feminism, and mystical activism she would become an international legend twice in her lifetime, and then in the mists of the Holocaust a forgotten Jewish heroine.

One balmy summer night, Bertha's consciousness started to undergo a series of transformations. As she watched her father attentively, the silence of the room was broken by the strains of music wafting from a dance at a neighboring house. Suddenly, Bertha was seized by a longing to be at the dance. She was immediately overcome with self-reproaches for desiring her own pleasure and thinking of abandoning her father. Then, she began coughing. After that night, every time Bertha heard rhythmic music, she would be overcome by *tussis nervosa*, a nervous cough.

The Pappenheim family had rented an entire floor of a large chalet in Bad Ischl, 130 miles from their home in Vienna. The center of the Salzkammergut region, Bad Ischl is surrounded by mountains, lakes, and lush valleys that lend a fairy-tale ambience to the Alpine town, famous for its beautiful vistas and its waters. The restorative powers of the many salt, sulfur, mud, and pine baths, as well as the saline and sulfurous drinking wells, were highly celebrated. As the summer home of Emperor Franz Joseph I and other noble families, Bad Ischl had become a chic vacation spot. Each summer the town burst into gaiety with a resplendent variety of bands, orchestras, and dances. The completion of a railroad connection in 1877 cemented its position as one of the most fashionable summer resorts in central Europe.

The self-conscious grandeur of the Court manifested itself in orchestrated, ornate parties, with dizzying, exhilarating, exhausting waltzes, combined with the ostentatious and flamboyant personalities of noble women, with their outlandish scandals and flamboyant theatrical gowns. The Court gave the illusion of the golden kingdoms in fairy tales. As the Court life mirrored the stage, so Bertha's inner life mirrored her environment. Her outer world and her inner world were both constructed of fictional fabric. Bertha's development of a melodramatic imagination and an enchanting personality mirrored the privileges of the external world to which she was privy.

The Pappenheims, unlike the majority of summer residents, were *haute bourgeois*, acculturated Orthodox Jews, tolerated by but not quite assimilated into the town's aristocratic society. Most of the parties and salons the Pappenheims likely attended would have been hosted by a rather influential circle of liberal-conservative financiers. Still, the emigrant, newly enriched Jews' perception of their acceptance into the "Vienna of Dreams" remained a most vulnerable illusion. True, they assimilated the manners, dress, cuisine, and culture of the Christians, whose behavior and soft Viennese dialect embodied the height of refinement and civilization—or so they believed. But underneath, Orthodox Jews like the Pappenheims vacillated between pride in their heritage and a secret desire to "pass" as established patricians.

In the 1880s, when Jews rose to prominence as never before, so did the latent strains of anti-Semitism from which they had never been immune. The Jewish desire for assimilation surged as much from terror of annihilation as it did from admiration of the Viennese aesthetic.

The Pappenheims had been summer residents of Bad Ischl since 1871. In the summer of 1880, Sigmund Pappenheim, a rich entrepreneur of fifty-six, accompanied by his wife, Recha, fifty, his daughter, Bertha, twenty-one, his son, Wilhelm, twenty, and several servants, arrived as usual. Aptly named Bellevue, the chalet Sigmund Pappenheim rented stood on the slope of a steep hill at Bremerstrasse 25, a ten-minute stroll from the center of town. The impressive four-story house boasted a magnificent view overlooking the town, a string of shining lakes, and wooded slopes. Striking yellow and brown wood walls and intricately carved balconies on each floor graced the building. Flowering fruit trees and purple and coral flowers burnished an elegant garden facing the mountains. The air was redolent with the scent of pine trees and wildflowers.

Anticipating a summer of pleasure, the Pappenheims arrived on June 23, but soon after Sigmund developed an acute fever caused by an inflammation of the lining of his lungs. The family was in a state of anxiety, fearing that he had contracted tuberculosis, the "Viennese disease," which had broken out like a plague in the capital. The only known cure was bed rest and pure mountain air.

Sigmund was confined to his bedroom, where he was nursed by his wife and a day nurse. His daughter, Bertha, on whom he doted and who adored him, slept during the day, taking on the night watches alone, thereby reversing her biological clock.

Sigmund was soon at a critical stage, suffering not only from bouts of fever but also from an abscess of the lung. On Saturday, July 17, a surgeon was summoned from Vienna to operate. Night after night, while she took on the lonely watch over her sick, sleeping father, Bertha's fantasy life started to overwhelm her. On one of these nights, as she gazed at her father with tears in her eyes, he suddenly asked her for the time. Her vision was blurred by her tears. As she brought the watch close to her eyes, she was shocked by how distorted and enormous its face had become. Later that night, while she anxiously awaited the train bringing the surgeon to operate on her father, Bertha's fantasies began to transform themselves from surrealistic images into nightmares. As she drifted into a kind of autohypnotic "absence," she imagined her father's face transformed into a "death's-head."

Seated by her father's bedside, her right arm over the back of her chair, Bertha was overtaken by a hallucination in which enormous black snakes slithered out of the wall. One snake seemed to plunge toward her father. She tried to reach out to protect him, but her arm was paralyzed. Staring at her hands, she saw her fingers transform themselves into little snakes with death's-heads on her fingernails. Then, as quickly as they had appeared, the snakes vanished. Horrified, Bertha desperately tried to pray but could find no language in which to speak until she thought of some children's verses in English. The shrill whistle of the train startled her but left her caught up in the spell of her waking dream so that she did not even hear the surgeon enter the room. The surgeon drained Sigmund's lungs and returned to Vienna. But Sigmund failed to respond to the treatment and before the family's eyes metamorphosed into a sad and debilitated invalid.

The next day, Sunday, July 18, in order to distract herself, Bertha played a game of quoits in the garden. Retrieving a quoit that had fallen into the bushes, she was stunned by the sight of a bent branch that reminded her of her "snake" hallucination, and her right arm became rigidly extended like a snake itself. From then on, whenever she saw a snakelike object, her arm would contract.

In one of her deep "absences," which increasingly overtook her normal consciousness and left her unresponsive to normal stimuli, she failed to recognize her father or understand him when he asked a question. She recovered somewhat when he jokingly addressed her in English, "Nuh, how are you, Miss Bertha?" She kept these and various other similarly distressing experiences a secret.

Indeed, she kept these experiences a secret from herself, for as soon as they had passed she retained no conscious memory of them. Had anyone questioned her about these fleeting episodes, she would have been unable to explain what had just happened.

In early September 1880, the Pappenheims returned to their

luxurious third-floor apartment in Vienna. The white stone building at Lichtensteinstrasse 2 was not far from the newly constructed Ringstrasse, the center of the capital's intellectual, cultural, and political life. In 1865, the old fortifications of the cramped city had been razed to provide space for the splendor of this new center. The newly built Parliament, the City Hall, the University, the Burgtheatre, the Imperial Museums of Art, History, and Natural History, and the Opera bestrode the two-mile-long architectural spectacle. Magnificent towers and spires in Gothic, Renaissance, and Baroque styles dominated the Ring. The Parliament building was designed to resemble a classical Greek temple and the University to emulate the grandeur of Renaissance architecture. All these elaborate buildings, parks, and squares were adorned with lime and plane trees. The surrounding formal gardens were created to echo the glory of the vast Austro-Hungarian Empire. This was a splendid public theatre, a stage decor, in which everyone vied to see and be seen.

Rich and fashionable Viennese like the Pappenheims chose to live nearby in large apartments rather than in private houses. These new apartments, with their highly decorative facades, were considered chic and modern. Although each social circle lived in its own district, everyone gathered for great festivities, in what the writer Stefan Zweig called "theatromania." All classes attended the opera and the theatre and, mirroring art, the streets themselves became a theatre where three hundred thousand adulated the "upper ten thousand" in their fancy carriages during the Flower Parade in the Prater, the Viennese amusement park, or with equal enthusiasm gathered for a funeral procession. Obsessed with aesthetics, the Viennese desired even in death to be "lovely corpses" honored with majestic spectacle. The Pappenheims like other residents of the Ringstrasse would take long promenades by foot or carriage rides through the Prater.

The famous coffeehouses where artists, dandies, and intellectuals met daily in lively colloquy added to the élan of the burgeoning Ringstrasse district. Jews were both the creators of and the audience for conventional and avant-garde art and ideas, helping to make Vienna the alluring and sparkling center of European cultural life. Among the Jews in the most prominent literary circle, *Jung Wien*, were Arthur Schnitzler, Stefan Zweig, Karl Kraus, and Hermann Bahr. In music, Gustav Mahler and Arnold Schoenberg, both Jewish converts to Christianity, achieved stellar reputations. In the "gay apocalypse" of fin de siècle Vienna, while the bourgeoisie waltzed and devoured their beloved pastries, the startling creativity that gave birth to modernism was born. This creative burst, as pointed out by historian Marsha Rosenblit, owed "its intellectual character for the most part to men of Jewish origin."

The Jewish contribution to Vienna was so enormous that public life everywhere was influenced by Jewish writers, bankers, artists, musicians, scientists, and physicians. This influence even reached the Court. As *haute-bourgeois* Jews, the Pappenheims intermingled with both leaders and amateurs of the city's artistic life. Surrounding themselves with exquisite art and ornate antique furniture, they eagerly participated in the active social and cultural life of the Jewish elite. In the fall of 1880, life as they knew it ground to a stop; they became housebound. Sigmund's illness left him unable to return to work or resume his social life. This formerly vigorous man continued to wither away in bed, his physical condition daily deteriorating. His wife and daughter continued to nurse him, Recha by day and Bertha by night.

By now Bertha's stamina had begun to weaken. She was

Recha Pappenheim, née Goldschmidt.
[Photo © Juedisches Museum, Frankfurt am Main]

increasingly fatigued and anxious and she started to lose her appetite. Although she appeared to be ostensibly her old self, her states of momentary distraction in the face of her father's decline were becoming more frequent. As she sat by his bedside, images of her heritage passed on to her by her father flittered across her mind.

Sigmund Pappenheim was born on July 10, 1824 in Pressburg, Hungary (today Bratislava, Slovakia) into an affluent Orthodox Jewish family. The Pappenheims had a formative influence both on Pressburg, the former capital and coronation city, and on the history of Hungarian Orthodoxy. His father, Wolf Pappenheim, was already a wealthy merchant when he married Katherina Calman, and from her brother he inherited another large fortune. In addition to his standing in the business community, Wolf was a leader of Orthodox Jewry in Hungary. As a young man Sigmund moved to Vienna, where he capitalized on his inherited wealth by becoming a grain merchant. Carrying on his father's religious activities, in 1864 he cofounded the Orthodox Schiffschul in Vienna, led by Rabbi Solomon Spitzer. This synagogue was dedicated to a "Torah true" *Yiddishkeit* (Jewishness). At the age of twenty-four he met eighteen-year-old Recha Goldschmidt, who became his bride in an arranged marriage.

Recha was born in Frankfurt, Germany, on June 13, 1830, and kept close ties with her family, which included famous Jewish bankers, philanthropists, and the poet Heinrich Heine. Her family marriage patterns were "traditional": exclusive and marked by a distaste for outsiders. These couplings were coerced, or arranged, with the preservation of both social and business capital in mind. Recha, the great-great-granddaughter of the family's powerful patriarch, Benedikt Salomon Goldschmidt (1738–1812), bearing a large dowry, should have married within a small circle of Frankfurt families of the first order. Typically, banking-dynasty marriages were made between cousins, uncles, nieces, nephews, or friends of equal status. If a member of the family married someone of equal prominence in Vienna, London, or Paris, the union's primary purpose would have been to expand a branch of the business or family there. Recha's family, originally of the "second order," had over the years united with the Homburgers, the Warburgs, and, their "crowning glory," with the Rothschilds.

The pattern of these couplings is easily seen by a casual walk through the old Jewish cemetery.

At a time when the Goldschmidt family was reaffirming its social position by merging with other German dynasties, Recha's family made an odd choice. Although her future husband's family had its origins in Bavaria, the Pappenheims, despite their wealth and status, were *au fond* Ostjuden, East European Jews, considered inferior, even alien, by the German and Viennese Jews. The hegemonious structure of Jewish society may have seemed superficial and irrelevant to the Christians, for whom all Jews constituted an alien race. Yet within Jewish culture the nuances of difference between the "authentic" German Jews and the outsiders constituted a point of extreme psychological and social awareness. Recha Goldschmidt's marriage beneath her social position, for example, was later apparent to her children and caused tension in the marital and family relationships. Sigmund and Recha married in 1848 in a small village in Burgenland, on the Austrian-Hungarian frontier. The ceremony was performed outdoors, according to local custom. The provincial surroundings were emblematic of the incongruousness of the match. Indeed, the formality of the ceremony, as Bertha, a born storyteller (her parents' description), liked to recount with amusement, was undercut by waddling, quacking ducks scampering to and fro among the very elegant, distinguished guests.

At the time of their marriage in 1848, the year of the European Revolutions, the Pappenheims were living in Leopoldstadt, essentially a Jewish ghetto named after Leopold I, officially referred to as the Second District, across the Danube Canal from the center. Although they lived on Praterstrasse, an elegant street, life among peasants, peddlers, and the provincial immigrant Ostjuden wearing caftans and observing "oriental" customs appeared in sharp contrast to Recha's staid Frankfurt milieu where she had been raised as an elegant European lady.

The narrow streets of the old city bustled with international trade and social activity. The Prater, the former zoological gardens of the emperor, was now a place of popular entertainment, bandstands, and a big Ferris wheel, all adding to the vibrant, bon vivant atmosphere. Leopoldstadt was used for Imperial Parades with music conducted by Johann Strauss, enterprising theatres, and enchantments like the Renz Circus.

The Jews' long historical attachment to Vienna dated from the twelfth century, and a flourishing Jewish community had existed there during the Middle Ages. In the thirteenth century an observer remarked, "There are more Jews in Vienna than in any other German city familiar to me." Vienna became known throughout the Jewish world as the center of scholars, referred to as the "sages of Vienna." In 1421, however, during a vicious pogrom, hundreds of Jews were publicly burned at the stake and the survivors herded into boats and deported to Hungary by way of the Danube. Jews who refused to convert to Christianity were either executed or exiled.

By the mid-1600s, valued for their commercial and financial expertise, the Jews gradually returned to Vienna. Approximately 500 families settled in Leopoldstadt, where the Pappenheims first installed their household 300 years later. Known in the seventeenth century as "court Jews," they circulated through the center of the city during business hours only and paid high taxes for residence permits. They nevertheless flourished, though in 1670 the envy and hostility of their patrons caused them to be expelled once again. By 1793, however, the financial loss had become painful to the city and a small number were "tolerated." Thus, in between grisly outbreaks of anti-Semitism, Jewish ghettos were formed, dissolved, and re-formed.

In 1781, Emperor Joseph II issued the Edict of Tolerance allowing Jews to settle freely. The resident Jewish population grew to 1,000 by 1800, and the number of visiting merchants swelled to 10,000 a year. In 1792, another anti-Semitic reaction surfaced, resulting in the establishment of a *Judenamt*, or Jewish Office, to control immigration and impose heavy taxes and other restrictions.

After the end of the Napoleonic Wars in 1815, five Jews were ennobled and the wife of one, Fanny von Arnstein, became the leader of one of the most intellectually powerful salons in Europe. Jews were admitted to public schools and universities, the civil service, and other professions, but were still prevented from trading, freely residing, owning land, and forming religious organizations. They achieved total legal equality only after the middle-class uprisings of 1848, in which they struggled and fought alongside other Viennese against the aristocracy and Baroque absolutism. During most of Bertha's life, Emperor Franz Joseph ruled the Austro-Hungarian Empire (1848–1916). The Jewish population of Vienna expanded to 6,000 in 1859, and to 147,000 in 1900, or about nine percent of the population. The first wave of Jews had come from Hungary; more recent immigrants hailed chiefly from Bohemia and Moravia.

Following the institution of constitutional reforms favorable to Jews and middle-class Germans, Jews like the Pappenheims began to integrate themselves into all aspects of Viennese culture. Many acculturated Jews quickly rose to prominence in commerce and finance, abandoning their traditional trades as peddlers, merchants, or shopkeepers. Many became apostates and/or converted to Catholicism in order to buy noble titles, marry gentiles, or attempt to obliterate their background. Vienna had the largest conversion rate of all the major European cities.

Sigmund and Recha, however, followed the rigorous precepts and rituals of Orthodox Judaism in their daily life. They kept a kosher kitchen and observed all the Jewish holidays and ritual celebrations. The couple also began a family. Their oldest daughter, Henriette, born in 1849, died at the age of sixteen of "galloping consumption." Their second daughter, Flora, born in 1853, died at the age of two. Bertha was born in Vienna on February 27, 1859. A year later, Wilhelm, the couple's only son, was born. Sigmund and Recha raised their two surviving children according to the conventions of the Jewish elite.

Bertha's intense nursing of her father continued to take a toll on her health. Weak and anemic, she survived on oranges and melons. Self-starving, then called "sublime tubercular emaciation," was the psychological precursor of twentieth-century forms of anorexia. As historian Elaine Showalter describes the process, "The body wastes, and the face has a thin anxious look, not unlike that represented by Rossetti in many of his pictures of women." Bertha started to rest in the afternoon, falling into a sleeplike state in the evening, followed by high excitement or agitation.

In November 1880, as Sigmund lay dying, Bertha became a second source of anxiety in the household. Her moments of distraction had been steadily increasing during the fall. She would stop in the middle of sentences, pause, and the repeat her last words and continue talking as though nothing had happened. Her mood was increasingly anxious and querulous. The complaints she now voiced about her momentary "absences" went unheeded. By the end of November she had developed a heavy, persistent cough. Her parents, fearing another case of tuberculosis, called in Josef Breuer, the family physician, for a diagnosis.

Breuer, a general practitioner, was celebrated by both fashionable Jewish society and gentile Viennese intellectuals. The thirty-eight-year-old doctor was known to have the "golden touch." He was also a medical researcher of some renown. While still a student at the University of Vienna, he had discovered (with Ewald Hering) the reflex regulation of breathing. Less than a decade later he demonstrated how the semicircular canals of the ear regulate equilibrium. In addition to his demanding practice, Breuer worked in the laboratory of the famous physiologist Ernst Brücke, where he later made the acquaintance of a young physician named Sigmund Freud, fourteen years his junior.

Breuer diagnosed Bertha's cough as having no physiological basis, identifying it instead as *tussis nervosa,* a symptom of "hysteria." Bertha's anxiety, fatigue, irritability, and complaints of distraction had reached the point where they were readily apparent to Breuer, even though no one in the family seemed to take them seriously.

Breuer's initial diagnosis of Bertha's cough as "hysterical" was a common one in 1880. For centuries, hysteria had been the quintessential female malady. Indeed, the word itself is derived from the Greek for "womb" and the condition was originally thought to result from a dysfunction of the uterus, also referred to as a wandering womb. The oldest description of hysteria can be found in a small number of surviving Egyptian papyri, dating from 1900 B.C., long before the term was coined. The Egyptians made no effort to physically manipulate the wandering womb, which they associated with disordered sexual activity and emotional instability. Rather, as the historian Ilza Veith describes, they used "precious and sweet-smelling substances to attract the womb; or evil-tasting and foul-smelling substances to drive it away from the upper part of the body where it was thought to have wandered." Among the Greeks, elderly virgins as well as widows were thought to be particularly vulnerable to hysterical afflictions caused by irregular menses; marriage was recommended as the speediest way of achieving a cure, and it continued to be among the standard prescriptions for more than two thousand years.

From 1870 until World War I, a period also known as the "golden age" of hysteria, doctors in England, America, France, and Germany found this phenomenon increasingly central to their work. Toward the end of the nineteenth century, hysteria became almost interchangeable with femininity. With no precise definition of this disorder, its vast repertoire of emotional and physical symptoms ranged from "fits, fainting, vomiting, choking, sobbing, laughing, paralysis—and the rapid passage from one to another suggested the lability and capriciousness traditionally associated with the feminine nature."

Having put all of her energy into nursing her father, Bertha began to collapse in earnest. Her momentary "absences" growing still worse, she complained more bitterly about "losing time" and suggested that she was going mad. In early December 1880, she developed a new symptom, a noticeable squint that caused her to be cross-eyed; the family called in both an eye specialist and, once again, Breuer. The previous spring, before her father became ill, Bertha had been troubled by transitory eye pain and facial spasms. The specialist now diagnosed her as suffering from a deterioration of the eye muscles, but Breuer was unconvinced. In any event, the result was that Bertha was prohibited from nursing her father, both for her own good and because her behavior was alienating his other attendants. On December 11, 1880, Breuer was called in again and from this date on he began to see her every day.

Although he lived only a short carriage ride away, Breuer's commitment to his ailing patient was unusual at a time when most doctors treated "hysterical illness" with disdain. Hysteria epitomized the cult of invalidism, affecting middle- and upper-class women almost exclusively. "It had no discernible organic basis, and it was totally resistant to medical treatment." When a hysterical young woman became sick, she no longer played the role of the self-sacrificing daughter, for example, but "instead she demanded service and attention from others. The families of hysterics found themselves reorganized around the patient, who had to be constantly nursed, indulged with special delicacies, and excused from ordinary duties." Unlike the sympathetic Breuer, most physicians saw the hysteric as a charading antagonist and were concerned that she was enjoying her new freedom and power over her family.

When Breuer began treating Bertha, medical concepts of emotional illness were crude and the treatments were physiological in nature. Mental disorders were thought to be a combination of disturbances of the brain and hereditary disorders of the nervous system. Therapy ranged from confinement in rest homes and sanatoria to various types of hydrotherapy and massage. Some physicians experimented with electroshock; others used sedatives and morphine. Experimentation in hypnosis and suggestion therapy was limited to trying to cajole patients to let go of their symptoms.

Breuer had treated many hysterical patients, and his visits were usually short and routine. But something about Bertha and her symptoms fascinated Breuer, causing him to devote an unprecedented period of a year and a half of daily visits to her.

Approaching his patient as if he were dissecting tissue, he assumed a Darwinian notion of the origin of her condition. He believed that Bertha had a hereditary tendency to mental illness because some of her distant relatives had suffered from psychosis. Until Bertha's father had taken ill, Breuer noted that she had been healthy and free of neurosis. He was impressed with Bertha's brilliance, finding her "markedly intelligent, with an astonishingly quick grasp of things and penetrating intuition. . . . She possessed a powerful intellect . . . great poetic and imaginative gifts which were under the control of a sharp and critical common sense." He was also moved by her intense instinct for sympathetic kindness. He specifically regretted that even though "bubbling over with intellectual vitality," she was forced to lead an "extremely monotonous existence in her puritanically-minded family."

According to Breuer, Bertha seemed to have accepted her situation and apparently had a happy, healthy, conventional childhood within the strictures of her class. She acted out the role of the "European lady," possessing the demeanor of the "angel in the house." As expected by her culture and family, she appeared to be a well-mannered and dutiful daughter. Because there were no schools in Vienna for Jewish girls, she had attended an exclusive Catholic finishing school, where she had revealed the brilliance and imagination noted by Breuer. She had mastered English, French, and Italian, and showed promise as an artist and writer. Although more intellectually and artistically gifted than her brother, who having attended a Viennese gymnasium had gone on to study law, she was, as a female, legally barred from higher education in Vienna. The intellectual stimulation that she craved was doubly denied her, as Orthodox Judaism considered scholarly work the sole province of males. Indeed, Orthodox Jews greeted the birth of a daughter with disappointment, proclaiming sadly, "It's nothing but a girl!" Having finished her formal education, Bertha, despite her intellectual gifts, was expected to live at home, protected by her parents from the outside world until she entered into an appropriate marriage with a distinguished gentleman of her class and religion.

Bertha always envied her brother's education, freedoms, and opportunities for meaningful work. Wilhelm had dominated and bullied her throughout their childhood, a situation that continued throughout her youth. It is not surprising then that with the onset of adolescence, with her desires and prospects often treated as secondary, undercurrents of sibling rivalry increased. As an exceptional young woman, she both accepted and raged against the role she was to assume. Still, at home Bertha dutifully learned all the skills of an *höhere Tochter* (an upper-class daughter of marriageable age). She added Hebrew and Yiddish to her other three languages in order to maintain the traditions and customs of Judaism, while learning the refinements of cuisine and feminine crafts from her mother. She was at this time apparently not at all religious but carried out all instructions for her father's sake; religion served only as an object of "silent struggles and silent opposition."

Bertha's typical day probably began with a horseback ride with friends. Since the Pappenheims had servants for the major care of the house, the rest of her day was devoted to light household chores—tatting lace, sewing, stringing pearls, and embroidering. These crafts were considered appropriate, decorative activities for women. She also read passionately, showing a particular love of Shakespeare. She played the piano but never attained the skill she desired. The loving-kindness of her character, combined with an instilled sense of duty, often led her to do charitable work for poor Jews living in other districts. In the evenings before her father's illness, formally attired, she might attend a concert, the theatre, or a party, all activities of which she was passionately fond. Expectations for her were small and superficial: She was to prepare herself for entry into high society by dressing in the latest fashion, attending tea parties, and learning the nuances of politesse. She moved easily in her social circle, and her gaiety and charm seemed to enchant everyone who met her. In the summer Bertha's daily routine changed somewhat. A sensitive lover of nature, she particularly enjoyed her sojourns in Bad Ischl. As a child, her governess, Fräulein Hoffmann, of whom she always retained fond memories, accompanied her on excursions. At Bad Ischl, Bertha probably whiled away the days swimming, boating, hiking, and daydreaming during walks in nearby meadows. Many years later, in a prayer, she recalled Bad Ischl, not Vienna, as her real home:

> . . . that I may once again tread the soil of my homeland among the hillsides and the meadows—not the great city—but Ischl! I want to see the little flowers along the path, the wild coral-red bloom whose name I don't know and which I love so much, and walk on shady paths amid the fir trees, where quite unexpectedly a tiny brook gurgles—the air, the exquisite air, moist, spicy, unspoiled—soil, resin, cyclamen, to breathe them in just once more in one's life—as in the days of one's youth—just once more!

Bertha's daily life whatever the season was not very different from that of other young women of her circle, whose intellectual and artistic talents and physical beauty were considered only superficial adornments for attracting proper marriage prospects. It did not matter that Breuer noted that she possessed a powerful intellect that was in need of "digesting solid mental pablum."

Like her peers, she was overprotected and isolated from everything that was not pleasurable or aesthetic. The author Stefan Zweig observed in *The World of Yesterday* that a middle-class girl "of good family had to live in a completely sterilized atmosphere from the day of birth until her marriage." Bertha herself later wrote: "Up to now, the common conception of women has consigned daughters from upper-class families to an educational realm in which they are 'finished,' a term justly worth noting but in an ironic sense."

It had been axiomatic that girls should be left in the dark, or at any rate given only the vaguest notions about everything that happened outside the circle of domestic life. "They were permitted to learn of the past as reflected in outlines of literature and history 'specially' written for girls; but ordinary life, with its great demands, its contemporary interests, was supposed to remain a mystery. These young persons, who had grown up with their eyes blindfolded, knew virtually nothing of the connection between poverty, sickness and crime. They knew poverty only in the form of the street beggar or on the stage, they knew sickness as something repulsive, and crime as a sin, to be avoided by the moral equivalent of crossing oneself."

Some of Bertha's female contemporaries showed extraordinary insight into their predicament. Rosa Mayreder (1858–1938), who was born in Vienna to a lower-middle-class family just a year before Bertha, became the founder of Austrian feminism. At the age of thirteen, she wrote in her diary, "I must believe in the emptiness of life of the woman today. I must believe in the folly of the so-called woman's place. . . . I found within me the rights of the female; I put together the parts of a new world." Already obsessed with this issue at the beginning of her adolescence, Rosa wrote: "Woman is a 'human being' and consequently half of

Bertha Pappenheim c. 1880–Vienna.
[Photo © Leo Baeck Institute]

humanity is treated in a servile, unfair manner. I am constantly coming back to this intolerable theme each day, each hour reminds me."

At the time of her father's illness, Bertha was twenty-one. Although a beautiful, charismatic young woman, she remained single. Many of her childhood friends would have been married or betrothed. Although Bertha exhibited an outwardly cheerful and energetic persona, beneath the outgoing and gracious conventions of a wealthy young woman, she embroidered her interior life with imaginings that she later described as her "private theatre." Ostensibly attentive, she actually lived through these fairy tales. Since she was always alert when spoken to, no one was aware of her withdrawal into the world of fantasy.

From December 11, 1880, Breuer visited her daily in an attempt to make a thorough study of the case. Bertha constantly surprised him with new and excruciating physical symptoms, seemingly proliferating from nowhere. She developed a headache around her left eye. She complained that walls of the room appeared to be collapsing over her. She had various complaints about her vision, which Breuer found hard to analyze. Her right arm cramped in an extended position, with her hand turned inward to the point where she could not use it effectively. Then her right leg became twisted inward in a cramped extended position. She developed stiffness and cramping in her shoulder joints and lost the ability to turn her head with her neck muscles. She could only move her head by nestling it between her shoulder blades and turning her whole back. The cramping spread to her left leg, then to her left arm. She developed areas of numbness over her body, but out of anxiety refused to allow Breuer to make a thorough examination.

Virtually all of these symptoms, so far as Breuer could later determine, represented the elaboration of symptoms Bertha had first experienced in fleeting fashion during her "absences" over the previous six months. In the early winter of 1881, he had yet not made this connection. However, he did observe that his young patient's mental state was deteriorating along with her physical condition. Her "absences" became prolonged and more agitated; she angrily threw cushions at anyone who entered the room.

Bertha's hysterical symptoms were rooted in a social oppression as deeply terrifying as her personal problems. In the 1880s, the image of woman suffered from the duality of being either the "angel of the house" or the demonic temptress of men. Misogyny, always present historically, was being vehemently written about and published. Misogynistic ideas, fashionable with the intelligentsia, were accepted a priori by the bourgeoisie.

Misogyny in the last four decades of the nineteenth century played itself out in the form of increasingly sophisticated parlor games in which the male rhetoricians of each generation tried to top the previous wits. There has been a recurrent historical connection between the modern misogynist and the dominant ancient Greek philosopher Aristotle, who codified women as being in all respects inferior to men. Aristotle justified the male as ruler over the female since she lacked reason. He also conceived that woman only provided a material body for the embryo, while the semen from a man contained the "soul." Schopenhauer condemned women to usefulness only in child-rearing, claiming that they were directly "fitted for acting as the nurses and teachers of our early childhood by the fact that they are themselves childish, frivolous and short-sighted." After a brief period of beauty necessary to capture a man, they grew ugly and lost all aesthetic sensibility. Only a young man overcome by his sexual urges could have given the name of "fair sex" to that "undersized, narrow-shouldered, broad-hipped, and short-legged race." Schopenhauer's attack was on the European concept of the "lady," which he felt bestowed undeserved honor upon her. "Women have . . . no love for any art, no proper knowledge of any; and they have no genius." Schopenhauer's solution to the false heights to which the "lady" had been raised was polygamy—replacing a barren, old, or ill wife with a new one. This would reduce woman to her true and natural position as a subordinate being; "and the lady—

that monster of European civilization and Teutonico-Christian stupidity—will disappear from the world."

"Woman as dangerous plaything" was the famous philosopher Friedrich Nietzsche's phrase for the natural inferiority of women. He insisted that women were natural slaves and men their masters. The sole goal of a woman according to his philosophical vision of evolution was to give birth to a Superman. In *Thus Spoke Zarathustra* he characterized women as superficial, a "tempestuous membrane on shallow water." Man, by contrast, possessed a deep soul which "thunders through underground caverns."

Schopenhauer and Nietzsche were influential voices, but the most far-reaching attack on women—which revolutionized all modes of thought of that era—was Charles Darwin's evolutionary presentation of them as an intermediate race in between those of children and men. He used a biological basis to reinforce the traditional characteristics of women as maternal, gentle, and affectionate, while postulating men as possessed of genius, courage, and physical superiority.

The most pernicious views of women, however, were expressed by Otto Weininger, a Jew, whose anti-Semitic self-loathing led him to the thesis that women were by nature possessed of a wanton sexuality and had no "soul." Weininger's Jews, depicted in his book *Sex and Character* as a defective race, were "feminine," as depraved as women within the perfect rationality and creativity of "masculine" German culture. Weininger triply demeaned Jewish women, first as women and secondly as Jews: "No one who had experience with them would find them lovable." He then further degraded women using their religion, "for the God in man is the human soul, and the absolute Jew is devoid of a soul." He shocked Viennese society twice, first with the publication of *Sex and Character,* and secondly, with his suicide in the same house where Beethoven died, which transformed him into a Romantic hero.

In this repressive culture it became increasingly difficult for an exceptional young woman like Bertha to remain the "angel of the house." As Bertha deteriorated, she tore her linen and the buttons from her bedclothes with her partially paralyzed fingers. She suffered terribly, thinking that she was going mad, accusing visitors of persecuting her and leaving her in a muddle. If something in her room had been changed, or if someone had entered or left while she was in the midst of an "absence" or altered state of consciousness, she complained of having "lost time." When people tried to placate her, to convince her she had not "lost time" or "gone mad," she would tear up objects and blame others for the untidiness. She also complained of a profound darkness in her head, of being unable to think, and of becoming blind and deaf.

The illness gradually consolidated into a distinct pattern. During the day Bertha was troubled by "absences" and hallucinations; steadily worsening in the late afternoon, by sunset she had completely fallen into a trance, which she called "clouds." Right before Breuer's eyes, her consciousness seemed to split into states. Bertha believed she had two selves—one "good," the other "evil." In her conscious state she oscillated between exaggerated high spirits and anxious melancholy; in her second state she was "naughty," hallucinating, and obstinate. Looking at her hair ribbons and strings, she saw snakes. She then would chide and convince herself that those were only her ribbons and strings. In the evening, at the time she used to nurse her father, her second state progressively worsened until she entered a condition of continuous trance.

Rather than calling in a consultant or sending Bertha to a sanatorium, Breuer felt compelled to spend even more time observing her. Given his bent for research, he was probably excited about experimenting with new methods of healing, particularly with this young woman, for whom he had such unusual respect and compassion. He called this period of her illness a "psychosis," noting: "It was in this condition that I undertook her treatment and at once recognized the seriousness of the psychical disturbance with which I had to deal."

Of all Bertha's symptoms none was so distinctive as the disturbance in her language. In the evening, when she had passed into the somnolent "clouds" of her autohypnotic state, her use of words became increasingly bizarre. It reached the point where Breuer had to consider, and then rule out, a diagnosis of aphasia, perhaps caused by tubercular meningitis. "Tormenting, tormenting," Bertha cried out during her somnambulistic state. Gradually, she lost her command of grammar and syntax, speaking only in infinitives. Personal pronouns were consigned to oblivion because everything was impersonal to her. All she was able to mutter were constructions like "to desire," "to torment," "to love," "to hate." Then for two weeks she withdrew into muteness and, despite her intense efforts, appeared unable to pronounce a syllable. For the first time Breuer imagined he understood the "psychical mechanism" of her disorder. He thought she once must have felt acutely offended and had determined not to speak about it. When he implored her to talk about it, she resumed speaking. Bertha, as this example shows, used language as well as her body as a signifier of her rebellion against her stifling existence.

As a result of this breakthrough, in March 1881 Bertha's apparent aphasia receded, and she began speaking only English, although she believed she was speaking German and understood

German when it was spoken to her. She had disputes with her detested nurse, who spoke only German and was unable to understand English. With Breuer's full complicity, English became their secret language. In moments of anxiety, however, Bertha would speak in a jumble of languages—French, English, and Italian. Speaking solely in the present tense, she withdrew to an infant state of babbling, identified by French feminist interpreters of Lacan as the "Imaginary" or "Mirror Stage," during which the child feels merged with the mother. When a female child enters into what they call the "Symbolic Stage," or into language, she enters into the language of "Patriarchal Law," and takes on the name of the Father and the laws of his cultural realm. Bertha's linguistic difficulties signify the repression of her father's German, and speaking it therefore became unbearable for her during the agony of her father's death, as Sander Gilman so insightfully describes.

He also notes that when Bertha hallucinated snakes she was unable to remember a prayer and substituted English nursery rhymes. The prayer she sought would have been in Hebrew, and in recalling it, she would have expressed her father's holy language. Her retreat into babble, according to Gilman, indicates that her identities as a cultivated European young lady and an assimilated, but religiously Orthodox, German Jew vanished. Her babble became a fantastic referent to Yiddish, the tongue of the Ostjuden, and Jewish women's religious literature that was to be despised and repressed as inferior. If the intersections of Bertha's contradictory selves met in language, constructing for her the boundaries of the Real, then her lapses into muteness refer to the void of a symbolic death-of-self, with her movement back into language and eventually German constituting both rebirth and transformation.

Between episodes of speaking gibberish and speaking English, Bertha suffered from total amnesia. By the time Breuer discovered the psychical mechanism underlying Bertha's aphasia, he had already conceived of a surprising means of pulling her out of her autohypnotic states. By chance observation he noticed that when she was attentive to an image she muttered and repeated it, and she grew calmer. The same held true if it was a phrase that a family member noted that she had muttered during a daytime "absence."

Consciously or unconsciously, Bertha was drawing Breuer closer to her, while Breuer, consciously or unconsciously, felt compelled to follow her lead. At some point during these encounters, they discovered a unique method of relating to each other. Breuer would repeat a phrase or a word that seemed charged with meaning, and she would begin to tell him a fairy tale. By now Bertha clearly recognized only Breuer and spoke English to him. She had effectively enticed him into her "private theatre," but they also created their own private theatre, isolating themselves from her family and servants. As Breuer often found it difficult to persuade Bertha to tell a story, he was "obliged to overcome her unwillingness by urging and pleading and using devices such as repeating a formula with which she habitually introduced her stories." He observed, for instance, that in the daytime she occasionally uttered words such as *Sandwüste* (sandy desert) and that when in the evening he mentioned the word *Wüste* (desert) as a cure, she began to tell a story about people who had lost their way in the desert. This was a momentous discovery. Bertha discovered the primacy of the imagination over the Real; Bertha's self as creator-artist became her healing-force when she was in a state of shattering pain and confusion. Imagination became her necessary angel. As James Hillman advises, there is profound, complex morality in taking fantasy life images seriously.

To know our fantasy life is to know ourselves most profoundly. Soul-making arises from image-making. Imagination "discovers and forms a personality by disclosing and shaping the multiple soul-personalities of the primary *massa confusa* of arguing voices."

Henri Ellenberger would call it the result of a "creative illness." The experience of "creative illness" is found in religion, philosophy, psychology, and literature. This concept is as ancient as the initiation rites of shamans, who consider themselves possessed by a curative madness from which they emerge as intermediaries between the world of humans and the world of spirits as healers. This "illness" is also similar to the dark night of the soul of Christian mystics. According to Ellenberger, after a long period of suffering, the "illness" begins to terminate in a euphoric feeling of liberation. A person enduring "a creative illness" then experiences a "durable transformation of the personality. He or she has the impression of rising into a new life." The interchange between Breuer and Bertha bears witness, for the first time in medical history, that the power of the "imagination" was being used to systematically to alleviate psychological suffering.

Bertha called this process the "talking cure" when she was being serious and "chimney sweeping" in her more playful moments. The pattern of telling these fairy tales lasted for over eighteen months, as long as Breuer continued to see her. Doctor and patient had reached an accommodation that allowed Bertha gradually to alleviate her symptoms through the use of her imagination, through her fairy tales.

According to Breuer, the stories were charming, though invariably tragic, and reminiscent of Hans Christian Andersen's *A*

Picture-book Without Pictures, on which he believed Bertha's tales were modeled. The title is a metaphor for the "imagination," Bertha's primary power in her powerless state. Andersen's thirty-three short tales are told from the point of view of the moon traveling around the planet. The tales are told to a lonely man who has moved to the city from the country; his only friend is the familiar moon, which magically speaks to him. "What a beautiful picture-book you would have," she (the moon) says on her first visit, "if you were to paint all that I relate to you." On hearing this, the man feels that he might paint a new "The Thousand and One Nights." In Bertha's dissociative states, Breuer recognized "an observing brain" still operative inside his patient. Bertha confirmed this insight by remarking that during her worst periods, an "observer brain" inside her brain observed with accuracy and acuteness, furnishing her with information. Distanced from herself, just as in Andersen's tales the moon is distanced from the man, she revealed her inner life as if it were a moonbeam illuminating small parts of the terrain. The moon, like Bertha's imagination, moved from one terrain to another, viewing fragments of tragic stories. In one of Andersen's tales, the moon illuminates a prisoner, tracing musical notes of farewell on the wall. The prisoner disappears, and the moon's rays are able only to "illuminate a small part of the melody and the greater part remained in perpetual darkness. Was it his death-song he had written, or had he flown on wings of love to meet the embrace of his beloved?" It was as difficult for Breuer to decipher Bertha's imaginings and to discern the source of her symptoms as it was for the moon to decode the melody on the prison wall.

Bertha's stories most frequently began with a girl anxiously sitting by a sickbed; Breuer mentions that she also created stories about many other topics. Speaking her aphasic jargon at the onset, she would progress toward a more polished and correct language, until by the end of the narration she was speaking perfectly. Strangely, not one of the stories is included in Breuer's case history, even though it is with these fairy tales that he and Bertha forged their important place in history.

Breuer never once had any doubt as to the reality of her symptoms. He never supposed she was malingering. As he later wrote in her file, her illness prevented her from satisfying her most passionate and genuine desire to see her gravely sick father. Breuer emphasized, "I am convinced that she would have made any sacrifice, renounced any merely capricious behavior, to achieve that end."

She was, however, close to gaining that end. By March 1881, the "talking cure" brought about the desired effect, as one by one Bertha's symptoms vanished. With the disappearance of aphasia, when at night she began talking solely in English, the paralysis of her left side also disappeared. Then she became able to support her head, to use her right leg, and to a slightly lesser degree, her right arm. Her squinting and the disturbances of her vision partially cleared. What continued were the daytime "absences," followed by a somnolent state in the evening, but both were more tolerable because the nighttime "talking cure" continued to provide its magical relief.

By April 1 Bertha was well enough to get out of bed. Four days later her father died.

During her illness, Bertha had seen her father rarely and only for short periods. Several days before her father's death, after rereading the gravedigger's scene in *Hamlet,* Bertha suffered from recurrent images of "death's-heads." Her anxiety for her father had increased and she was convinced that "people had told her nothing but lies." She stopped recognizing anyone but Breuer, who identified what she was now going through as "blindness of the soul as described by Munk." She would not even speak to Breuer without touching his hands and reassuring herself that he was indeed her beloved doctor. As if like Saint Joan she were possessed by voices, Bertha also physically acted out her tragic stories, calling them "hearing hallucinations." Breuer was convinced that the phenomenon he witnessed during the winter of 1880–1881 was genuine. The illness had prevented her from satisfying her most passionate and genuine desire to see her gravely sick father; and Breuer emphasized, "I am convinced that she would have made any sacrifice, renounced any merely capricious behavior, to achieve that end."

Sigmund Pappenheim died on April 5, 1881 at the age of fifty-seven. He was buried at his birthplace in Pressburg, but in Bertha's debilitated condition it would have been impossible for her to accompany her family to the funeral.

At the very moment of her father's death Bertha cried out to her mother in terror and begged to be told the truth. Her clairvoyance points to her special gifts and extraordinary sensitivity, as well as to her psychic ties to her father. She also demanded permission to write to her father, believing that she would not be allowed to do this if he were really dead. Having been forbidden to see him for months, she felt cheated of his last words. Furious at having been kept from him, she severed her emotional ties to her family. Her isolation from her father coupled with his death was the origin of her disturbed relationship with her mother. The night of her father's death she called for Breuer, and before he arrived she wrestled with others in profound agitation.

Whenever her mother and brother came near her, she experienced waves of uncomfortable warmth that she called "stoves." When Breuer entered, she allowed him to put her to bed quietly, repeatedly cautioning him, "Don't tell me any more lies, I know my father is dead."

The day after her father's death, Bertha was in a stupor until she confronted Breuer in Italian. "*Buona sera, dottore,*" she cried, suddenly leaping up. "*E vero che il mio padre e morte?*" ("Is it true that my father is dead?") Breuer told her she had already known it was so and now must learn to accept it. After an initial violently excited outburst, she subsided into a deep stupor. Two days later she emerged in a greatly changed state.

Chapter Two

THE TALKING CURE (1881-1882)

Devastated by her father's death, Bertha, now twenty-two, was seized by moods that swung between violent agitation and profound stupor. Her vision became strangely distorted and she was unable to recognize people, perceiving them to be "wax figures" and not individuals familiar to her. Everything was so blurred that only through laborious "recognizing" work was she able to identify people. She recognized her mother by her dark hair; a shock of red hair represented her brother. In a vase filled with spring flowers she perceived but one. Breuer was the only person Bertha recognized; she would confirm his presence by feeling his hands. Her behavior turned infantile; her dependency on Breuer became total. She refused to eat unless he fed her, and after eating she would obsessively wash out her mouth in a ritual cleansing. After sunset she continued to fall into a deep sleep. If Breuer was there when she awoke to let her talk herself out in the autohypnotic state, she became clean in her mind, calm, and cheerful. She would sit down to work, write, and draw until four in the morning, when she again went to bed. This substitution of day for night replicated Bertha's nursing schedule with her father. She continued to speak only English, though she understood German.

The agony of her father's death so devastated her that on

April 15, 1881, ten days later, Breuer brought in a consultant. Like Jean-Martin Charcot theatrically displaying his hypnotized hysterical patients at the Salpêtrière clinic in Paris, Breuer showed off Bertha's peculiarities to Richard von Krafft-Ebing, the renowned psychiatrist and sex researcher. First, he permitted Krafft-Ebing to observe Bertha as she was writing. She had begun to write in a strange fashion, using Roman printed letters from the alphabet of her edition of Shakespeare. Then she quickly translated a French text into English, and laughing, exclaimed, "That's exactly like an examination!" She completely ignored Krafft-Ebing, who was trying to get her attention. He became so frustrated that he held a flaming piece of paper in her face. Startled and terrified by the sight of a stranger, her status as patient suddenly and humiliatingly brought home to her, Bertha ran to the door to remove the key and collapsed unconscious. After Krafft-Ebing left, Breuer spent considerable time calming his angry, despondent patient down.

That evening Breuer left Vienna for a three-day trip to Berlin and Bertha's condition worsened. In his absence, she did not eat, her anxiety returned, and her daytime "absences" became dominated by death imagery, hallucinations of death's-heads and skeletons. In this dark "private theatre" she acted out these dread experiences, occasionally putting them into words. Her "private theatre" had become a stage as she bodily acted out her visions.

Upon his return, Breuer resumed the "talking cure" in the evenings. He noticed that Bertha's poetic imagination was beginning to dry up. Her stories were neither as fresh nor as charming as before. Instead, they were accounts of her frightening hallucinatory experiences during the "absences" of the day. By observing her daytime behavior, Breuer was able to anticipate their content. Once she had given vent to them in the evening, all the while shaking with fear and horror, Bertha grew relieved and was again cheerful. On the few occasions when an evening session had been incomplete, Breuer gave her chloral hydrate, a calmant, to help her sleep. Still, Bertha's condition continued to deteriorate.

Bertha suffered such unrelenting inner torment that she became actively suicidal, smashing windows and committing other violent acts. In addition, she suffered from a painfully neuralgic jaw and intense convulsions of the whole left facial area. Breuer despaired that in spite of frequent alleviations of her agonies, Bertha required additional urgent help that he could not provide alone. On June 7, 1881, fearing that Bertha might jump to her death from her third-floor bedroom, her mother and Breuer transferred her by force to a small villa on the grounds of the Inzersdorf sanatorium directed by two physicians, Hermann Breslauer and Emile Fries, where Breuer continued to supervise her. Breuer lied about this when he later wrote her case history for *Studies on Hysteria,* claiming that she had merely been taken to a "country house." At the sanatorium she went for three days and nights without food and sleep. She started consciously hallucinating, unaccompanied by "absences." She then became peaceful and even agreed to continue taking chloral at night. Breuer, or in his absence Breslauer, would administer five grams of chloral, which allowed her to sleep, but did not affect her overall condition. When Breuer was present she was euphoric, but in his absence her state was highly disagreeable and anxious. Since earlier the verbal utterances of her hallucinations had calmed her, Breuer had avoided the use of narcotics.

The sanatorium in Inzersdorf, about five miles south of Vienna, was established in 1872 in a mansion that had once been the residence of Prince Ferdinand von Lobkowitz. The sanatorium's practices reflected the paternalistic methods of S. Weir Mitchell's famous "rest cure." His "cure," which he first described in 1873, called for seclusion from family, massage, electricity, immobility, and diet. Bertha was confined to bed, but unlike her American and English counterparts, was allowed to read and write. In effect, under the illusion of being healing guardians, these doctors "cured" women by restoring them to the stereotypical concepts of "femininity" by subordinating them to an ostensibly benevolent male will. Forced back into "womb-like dependence," the patient was "reborn, re-educated by the parental team of a subservient female nurse and a godlike male doctor."

Under Breuer's instructions Breslauer tried unsuccessfully to continue her "talking cure." Instead, in the name of humane treatment she was tortured. Electric eels were applied to her face, currents of electricity were shot through her body, and she was treated with arsenic for several weeks. All of these techniques proved ineffective.

According to Dr. Wilhelm Orb, professor at the University of Leipzig and one of the early scientists of electricity, the treatment of hysteria, which he considered a morbid disturbance of the nervous system, is the removal of the disease itself through electrical shocks to the body. He proposed a combination of general faradization, electrical baths, and galvanization of the spine and ovaries as the most effective method to accomplish the elimination of hysteria.

Bertha deprecated the inability of science to alleviate her suffering and snappishly emphasized the uselessness of her stay in the sanatorium. She continually fantasized about projects for her life and then forgot them, before obsessing about them with renewed energy. The one project that frequently occupied her was the idea of dedicating herself to practical nursing. She also became preoccupied with visiting her father's grave in Pressburg and often spent hours in tearful worship in front of his picture.

Over time Bertha became very attached to Dr. Breslauer and for a while her condition seemed to improve. She was passionately fond of a Newfoundland dog she had been given. One day, when the dog attacked a cat, Bertha, although frail, was able to take a whip and beat the dog off its victim. Her compassion for others also led her to look after the poor and sick people in the neighborhood.

During Bertha's stay in Inzersdorf, Breuer was unable to visit her every day. When he did visit, she recounted her stories until he felt like the "sultan with Scheherazade." When she finished, she felt calmer, or *gehaglich* as she called it, from the German *behaglich,* meaning "comfortable" or at ease. If Breuer absented himself one night, she remained anxious, moody, and unpleasant until he reappeared. The next night Breuer often found it difficult to persuade her to resume her storytelling and he was often obliged to plead with her or to begin the stories himself.

In mid-July 1881, Breuer left Vienna for a five-week holiday. He returned in August to discover that, despite Bertha's trust of Dr. Breslauer, she had refused to tell him any stories and had fallen into a wretched, ill-tempered, and malicious state. Breuer found her in low spirits, "intractable, moody, spiteful and indolent." In his absence, she had added a series of "caprices" to her panorama of symptoms. Lying in bed in her nightgown, she would refuse to take off her socks but would later pull them off in the middle of the night. Breuer discovered that this "caprice" was directly related to an event Bertha perceived as shameful. After she had been forbidden to visit her ailing father, Bertha would sneak into his room at night in her stocking feet. One night her brother, Wilhelm, caught her watching over her sleeping father and scolded her. She felt guilt and shame. After she told Breuer this story, the sock caprice never recurred.

The other incident that now caught Breuer's attention was Bertha's inability to drink water. In July 1880, during a period of extreme heat in Bad Ischl, Bertha had suffered from terrible thirst, but was unable to drink. She would hold a glass to her lips and then push it away in disgust. She suffered from this thirst for six weeks, and later her hydrophobia reappeared periodically.

One day Bertha grumbled to Breuer about the English lady who had accompanied her to Bad Ischl. Her memory may have been triggered because they were speaking English. Her companion had apparently allowed her "horrid" little dog to drink out of Bertha's glass. Though outraged, Bertha repressed her response at the time, replacing her anger with "politesse." This was an expression of the "ordeal of civility" that she performed in the presence of her gentile "nanny," but was able to overcome in the permissive company of her Jewish doctor. While recounting the story to Breuer, the most dramatic episode of their "talking cure" occurred. Bertha expressed her repressed rage. After Bertha finished giving vent to her fury, she asked Breuer for something to drink, and then drank a large quantity of water from the glass. She awoke from her autohypnosis with the glass at her lips, and "thereupon the disturbance vanished, never to return."

Bertha demonstrated not only that suppressed rage had enormous power over human behavior, but also that the dysfunction it caused could be permanently "talked away." This was an historic moment, the first instance of what Breuer and Bertha would subsequently call the "cathartic" method, later acclaimed by Sigmund Freud as the germinal method of psychoanalysis.

The "cathartic method" was a direct allusion to Aristotle's theory of "catharsis" in Greek tragedy. Aristotle argued that by witnessing an actor's deep suffering, an audience was cleansed of its "eleos" and "phobos," its pity and fear. Aristotle's theory dovetails perfectly with Bertha's "cathartic" method of cleansing her own psyche. Although the Aristotelian term referred to purging the emotions of the audience, Bertha was both actor and spectator in her "private theatre": Bertha's self was apparently divided as if she were viewing herself on a stage.

However, this divided self can be viewed as the opposite of a pathological state. Bertha can also be conceptualized in Zen Buddhist or Transpersonal terms as transcending the "ego" and becoming her "inner witness." The emergence of this "witness" might be viewed as going beyond her "self" to release her "self" from the constricting boundaries and illusions of her feminine cultural "personae." While Bertha witnessed her suffering and pain she would begin to transcend it and free herself from its source in false identities which had been forced upon her by her family and the culture. What distinguishes the tragic from the pathetic is the courage to enter into the core of immense human suffering and to go wherever it leads. Bertha's courage in revealing the images of her "private theatre"; her deepest "truth"; and her endurance in continuing to engage in an unchartered healing process while living in desperate despair could be compared to Greek tragic heroines. Bertha's symbolic action of following every symptom to its source made Breuer renowned as both a psychological and medical pioneer. Bertha's fame as the co-creator of the "cathartic method" must be acknowledged by future histories.

The choice of the concept of "catharsis" was no accident and came out of both Breuer's and Bertha's education. Aristotelian "catharsis" had become the rage in Viennese intellectual circles and salons, due to a book by Jacob Bernays, the uncle of Freud's future wife, and Bertha's friend, Martha Bernays, which had just been reprinted in 1881. Both Breuer and Bertha would have been aware of this idea, which must have contributed to their mutual creativity.

Improvising with Bertha, Breur elaborated a hypothesis from the drinking glass incident: that all of her symptoms were created by emotions suppressed during traumatic experiences. The release of these emotions was termed "abreaction."

At the end of August 1881, Breuer accompanied Bertha from the sanatorium to her home in Vienna for an eight-day visit. In Vienna he cajoled her into telling him three to five stories a night. Although Bertha had improved again in Breuer's care, she was sent back to Inzersdorf at the end of the visit. Upon her return, a new pattern emerged. After an evening's "talking cure," Bertha would be cheerful and agreeable most of the next day. The second day, if Breuer did not visit, she would become moody. By the third day of his absence she would turn angry and nasty. Breuer again grew hopeful that with his continuing involvement her state would become manageable. Her physical symptoms seemed to be abating. Her daytime "absences" were less frequent and less agitated. In the evening, however, the "clouds" kept emerging, and in the morning her memory of her nighttime activities waned.

By the beginning of November 1881, Breuer decided it was time to try to reintegrate her with her family. He realized that this would be difficult. Bertha had been estranged from her mother and brother ever since they deceived her about her father's death. She restrained her rages against them in their presence with false politesse. As a precaution, Breuer contacted a colleague, Dr. Robert Binswanger of the Sanatorium Bellevue in Kreuzlingen, Switzerland, and explored the possibility of having

Bertha transferred there if the move home led to a worsening of her state. With Bellevue looming as a safety net, she returned home in the beginning of November and was discharged from Inzersdorf diagnosed "cured."

When Bertha returned to Vienna, she found herself in new surroundings. After Sigmund's death, her mother had moved to Neuer Markt 7, a half mile from where the family had lived before. Breuer wrote that Bertha's condition at this time was "bearable, both physically and mentally." He hoped for continued improvement, but was disappointed. December 7, 1881, marked the first anniversary of Bertha's separation from her father. On that day her condition began to deteriorate. She no longer had "good days," despite Breuer's visits, but remained gloomy and irritable. Nor could Breuer discern any new experiences that she might have retained during the day. Throughout Hanukkah, she was particularly restless. Breuer observed that instead of telling him new stories, she recounted the same ones she had told him during Hanukkah the previous year.

At this time an extraordinary change in her consciousness occurred. By evening Bertha seemed almost supernaturally possessed by her "second condition." In her daytime state, Breuer later wrote, she "lived like the rest of us in the winter of 1881–82, whereas in the second nighttime state she lived in the winter of 1880–81. She imagined that she was still living in her old room, so that when she wanted to go to the door she knocked up against the stove which stood in the same relation to the window as the door did in the old room." Bertha's return to the past was amazing for its accurate recall of day-by-day events, which Breuer confirmed through her mother's private diary. (Breuer does not quote extensively from the diary, nor has it ever been found. Neither has there been any mention of Bertha's own diary, which a young lady of her station and era would most likely have kept.) It was also extraordinary as it showed that Bertha's suffering differed markedly from the stereotypical hysteric illness of the time.

Breuer first discovered that she was living in "double time" when Bertha told him laughingly that she was angry with him. Through her mother's diary he learned that she had been angry with him exactly one year before. Though she was wearing a brown dress, she protested to Breuer it was blue. Breuer was also able to verify that she had been wearing a blue dress on that day the previous year.

Breuer discovered that this bizarre state not only appeared spontaneously, but could also be induced. During the first phase of Bertha's illness, when she could not eat, she had survived by eating oranges and melons. Breuer could make Bertha believe that she had gone back in time merely by holding up an orange before her eyes.

Bertha's emotional disturbances of the previous year became the focus of their attention, and they found themselves immersed in past events. What they created together was a tedious but consistently successful method of achieving a permanent "cure." They examined each of Bertha's symptoms in reverse chronological order, from its present-day appearance to its origin. Bertha would try to recall every instance of the symptom in order to trace it to its beginnings. Breuer concentrated on recent traumatic events without leading her back to her childhood; nor did Bertha spontaneously recall events prior to her father's illness.

Bertha and Breuer developed a new procedure for working together. He would visit her in the morning and after hypnotizing her, would ask her to concentrate only on the symptom being treated. In the evening he would return and they would resume work. As Bertha began to narrate its origins, the symptom spontaneously disappeared. Each symptom was examined, and "all the occasions on which it had appeared were described in reverse order." Breuer became progressively more excited as each paralytic contracture, speech disorder, and dysfunction of vision and hearing, cough, and tremor was talked away. The tedium of the method was lessened by the exhilaration of relieving the symptoms. This methodical and lasting cure for hysteria had never before been codified.

Bertha's cough, as previously described, for which Breuer had originally been summoned, began while she was taking care of her father on the night in Bad Ischl when Bertha heard dance music from a neighboring house. Thereafter, every time she heard sharply rhythmic music, she had fits of nervous coughing, or *tussis nervosa.*

On another night in Bad Ischl, while she was tending to her father, he asked for the time. Her grief over his condition brought tears to her eyes, and as she looked at the watch it seemed to become too large to be read. Because she stopped herself from coughing, so as not to let her father see her despair, Bertha developed a squint. On a third occasion, again while nursing her father, Bertha hallucinated that a death's-head had replaced his face. Later, when she appeared to be in good health, she visited a relative. As she entered the room, she saw her "pale face reflected in a mirror hanging opposite the door; but it was not herself that she saw but her father with a death's-head."

Her periodic inability to read began when she went to the theatre for the first time during her father's illness and, fraught with guilt and crying, denied herself the pleasure of reading.

Bertha's dread of a memory often inhibited its emergence, but with Breuer's encouragement she made a great effort to recall even the most appalling images. Her progress was frequently halted because of a particularly horrifying hallucination or because many symptoms elicited the recall of hundreds of incidents. Breuer documented the exhaustive manner in which they alleviated her hearing problems as follows:

(a) Not hearing when someone came in while her thoughts were abstracted, 108 detailed instances. First instance, not hearing her father enter the room.

(b) Not understanding when several people were talking, 27 instances. First instance, her father and an acquaintance speaking together.

(c) Not hearing when she was alone and directly addressed, 50 instances. Origin: Her father vainly asked her for some wine.

(d) Deafness brought on by being shaken, 15 instances. Origin: having been shaken angrily by her young brother when he caught her one night eavesdropping at the sickroom door.

(e) Deafness brought on by fright at a noise, 37 instances.

(f) Deafness during deep absence, 12 instances.

(g) Deafness brought on by listening hard for a long time, 54 instances.

Eight months after beginning the "cathartic" method, the only vestige of Bertha's hysterical symptoms remaining was her stiff right arm. Clearly, the cure was not complete. During the spring of 1882, while she and Breuer were working hard to clear up her symptoms, Bertha developed a new facial neuralgia and, more ominously, convulsions. Breuer treated the convulsions with morphine and administered chloral hydrate to help her sleep; his initial attempt to wean her off the drug had to be discontinued when she became delirious. The period of "clouds" in the evening also persisted.

In early June she brought up a number of childish fears and reproaches. She told Breuer that she had not been sick at all, but had pretended to be an actress and simulated the entire illness. Breuer convinced her that this was not an uncommon thought, that once her divided consciousness had unified, she would look back on it as having always been thus. Bertha's delusion of pretense quickly passed. She became determined to terminate the treatment by June 7, 1882, the first anniversary of her forced removal to Inzersdorf, and entered into the final act of the "talking cure" with great energy. It was time for her to act out the terrifying hallucination that apparently lay at the root of her illness.

Bertha staged her memory of her hallucination of a snake attacking her dying father as if it were to be represented in an actual theatre. Bertha once again became the witness of her "self," of a past "self" that had been free of her hysteria. She rearranged her new room so it resembled her father's sickroom at Bad Ischl. Seated in a chair, she placed her right arm over its back. Psychodramatically, she re-created for Breuer the terror of her hallucination of the snake. Miraculously, after reproducing this intense experience from the past in the present, she again spoke her primary language, German, and finally was able to move her right arm freely. Bertha's reenactment of her struggle with an illusory image, acted out like a medieval passion play, ended triumphantly with the illusory demon that had possessed her being exorcized. Breuer was now convinced that she had relieved her anguish and had completely regained her mental and physical health. Bertha's "cure" gave birth to a new self with a higher awareness of the nature of her being than before she became ill.

In the classical era Bertha might have been described as having been in a divine frenzy and thus a prophetess, like Cassandra.

With the advent of Christianity, however, hysterical states in which a woman appeared to exist in an altered state of consciousness were explained as evidence of demonic possession. The woman in question would have been accused of witchcraft and most likely been put to death. In the Middle Ages theologians explained these manifestations of hysteria as proof of an individual's alliance with unholy powers that inhabited the shadows of the world. Hysteria ceased to be considered a disease, and hysterics often became victims of the witch craze, that long and dreadful mass delusion that held Europe in its sway for many centuries. Under inquisition many hysterics confessed to sexual intercourse with the devil, wild orgies, and practicing witchcraft on men who spurned them. The most extraordinary document from this mania was *Malleus maleficarum* (1494), known in English as Witches' Hammer. Although written in the Renaissance, it remains medieval in tone. A careful study of this fantastic document reveals that most of the accused witches were hysterics who suffered from partial anesthesia, mutism, blindness, convulsions, and a variety of sexual delusions.

In the early part of the nineteenth century, however, Bertha would have been considered an exemplary case of "magnetic" illness. The unusual coexistence of one personality living in the present and one living on the same day of the year before was first stressed by Henri Ellenberger in *The Discovery of the Unconscious*. Bertha's recollections were reminiscent of the "prodigious mnemonic feats" of Anna Katherina Emmerich (1774–1824) and particularly of Friedericke Hauffe (1801–1829), called the "Seeress of Prevorst."

Clemens Brentano, a prominent German poet and novelist who was a friend of Breuer's, and also the uncle of philosopher and ex-priest Franz Brentano, documented "magnetic cases" in no fewer than twenty-four volumes. The best known, Anna Katherina Emmerich, a peasant woman and former nun in Westphalia, had nightly visions, and while in cataleptic states of great suffering, she bore all the stigmata of Christ's passion. In her trances she witnessed the unfolding of the lives of Christ and the Madonna and described the final home of the Virgin Mother in Ephesus. This vision was verified as accurate when archaeologists later excavated such a house. As Ellenberger notes, Bertha's hallucinations of what happened to her "day by day, one year previously, could be compared to Emmerich's nightly visions that coincided exactly with the Church calendar."

These hallucinations are also comparable to those of Friedericke Hauffe, the uneducated daughter of a gamekeeper in Prevorst, who had visions and premonitions as a child. Following her marriage, Hauffe fell ill with convulsions, catalepsy, hemorrhages, and fevers. She was taken to a famous exorcist, magnetist, and poet, Justinus Kerner, who brought about some improvement in her state through magnetism. Kerner documents her remarkable capacities as a visionary who could describe the world of spirits, foretell the future, and give advice and exhortation. She spoke in a private language, allegedly an Ursprache, and prescribed self-medication, which cured her as she predicted.

To these older magnetizers, or hypnotists, Bertha's illness would not have seemed as extraordinary as it did to Breuer. As Ellenberger notes, "It was one of those cases so frequent in the 1820s, yet so scarce in the 1880s, in which the patient dictated to the physician the therapeutic devices he had to use, prophesied the course of the illness, and announced its terminal date." Clemens Brentano and Justinus Kerner were of a religious disposition, and saw in magnetic illnesses a possible meeting place between the profane and the divine. Breuer, by contrast, was a committed advocate of what William James would later dub "medical materialism," the "secularization of the spiritual and supernatural."

Bertha's attendance at a Catholic girls' school would have familiarized her with the lives of the Christian saints and the stories of visionaries, tortured magnetic illnesses, and the religious feats of saintly women earlier in the century. Although Breuer codified their process in scientific realms, perhaps Bertha's attempt to purify herself from traumatic images of the past opened her heart to what were to become her transcendent spiritual, almost mystic experiences that guided her later life, reworked through her increasingly devout Judaism. Bertha's extraordinary gifts of imagination may have begun to free her to dissolve the boundaries that connected the secular to the imagination of the divine.

After almost two years of daily closeness, Breuer knew Bertha "to an extent to which one person's life is seldom known to another." Breuer had learned more about Bertha's interior life than that of his own wife—and probably more than he knew about his own. His unswerving persistence in listening to Bertha, and her unflagging honesty and trust, united them in an extraordinary intimacy. Although Breuer had immersed himself in Bertha's psyche, there are no precise records of their emotional responses to each other, nor any records of dialogue between them.

Although Breuer appeared to be a happily married middle-aged man with four children, Bertha's confessions of her innermost secrets were undoubtably precious and special to him. He never spoke of his attachment to her, nor did he discuss the question of love or erotic feeling. In fact, Breuer claimed that throughout their exploration of Bertha's numerous hallucinations, memories, and fantasies, the element of sexuality never emerged and was "astonishingly undeveloped in her." He also claimed that she had never been in love.

The bond that harnessed them on this long, uncharted journey remains mysterious. Bertha's genius in creating the "talking cure"—and Breuer's in understanding its revolutionary implications—set their relationship apart from all others. In the 1920s, the surrealists Aragon and Breton declared that hysteria was not a sickness or a pathological condition but a revolutionary rebellion and a supreme means of expression. Bertha could claim to have been just such a revolutionary and artist. She used her body as a signifier of her affective languages, similar to an actor's physicalization of an internal state. Bertha had an enormous need for a special relationship to sustain her while she watched her father die. Indeed, there were two Breuers, just as there were two Berthas: the Breuer present during her father's illness, and another, fully present, who relived these events with her. The "talking cure" helped Breuer become a healer in an inventive fashion he had never previously imagined. Moreover, he might not have been entirely without his own reasons for identifying with Bertha, for in doing so he could bring his own repressed sorrows to the fore. His mother, also named Bertha, died when he was four, and Bertha Pappenheim may have evoked the memory of his mother when she was about Bertha's age. Like Bertha, Breuer had lost a sibling, a brother who had died of tuberculosis at the age of twenty-four. He also knew the impact of a father's death. His own father, a teacher of religion employed by Vienna's Jewish community, had died at the age of thirty and, like Sigmund Pappenheim, was also from Pressburg. Breuer, like Bertha, was close to his father, who was also his mentor. Bertha may well have been aware of the traumatic events in Breuer's life; the

Breuers and the Pappenheims had known each other for decades and Breuer probably had no compunctions about revealing certain aspects of his personal life to his patient.

Breuer and Bertha culminated their "talking cure," as Bertha had wished, on June 7, 1882. Breuer considered this a successful end of the treatment. In *Studies on Hysteria* he described Bertha as being free from the innumerable disturbances that she had previously exhibited. Breuer wrote that after this cure "she left Vienna and traveled for a while, but it was a considerable time before she regained her mental balance entirely. Since then she had enjoyed complete health."

Was Bertha really cured? Or did she have a relapse that evening after they bade each other farewell?

A legend has persisted that Bertha's mother called Breuer back in desperation; that he found her in the throes of a hysterical childbirth, crying, "B's baby is coming!"; that he managed to calm her down by hypnotizing her and then fled from her phantom pregnancy in a cold sweat. According to the legend, Breuer then went on a second honeymoon with his wife to Venice and fathered a child named Dora, who committed suicide sixty years later in New York.

However, Breuer did not abruptly abandon his patient. Nor did the second honeymoon and birth of Breuer's child occur in June 1882. Henri Ellenberger has extablished that Dora was born on March 11, three months before the legendary event. Yet, other documents make it plain that Breuer's wife had become so jealous of the amount of time her husband spent with his young patient that she became despondent and attempted suicide. Two years later a rumor circulated among the physicians at Inzersdorf that something untoward had indeed happened between doctor and patient. Much later Breuer himself confided in the

Swiss psychiatrist August Fore that after his own involvement in the case ended, he resolved never again to undertake so time-consuming and arduous a treatment.

It is, finally, an incomplete archive. Breuer himself left posterity a fairy-tale ending to the case. Although Bertha and Breuer were locked in the doctor-patient relationship, theirs was a love story. Conscious or unconscious, the question of an "erotic" element between them trivializes the profound intimacy and trust they shared. Together they created a new method of healing. The intensity of their relationship and their unrelenting mutual devotion to the creative mysteries of healing, transcended possessive love, and can only be defined in the metaphysical realm of soul-love, or transpersonal spiritual love. Their love is best described by Plato in the *Symposium:* "Men whose bodies are only creative, betake themselves to women and beget children . . . but creative souls . . . are bound together by a far nearer tie and have a closer friendship than those who beget mortal children . . . for the children who are their common offspring are fairer and more immortal."

To Breuer's dismay, Bertha's recurrent disorders led her on an arduous journey without him. In mid-June, Recha and Breuer decided to send her to the famous Sanatorium Bellevue. Breuer wrote a second letter to Dr. Robert Binswanger at Bellevue, stating that he hoped "my patient, who has always meant a great deal to me, will soon be safely in your care."

Chapter Three

ASYLUM AND FIRST STORIES (1882-1887)

In July 1882, Bertha journeyed to Sanatorium Bellevue in Kreuzlingen, on Lake Constance near the Swiss-German border. On a hot, tedious carriage ride, Bertha and her entourage stopped at her maternal aunt's home in Karlsruhe. Unlike her childhood friends, who might have been visiting relatives for a potential betrothal, or in Kreuzlingen, strolling the spacious promenade winding along the foothills that cup the eastern end of central Europe's largest lake, mingling with other tourists of Lake Constance for a sparkling holiday from the torpor of Vienna, Bertha was traveling to a second sanatorium. Karlsruhe fortuitously was destined to become a home away from home for Bertha, a refuge where over the years she would be free to experiment with her identity and with the various options life offered her. In Karlsruhe her mother's sister, Bella Homburger, took a compassionate interest in Bertha, who also formed a sympathetic bond with Bella's son, her cousin Fritz. Later, they both benevolently did not remind Bertha of the hysterical illness which had led to her stay in Bellevue.

At the same time Bertha was making her way to the shore of Lake Constance, Jean-Martin Charcot was plunging into the mysteries of hysteria from his lecture hall-cum-theatre in Paris.

For Charcot the hallmark of the disorder was a diffuse anomaly of the nervous system, which allowed physical and emotional stresses to express themselves in typical symptoms, including painful contractions of the limbs, trances, seizures, and deliria, all of which could be called forth at the doctor's command through the use of hypnosis. Before a weekly Tuesday audience of physicians, many from foreign cities, and Paris's literary elite, Charcot presented his findings using dramatic case material drawn from the Salpêtrière, a women's workhouse turned asylum that had become a kind of hyperfeminine hell by the last third of the nineteenth century. Four thousand women, poor, ill, or mad, were housed there. It was a nightmare made newly accessible to the curious underbelly of the "belle époque," as Charcot turned his clinic into a theatrical spectacle. Charcot did not allow his "hysterics" to speak, nor did he listen to them. To him the "hysteric" was an actress who, under Charcot's direction, played the role of "woman," a creature of frailty and despair, who permitted man to be the strong protector and the superb lion.

According to Michel Foucault, the confinement of the "insane" to institutions was a product of the seventeenth century. Madness was torn from the "imaginary freedom which still allowed it to flourish during the Renaissance horizon . . . it had floundered about in broad daylight: in *King Lear,* in *Don Quixote.* But in less than a century, it had been sequestered and, in the fortress of confinement, bound to reason, to the rules of morality and to their monotonous nights." The poor, whether insane or merely beggars or vagabonds, were punished and incarcerated as criminals in hospital prisons. In 1792, during the French Revolution, soldiers massacred innumerable women in the famous Salpêtrière hospital. A painting of this massacre, dominated by torches and swords looming over the corpses, hangs in the Musée

Carnavalet. A contrasting painting by Antoine Fleury depicts the famous act of Philippe Pinel (1745–1826) unchaining the madwomen held captive in Salpêtrière during the Revolution.

Owing to her wealth, Bertha was spared the traumatic extremities of her penurious sisters. Bellevue was a luxurious mansion, which gave the impression of a resort. The treatment of the rich at private asylums, however, paralleled the "moral" treatment in public asylums.

The age of "Enlightenment" and industrialization required the regulated movement of people, which was incompatible with the "nomadic character" and romanticization of madness. Mental health specialists, indignant at the practice of isolating the insane in prisons, emphasized the progress in philanthropy the asylum represented. However, they unwittingly invented a scenario of incarceration and confinement that, ironically, was structured like a prison. According to Castel, the "moral" treatment was for the most part "physical" maltreatment.

The patient's *Weltanschauung* was neither interpreted nor given credence. The doctor was the law and the asylum was the "world constructed in the image of rationality that he embodied." The asylum's requirement of obedience to the predominant "norms" reproduced the paradigm of a child's subservience to the absolute power of an adult. The patient, forced into the doctor's concept of "reason," could therefore only consider herself "evil" and the doctor "good," unless she capitulated. The emphasis on "moral" causes and "moral" influences was balanced, and in severe cases ultimately undermined, by an etiological belief in hereditary degeneration. This degeneration, at once moral and neurological, was thought to grow like the proverbial green bay tree through successive generations. The first generations would reveal relatively milder conditions, like hysteria and arthritis, as its first buds in the family lineage. The following generations were cursed with a destiny of increasing degeneration, leading to full-blown madness, alcoholism, and criminality.

"Hereditary degeneracy," supported by social Darwinian theories, was the reigning paradigm in Western psychology and neurology, and "hereditary taint" and "psychopathic disposition" were routinely considered the primary cause of neurosis or insanity, although autopsies of "hysterical" women revealed no physical deformation in the brain.

Breuer had noted at the outset of Bertha's treatment that she had a "moderately severe neuropathic heredity, since some psychoses had occurred among her more distant relatives." Bertha was conscious of her hereditary vulnerability. On a family tree constructed by her brother and a cousin, marks appear next to ancestors who had married close relatives and had nervous breakdowns or been mentally ill. Under the prevailing theory, Bertha was triply vulnerable, having an inferior nervous system through heredity, her status as a "virgin," and as a member of an "inferior" Jewish race. A woman's sexuality, whether it was a lack of sexual intercourse or hyperactivity, was thought by many doctors to be a trigger for hysteria. Breuer had dutifully noted that the element of "sexuality was astonishingly undeveloped in her."

By sending Bertha to Bellevue, Breuer at least protected her from the more draconian physical treatments, some of them surgical and many pernicious, that many prominent doctors prescribed. Had they not been documented, some of the medical practices performed on intractably ill women of a century ago would seem preposterous today. In the second half of the nineteenth century, gynecological atrocities were performed on wealthy and poor women alike. In 1858, English gynecologist Isaac Baker Brown invented clitoridectomy as a "cure" for female masturbation. In the 1860s, Dr. Isaac Ray proclaimed that women were susceptible to "hysteria, insanity, and criminal impulses by reason of their sexual organs." As Mary Daly reports in *Gyn/ecology: The Metaethics of Radical Feminism*, in 1873 Dr. Robert Battery invented "female castration" by removing the ovaries to cure "insanity." Hysteria linked with nymphomania and erotomania gave birth to innumerable literary works and paintings, each depicting woman as a devouring and insatiable sexual organ.

Although Bertha had been treated with "electrotherapy" and "eels" at Inzersdorf, she was spared from "hydrotherapy," perhaps the most common treatment for "crazed" women. "Hydrotherapy" was a "shower" consisting of jets of water aimed at the patient. Depending on the diameter of the pipe, the coldness of the water, and the pressure of the water, the experience was more or less violent. If the treatment went on too long, it could cause fainting and occasionally death. Dr. Marvario of Mareville asylum describes the "moral" cure of Miss "E.P.": "The doctor made a sign, and the fatal tap was opened; the water burst out and fell on Miss E.P.'s head. . . . She screamed with fear and begged us to stop. She promised to give up all her delusions of grandeur. We read her story back to her . . . and emphasized each of her fantasies. She recanted everything she had said and assured us she had been mad but was not mad any longer."

In selecting both Inzersdorf and Bellevue, Breuer had chosen the most innovative and humane care for Bertha then known.

Ludwig Binswanger founded Bellevue with what he considered a pioneering idea, as a patriarch of a large family of both patients and doctors. He gathered his patients around him with the understanding that only a "plus" or "minus" on a continuum distinguishes the symptoms of the "mentally ill" from the passions that move the hearts of normal people. In contrast to state insti-

Main Building of the Sanatorium Bellevue c. 1882.
[Photo courtesy of the administration of the former Sanatorium Bellevue]

tutions, patients at Bellevue could move about freely, and only relatively harmless patients were accepted for treatment.

Robert Binswanger continued his father's efforts to humanize the care of the mentally ill. Bertha, stigmatized as "mentally ill," would one hundred years later have been considered a victim of the myth of mental illness, during the height of the antipsychiatry movement, where "insanity is . . . (conceived) as a social and cultural phenomenon. Experiences which are considered 'normal' in a particular culture or subculture may be defined as 'mad' in another cultural setting." The same critique is true of psychiatric concepts of "reality" and the "self." All states of altered consciousness, or expanded consciousness, were labeled aberrant except those that were consensually validated by primarily white, male psychiatrists.

When Bertha arrived, the sanatorium had grown to forty

Bertha in Riding Habit at Lake Constance, near the Sanatorium Bellevue c. 1882. [Photo © Leo Baeck Institute]

patients, and its fame had spread thoughout Europe. Bellevue had a reputation of providing discreet care to renegade or feeble-minded family members of Russian, German, and Italian nobility. Many of the patients stayed there for the majority of their lives. Until its recent conversion into condominiums, the magnificent grounds were dotted with private houses built by patients' families. The villas represent an aesthetic mixture of architectural styles, from a miniature Russian palace to an English cottage to an enormous glass greenhouse that housed tropical herbage and flowers.

Although the details of Bertha's treatment are not known, it surely included work therapy, gardening, and athletics, such as swimming. She also would have been required to attend classes in ancient and modern languages, literature, and history. All of these practices were instituted by Robert and were considered controversial at the time by psychiatrists who saw them as potentially problematic for women. During periods when she was feeling well, Bertha took long walks in the shadowy groves and gardens, enjoyed bathing in Lake Constance, excursions in town, and spending time horseback riding. In a photograph taken during her stay there, Bertha is in full riding habit. She appears plump and calm, standing stolidly on an oriental carpet; she carries a riding crop in one hand and a pair of gloves in the other.

Bertha's healthy appearance belied her continuing invalidism. The "talking cure" had not been permanent. Most of her symptoms had returned, and her jaw caused her such excruciating pain that she found it impossible to wean herself from the morphine to which she had become addicted.

During her stay at Bellevue, Binswanger asked her to write an account of the strange occurrence of her aphasia. The following narrative is the only extant autobiographical account of her

Sitting Room at the Sanatorium Bellevue c. 1882.
[Courtesy of the administration of former Sanatorium Bellevue]

illness. She wrote down her thoughts in rudimentary English, her secret language with Breuer, since she continued to lose the ability to communicate in German in the evening:

> Undated, Summer 1882.
>
> I, a native German girl am totally deprived of the ability to speak, to read, or to write German. This symptom lasted during the time of a heavy nervous illness I had to go though in permanence longer than a year; since about 4 months it only returns regularly every evening. The physicians point it out as something very strange and rarely to be observed; therefore I will try to give, as well, as a person who has never made any medical studies can do. A short account of my own observations and experiences considering this horrible state.

It appears quite suddenly without the slightest transaction in the very moment I recline in my bed, independent from the hour, which I have named already between 9 o'clock in the evening until 1. Two days I had been obliged to stay in bed for some other little increase, and then this phase began at 10 o'clock. For some hour then I am perfectly unable to communicate anything in German, while the other languages, I have learned later, are present to my mind, and the English I can use nearly to perfection. When the strong neuralgic pain from which I am suffering allows it, I mostly read a French or English book til the happy moment of my recovering my German arrives (what never occurs before midnight, seldom past 2 o'clock in the morning.) The whole going on is not accompanied from the slightest physical sensation, no pain, no oppression or giddiness are to be felt. From the point of any such symptoms the whole thing could pass very well without its being from me remarked at all, but as I do not understand my servant nor am I understood, I dayly must learn anew to find myself in the sad, bitter fact.

Considering my humour, my mental and psychic state during this time, there are some observations to be told. In the first 2 months of my sojourn here, I had shorter or longer absences which I could observe myself by a strange feeling of "timemissing"; one told me that I used to speak with great vivacity during these absences, but since some weeks, there have been none. When I do not read I am laying, not always very quiet, occupied with my thought, and am quite well able to govern them; I can reproduce the past and make plans for the future; I only get really nervous, anxious and disposed to cry, when the but too well motivated fear to lose the German language for longer again takes possession of me. When I have society during this phase I feel much easier,

Dining Room at the Sanatorium Bellevue c. 1882.
[Courtesy of the administration of the former Sanatorium Bellevue]

> but also when I am quite alone I dont fall into heavy melancholic or hypochondriac thinking.
>
> When during this phase two other persons are talking in German, I must take trouble to fix my attention to the conversation, which is quite indifferent to me. I feel sorry not to understand; but am not interested in it. I have bin told that after some hours I get my German language through speaking it very badly.

During Bertha's stay at Bellevue, she refused to see her mother and brother. Nor did Breuer, who had referred several other patients there, visit her. Bertha's archival file at Bellevue, discovered by Ellenberger in 1972, contained a text, similar to the published case history, which had been submitted to

Binswanger by Breuer and transcribed by a secretary, because Breuer asked that the original be returned. Dr. Laupus, assistant physician at Bellevue, corrected this text and added his own report. In 1978, Albrecht Hirschmuller discovered an incomplete but valuable correspondence, including letters written by Bertha, various relatives, and Breuer. Eight letters in all have been published. Binswanger's letters, reports, and replies, which are alluded to in the correspondence, are not included. Hirschmuller found additional case histories by Breuer about other patients he had referred to Bellevue, and two poems by Bertha, which have been added to the archive.

The first letter, dated June 19, 1882, in Vienna, is a reply from Breuer to Binswanger, advising of Bertha's probable arrival after a short stay in Karlsruhe, and his promise to send her case history if she entered Bellevue. While forwarding the case history at the end of June, Breuer angrily responds to Binswanger's charge that Bertha was a fake: "Your present contention that her entire illness is an invention is quite certainly false, even if individual elements are not genuine." He admits to giving Bertha large doses of morphine for "rolling convulsions," and believes that she can be weaned from it with little difficulty if she desires it.

Bertha's letters to her mother and other relatives are respectful and formal, with the exception of those to her cousin Fritz in whom she confided her deepest feelings.

On July 23, 1882, Fritz Homburger wrote the following letter to Robert Binswanger:

> Dear Dr. Binswanger,
>
> Your report to my aunt (Recha) concerning my cousin Bertha has arrived safely, and I am happy to learn from it that her morphine dosage has already been de-

creased by half. The letters from Bertha to her mother and to her other relatives are always perfectly lucid and cheerful, betraying not the slightest trace of disturbances. As she had promised, she gave me yesterday a confidential account of her health; perhaps the following extracts will be of interest to you:

". . . Being in unfamiliar land, particularly when having a taste of it for the first time in one's life, is not a substitute for home. As far as the morphine is concerned I received doses in the evening and the afternoon. As a result had bad hours from 1 to 5 o'clock, and could not bear lunch or coffee. . . . Since Dr. Laupus believed to notice a weight loss, he switched the injection . . . to midday. During the day I have really nothing to complain about, with the exception of the facial pains. Only in the evening the speech disturbance occurs regularly, and also the absences, which augmented by homesickness do not exactly help to make my nights comfortable. I seem to get through the bad hours as well as possible by rational argument and reading. At the start, I wanted very much to have Anna (Ettlinger) with me; however, Dr. Binswanger thought that I could stop the recapitulation of past times by completely forgetting about them, and this state of affairs could only be ameliorated . . . so long as I was completely isolated from everyone and everything connected with those events. Eventually! . . . the weaning from the morphine is so slow and scarcely perceptible. I shall not speak of this or of my not being allowed to receive a visit before six weeks have passed. I am perfectly satisfied with food and drink, care in general, and the medical treatment. I remain in company until 10 o'clock, associate with those whose company pleases me, retire whenever I please, in a word, live completely '*à mon aise*.' . . . I hope that I will not have to continue this life, which in the long run might become absolutely intolerable to me."

In one letter she expressed the wish to her mother, tactfully, but firmly, that she should not yet have a visit from her.

At this point I ought to mention that she is deeply attached to her mother, and loves her very much, however for the present—and for some time now—only at a distance. As soon as she is in her company a certain shyness and reserve is apparent, which perhaps has its roots in the fact that Bertha is very well aware of the inadequacy of her upbringing. She is also more attached to her brother when she is separated from him; he thinks that he has the right to dominate her, and has often provoked her by his inconsiderate behavior. . . . I should like to suggest that visits from her mother and brother be delayed as long as possible.

Yours sincerely,
Fritz Homburger

When the pain in Bertha's jaw became intense, her morphine doses were increased again. she was also treated with quinine and electrotherapy, as she had been at Inzersdorf. The doctors wanted to operate, but her mother intervened, obviously concerned with her daughter's well-being, but also with a "sang froid" desire to control her daughter and her treatment. In writing to refuse permission for Bertha's operation, Recha Pappenheim reveals her understanding of the relationship between Bertha's physical and psychological problems.

July 24, 1882:

Dear Dr. Binswanger,

Your welcome letter of the 21st of this month brought me your first report on my daughter's health. . . . As for the loss of her mother tongue and the absences you mention, judging from my own experience, I fear that these will increase in intensity when the present circumstances of her life are no longer a novelty. . . . I am quite convinced that everything is being done on your part to relieve the patient's situation, to make her disease tolerable not only by rational physical treatment but also by moral influence, and to bring about a final complete recovery. Because of circumstances of which you are not unaware, I was not able to hand over my child to you personally. Even though the pleasure of your acquaintance has not yet been granted to me . . . I ask you only to send me further detailed reports. You will certainly forgive this inmost request, when you consider that it comes from a mother, who cannot nurse her sick child with her own hands, nor can check for herself on her progressing recovery. . . .

You are considering the possibility of surgical treatment, as the facial pains can not be gotten at with electricity and quinine. I understand that you wish to make the painful nerve insensible by means of an operation. As a layman I do not presume to be able to judge this but I take the liberty of calling attention to the fact that according to all the experiences so far furthered, this neuralgia is not an isolated matter. Rather, it exists in close connection with the psychical processes . . . visible relief came always subsequent to the recounting of . . . earlier times and events, which were reproduced in a sort of dreamlike state, and with renewed brainwork the pain increased and was finally accompanied by the most violent convulsions, of which you have seen a pale sample during the morphine withdrawal. . . . You will understand that I cannot easily come to a decision where there is so much at stake, and that I consider it thoroughly, even though it is no little thing to know my child to be

> suffering so much . . . where Bertha's longing for me was only temporary and, whether if it continues, it may possibly be satisfied, I leave to your discretion. . . . The idea of nursing for the moment at least, would be best toned down . . . it would not be the worst to allow her to begin the theoretical course. I believe that upon a closer look she would drop it of her own accord. You have not mentioned whether her period this week was on time!

Recha's query about the regularity of Bertha's period was typical for the time. During the nineteenth century, doctors at asylums would observe a woman's period, its quantity, and the color of its blood. Menstruation, paradoxically, was considered both a purifying agent that cured and a breeding ground for madness.

The pioneering English psychiatrist, Henry Maudsley, observed that menstruation may become an important "cause of mental and psychical derangement," but also that in some cases, "a sudden suppression of the menses has produced a direct explosion of insanity."

Recha Pappenheim's almost belabored respect for Robert Binswanger reflects the exaggerated awe of doctors and professors that was part of the German value system and was compounded by all the nuances of a patriarchal tradition. In her next letter, dated October 7, 1882, in Karlsruhe, Recha wrote that she was frankly disheartened by Bertha's continued dependency on morphine and her rebelliousness. Morphine was obviously not proving a salubrious substitute for her "talking cure." Moreover, Bertha, in spite of the doctor's advice, was now refusing to remain at Bellevue. Succumbing to her insistent daughter's wishes, Recha conceded that a change of residence was unavoidable. Since Bertha had begged to spend time with the Homburger

Exercise and Arts Recreation Room at the Sanatorium Bellevue c. 1882. [Courtesy of the administration of the former Sanatorium Bellevue]

family in Karlsruhe, she would be allowed to stay there for a few weeks. Recha felt that Karlsruhe was a good halfway point to Vienna and that "Her own unfulfilled wish for many years has been to spend a few weeks at Karlsruhe . . . one has the opportunity of enjoying theatre, concerts, etc. without the noise of a large city."

Recha also deviously suggested a secret meeting with Binswanger: "May I suggest that we meet in Villingen . . . we have 2 hours in which to confer. My visiting you could cause Bertha some agitation, and this is to be avoided under any circumstances. . . . I trust that Bertha will not learn of the contents of this or any letter I may write you." During Bertha's entire stay at Bellevue—over three months—neither her mother nor her brother ever came to visit.

On October 29, 1882, Bertha left Sanatorium Bellevue for Karlsruhe, and on November 6 she sent Dr. Binswanger a letter of thanks:

> Esteemed Doctor:
>
> If you have thought of me during the past week, you have perhaps sought the reason for my silence until now in the belief that the whirlpool of city amusements had swept me away and had weakened my remembrance of all those who have met me with kindness and good will. This is not so. The court of Baden cannot be reproached with having such a demoralizing effect, and if I still failed to write to you immediately upon my arrival here, the reason keeping it has to be sought within the family circle. The purpose of my letter today is to thank you once again for the friendly, loving reception which I was given in your house. At the moment of departure, it was impossible for me to express my thanks to everyone, but particularly to Dr. Laupus, as I would have liked it, but I could not have found the right words if I had tried. When I consider with how much suspicion I entered your house and how sorry I was to leave it, then I see that I have gained, if nothing else, the conviction that there are many very kind people in the world. About my health, here I can tell you neither new things nor good things. You can imagine that a life shadowed by an ever ready injection need is not enviable. But I am glad to attend the nursing course, which since Friday, takes place at three o'clock every afternoon. I also have such good news from my mother and brother that reasonably I ought not to be homesick at all, such great efforts are made to make this a comfortable home for me. The theatre alone can provide everyone with very pleasant and delightful hours. Yesterday, by listening to "Carmen" I became in part fit for society, a process which I

> hope to complete in the next few days through "War and Peace." I often think of Miss Louise [a friend in Bellevue] and how sad it is that she has no telephone linking the theatre here with Brunneg [a house in the country connected to the sanatorium]. Since it would be too much to ask you for news of all those in whom I am interested, I shall wait until Miss Kreuser or Miss Hedwig [companions in Bellevue] send me some news; you only I ask to give my regards to Mrs. Dr. Sr. [Ludwig] and Mrs. Dr. Junior [Robert] . . . and all those who hold me in good memory. I repeat my thanks to you, and to Dr. Laupus, and remain respectfully yours,
>
> *Bertha Pappenheim*

Bertha's cordiality to the Binswangers, like her interest in her former fellow patients, is more indicative of her good upbringing than her mental state. By mid-November 1882, Bertha's facial neuralgia had worsened and she once again began spending her evenings speaking exclusively English.

Bertha's sojourn with her relatives in Karlsruhe encouraged her literary ambitions and exposed her to heightened concerns for social welfare and the budding women's movement. These three influences resounded at the core of her being for the rest of her life.

In Karlsruhe Bertha attended a nursing course and, in the evenings, frequented the theatre, concerts, and parties, which kept her very cheerful despite her continuing pain and whatever cloudy periods the morphine caused. She also acted in a theatre piece, performed in Anna Ettlinger's home. Her relationship with Anna, Fritz's cousin, and her milieu profoundly influenced Bertha's evolving perceptions of the possibilities available to her.

Anna was one of six daughters of the lawyer Vedit Ettlinger. In contrast to Bertha's parents, Anna's father had elected to give his daughters the best education then available to German women. Two of his daughters became translators of novels and Anna became a teacher. Anna also taught literature privately, produced plays in her home, and went on lecture tours. Although she refused all offers of marriage and had decided to remain single, she believed that in the future "education will help rather than hinder a woman in making a suitable marriage." Bertha read some of her fairy tales to Anna, and Anna advised her to forgo nursing and concentrate on her literary work. Bertha's cousin Fritz also believed that she should devote herself to writing and urged her to spend as much time as possible with Anna for encouragement. Anna and Bertha's relatives provided her with sensitive, serious role models and helped to counteract the prevailing theories that education, athletics, and the arts were not conducive to women's mental balance.

The Karlsruhe Women's Association organized the three-month nursing course that Bertha attended during her stay. The Women's Association had been founded in 1859 by Grand Duchess Louise, who was active in promulgating welfare measures. In addition to providing nursing training, the Association also established an adoption agency and embroidery schools, which were models for Bertha's later philanthropic work. In Karlsruhe, Helene Lange founded the journal *The Woman*, which several years later would greatly influence Bertha's intellectual life. Lange later founded the first German gymnasium for girls, again in Karlsruhe, in 1893.

In January 1883, breaking off her nursing course after only two months, Bertha spent three days with her relatives in Frankfurt and then rejoined her mother and brother in Vienna. On January 4, 1883, in a reply to Robert Binswanger's New Year's wishes, Fritz Homburger wrote, "as far as I was able to observe, I thought I detected an improvement of late . . . she was often in the company of my cousin Anna Ettlinger . . . and . . . will come here again in the not too distant future to cultivate her acquaintance with Anna."

Bertha was not to enjoy the mental health she had first achieved with Breuer for several years yet. Nor did she marry, although women of her generation often had arranged marriages.

We know little of Bertha's actual life in Vienna from 1883 to 1888. Indeed, what little we know is tied to her continuing bouts with illness. She was hospitalized at Inzersdorf four more times, her first stay beginning eight months after her return home on July 30, 1883, when she was again diagnosed with hysteria. Dr. Breslauer was assigned to her case and Breuer visited her there in early August 1883. By this time Dr. Breuer had become the friend and mentor of a young neurologist named Sigmund Freud. The two met while doing research at the famed physiology laboratory of Ernst Brücke. The Pappenheims were known to Freud: in February 1880 Sigmund Pappenheim had been appointed legal guardian of Freud's wife Martha's family.

In a published letter dated August 5, 1883, Freud confided to his fiancée that Breuer had visited Bertha and found her in an appalling state. Breuer was so disturbed by her disintegration that he wished she would die and so be released from her suffering. On October 31, 1883, Freud wrote to Martha:

> It will surely interest you that your friend Bertha P. is doing well . . . is getting rid of her pains and her morphine poisoning, and is rapidly gaining weight. This I know from a colleague . . . who is very taken with the girl, with her piquant looks in spite of the gray hair, her wit and her intelligence. I believe that, were it not that, as a psychiatrist, he knows so acutely what a cross is the

> disposition to hysterical illnesses, he would have fallen in love with her. But discretion *all around,* Marty . . . Breuer, too, has a very high opinion of her and has given up her care because his happy marriage threatened to come unstuck on account of it. The poor wife could not bear it that he devoted himself so exclusively to a woman about whom he obviously spoke with much interest, and was certainly jealous of nothing else but the engrossment of her husband by a stranger. Not in the ugly, tormenting way, but in a quietly resigned manner. She fell ill, lost her spirits, until it dawned on him and he learned the reason for it, which of course was a command for him to withdraw completely from his activity as B.P.'s physician. Can you be silent, Marty?"

On January 13, 1883, five and a half months later, Breuer wrote to Robert Binswanger, "I have seen the little Pappenheim today. She is totally healthy, without pains, or anything else." Four days later, Bertha was again deemed "cured" and released from Inzersdorf. Beginning on March 4, 1885, she spent four months at Inzersdorf for "hysteria" with "somatic disorders." In September 1886, Freud and Martha were married; one of their first visitors was Bertha Pappenheim. On both January 2 and May 31, 1887, Ernest Jones reports in unpublished letters that Bertha had visited Martha on more than one occasion, and that, while feeling fairly well in the daytime, she still suffered hallucinatory states at night. On the referral of Karl Bettelheim, a Viennese surgeon, Bertha was again readmitted to Inzersdorf on June 30, 1887 with "hysteria" and "somatic symptoms," and remained there for eighteen days before again being diagnosed "cured". Bertha was never again hospitalized.

In 1888, Bertha published her first book of fairy tales, *Kleine Geschichten für Kinder*, anonymously and at her own expense.

These stories are the closest examples of the fairy tales she had embroidered for Breuer. Breuer, unfortunately, never documented an image or plot of the stories she had weaved for him, so it is unclear how closely these tales resemble the stories she told him during her treatment. Bertha's fairy tales have never been translated into English before, nor have they appeared in German since their original publication. Amazingly, they not only cast tantalizing reflections on her treatment but hauntingly prophesy her future and clearly reflect her life history.

Of the five short stories, several merit exegesis. In "The Pond Sprite," the title character is drawn out of her pond by the almost hypnotic enchantment of the music of a country dance. As the pond sprite leaves the water, she encounters an angry, evilly grinning stone head. The sprite's yearning to "dance" is reminiscent of Bertha's guilt-ridden yearning to attend a neighboring dance as she sat nursing her father. The stone head conjures up her "death's-head" imaginings. The story, in both its form and symbols, is a version of the well-known Ondine story. It also contains the split of Thomas Mann's Tonio Kruger, in which the world is divided into those who participate in life and those shy, sensitive ones who observe.

Interpretations of similar tales of agony and of birth, death, and rebirth have numerous permutations in Western culture, beginning with Ovid's *Metamorphoses*. Both Bertha's terror of death and her yearning for transformation are contained within the images. The sprite is alienated from both the realm of the pond and the realm of ordinary life, just as many assimilated Jewish women found themselves alienated from both the male and gentile worlds, and just as Bertha herself was caught between the world of imagination and the world of experience.

Overcoming her shyness, the sprite hopes that someone will

ask her to dance. She stands in her "long white dress, with flowing hair in which drops of water still sparkled" among the rows of girls. A large, handsome man with a long beard approaches. His "dark blue eyes bespoke love and kindness." This portrait suggests Breuer; it is almost a perfect description of him. The man embraces the sprite, and they dance, repeatedly hurling themselves into the dance until the music stops. The sprite turns to thank her dancing partner and looks shyly into his eyes. He then notices that she has green eyes, "eyes as green as the reeds at the edge of the pond," and knows with whom he has danced. He shudders and flees. The sprite rushes back to the pond. While she was dancing, the pond has frozen over and she is unable to rejoin her sisters. The stone head mockingly laughs at her despair while, exhausted, she is buried by the snow. When the sun melts the snow, the stone head sees in her stead a snowdrop, the first sign of spring. The story is almost a history—a history and a testimony of faith.

Bertha's tales, meant for children, are also meaningful as parables and visions of adult desire. Bertha endured the deaths of a sister and her father, and the deathlike paralysis of her own mind and body. With the publication of her tales she underwent a rebirth of sorts, a self-transformation. The "talking cure" became the "writing cure."

"In Storkland" is a premonition, a prophetic dream. Bertha, as Breuer noted in the case history, was always charitable, and even during her worst moments, she was filled with sympathetic kindness for the poor. In "In Storkland," a young woman named Camilla is engaged to a young man of small means. He goes to seek his fortune before marrying her and disappears without a word. Years pass. Camilla feels she has lost her beloved and, more cruelly, now she must also give up her passionate desire to have children. Seeing the storks pass over her house as they deliver babies to others, she aches with longing. Mean boys in the neighborhood mock her with satirical songs about an "old maid." Suddenly she is transformed into an "angel" and takes care of other people's children with great gifts and good will. When the old Storkmother dies, chaos breaks out in Storkland. As conventional males, the Storkbrothers spread dreadful disorder. A black baby is brought to a white family and a white baby to darkest Africa. They decide that since "Auntie" Camilla loves all children she should replace the Storkmother. Camilla agrees with some fear and is flown to Storkland, bound by storks with swaddling bands. She is carried like a baby to be reborn in a new world. Camilla finds herself in a beautiful land, a velvety soft meadow covered with millions of little flowers and a grove of thick trees. She thinks that birds live in the low-lying branches, but on closer inspection, she finds they are filled with distraught babies. In the middle of the grove is a lake of sweet milk for the babies' nourishment. Camilla now cares for the babies. A year passes quickly. Both the storks and the humans are happy with Camilla's work. She decides to stay in Storkland forever. She always becomes a little sad when the storks carry away her charges, but she is consoled with new ones. The ending carries with it a hint of immortality through love. The narrator states at the end that "those who deal with children never grow old."

"Summer Snow" is one of Bertha's few stories which ends with a happy marriage. A farmer's wife finds a girl orphan, named Rosel, and keeps her, much to her husband's wrath. After the wife's death, their son falls in love with Rosel, who is exiled to the top of the mountain. The farmer doesn't want his son to marry a young woman with no background or money. He taunts his son with the sarcastic promise that if it snows in the middle of summer, on Peter and Paul's day, the son can bring his love home in a sleigh. Rosel, surrounded by flower-fairies, is treated with tenderness because of her goodness. And the most powerful oracle-fairy, Edelweiss, promises to help her. That night it snows, and John comes for her with his sleigh. Rosel and John are united and John's father's crops are ruined as a punishment for his lack of compassion.

With the creation of *Little Stories,* Bertha began making her "private theatre" public. Although she published the book anonymously and at her own expense, it marked a decisive transformation for Bertha. After the book appeared, Bertha was never again so ill that she had to be hospitalized.

Bertha had suffered from hysterical illness from the age of twenty-two to twenty-nine—the traditional marriageable years for a *höhere Tochter.* Whatever happened to scar Bertha internally during her years of mental torment did not disfigure her beautiful face. Perhaps the only visible trace of her anguish was that her hair had turned prematurely white.

Chapter Four

"THE POND SPRITE"*

It was a bleak February night and the promenades which surrounded the city with a bright frame now lay lost and abandoned. Wind stirred the surface of the pond and snow clouds racing through the sky were mirrored in the restless waves. Once in a while, the solitude was disturbed by a scraping in the sand, the muffled footsteps of a passerby, and a dance tune sounded clearly from a house across the street. Then the waves suddenly grew more turbulent and a little sprite emerged, her face intent with listening. Lured to the surface of the pond by the intriguing sounds, looking timidly around her, she met the stony gaze of a head carved into the fountain at the edge of the pond. It sneered at her even more maliciously than was its wont whenever she dared leave her dark home. Shuddering with fear, she again plunged into the water. It was not her fate to remain for long. Someone opened a window in the ballroom and the joyful tune spread even more insistently over the pond, drawing the little sprite from her home.

Hidden from the eyes of her stony observer by a cluster of reeds, the little sprite gazed her fill of the house, where swaying

*Text by Bertha Pappenheim. "The Pond Sprite" first appeared in a collection entitled *Kleine Geschichten für Kinder* (Short Stories for Children), which Bertha published anonymously in Karlsruhe in 1888.

figures glimpsed through brightly lit windows left no doubt that humans were abandoning themselves to the pleasure of dance. The little sprite thought how wonderful it would be to leave the cold world just once, for just a little while, and to fly through a brightly lit room, lost in an intoxicating whirlwind of music, led by a warm hand.

She forgot the dread punishment which awaited any daughter who dared leave the Realm of the Sprites and was recognized by man.

Moved almost unconsciously by her longing, yet still holding herself back, the sprite drew slowly closer and closer to the shore. Then forgetting everything, her mind a blank, she left her realm and whisked like a streak of fog over the street to the terrace of the winter garden whence the sounds poured into the night. She slipped in noiselessly, hid behind a cluster of palms and flourishing camellias, and watched the ebb and flow of the ballroom.

Humans eddied past her, beautiful and still more beautiful in their radiant colors and the feverish joy of celebration. They smiled, nodded, spoke, fanned themselves, and beckoned. It all seemed so incomprehensible, yet understood. For a long time, the little sprite stayed in her hiding place, unobserved. The strange atmosphere, the torrid heat, the light, the flowers' perfume, everything conspired to stun her, leaving her incapable of thought, prey to the one desire which possessed her in all its strength—only for someone to come and lead her in the dance.

She forgot how shy and awkward she felt. All of a sudden, she found herself, dressed as she was in her long, white gown, with loosely flowing hair in which drops of water still shimmered, standing in a row of young girls eager for the dance.

He was a tall, handsome man; a long beard framed his face in which dark blue eyes bespoke love and kindness. The sprite didn't look up. He clasped her in his arms and they sped away to melodies more beguiling than any she had heard before. Could this man possibly suspect with whom he danced? Did he have an inkling that she belonged to a cold, hostile world which she could not leave without punishment?

She danced for a long time, speechless and at peace, again and again plunging into the whirl until the last couples trailed off and the music finally died away.

When the sprite again neared the winter garden, she decided to gather all of her courage and thank her partner. She looked up at him and tried to say a few shy words. Then he saw that she had green eyes, eyes as green as the reeds at the edge of the pond. The man was overcome with shuddering and turned away from her. Now he knew with whom he had danced and the sprite knew that everything was over and done. She fled, hoping to return as quickly as possible to the pond, her birthplace.

But, to her dismay, she found that she had stayed with the humans far too long. For hours and hours, the north wind had raged in fury and cruel frost spread his icy blanket over the water. The little sprite was barred from her home. Now the stone head carved into the fountain had something to laugh about as he watched the sprite stray around the shore in despair.

She was so weary. The storm raked through her hair and the wind tore through her gown. The layer of ice separating her from her sisters grew thicker. With the gray light of dawn, snow began to fall and the little sprite sank weak and exhausted to the ground, her head cradled against a rock. Softly, the snowflakes drifted downward, covering everything and, as if with pity, the little sprite as well.

Frost and cold reigned for a long time. After many weeks, the sun began to regain its strength, and the snow melted away. Then the stone head carved into the fountain saw something delicate, a little green plant flowering near the rock at the edge of the pond: a snowdrop.

Chapter Five

FRANKFURT (1888–1899)

Bertha and her mother moved to Frankfurt at the end of November 1888. Frankfurt was Recha's birthplace and her family, the Goldschmidts, were among the most prominent Jewish families in the city. As a widow, Recha preferred to live among her tightly knit family than remain in faraway Vienna. She also believed Frankfurt would be a propitious new beginning for Bertha, whose last years in Vienna had been a nightmare.

As a Jew, Recha would have considered Frankfurt a safer city. In 1882, while Bertha was harbored in Sanatorium Bellevue, George von Schoenerer organized German nationalists in Austria into an extreme anti-Semitic, lower-middle-class German Liberal Party, which in 1887 proposed that Jews again be confined to a ghetto and restricted to certain occupations. Although he failed to establish a viable party, he formulated a pan-German ideology and elevated anti-Semitism again into a major force in Austrian political life.

Recha knew that Prussian anti-Semitism differed radically from its Austrian equivalent. In Austria anti-Semitism followed the fate of the consistent anti-Semitic policies of political liberalism, while in Prussia the politics of prejudice were a reflection of the vagaries of economic prosperity. It was difficult to be a Jew in Imperial Austria at the end of the century. In Vienna anti-

Semitism was not merely the cry of pathological extremists, it colored social relations on all levels. However, whatever ideological or economic self-interests differentiated Austrian from Prussian anti-Semitism, the experiential results were almost identically cruel in their treatment of the Jews. Prussian universities utilized the same anti-Semitic stereotypes as their Viennese counterparts.

Bertha had difficulty relocating to Frankfurt and continued to take trips back to Vienna and, perhaps more important, to Karlsruhe, where her cousins loved and inspired her. On a visit there in early January 1889 she played King Priam's daughter in *Holy Day Eve Play of Troy of 1463,* performed at her cousin Anna Ettlinger's house. Later that year she appeared in a second theatrical there, this time taking on the role of an audience member in the *Comedy of Craftsman.* In Karlsruhe she continued to find sustenance for her budding career as an author: a year later there she published her second book, again a collection of fairy tales.

Stephanie Forchheimer, a Viennese woman who had made her second home in Frankfurt, felt a special bond with Bertha because of their common nationality. Stephanie recollected how in the early days she and Bertha often happily traveled to Vienna, how Bertha, filled with pleasure and excitement, revisited museums and wandered through all the old streets, just to "scrounge" in the junk shops for her collections of lace, glass, and porcelain. Bertha loved to visit an old childhood friend. They would speak of the times when they had "both been young," and Bertha felt at home in the friend's comfortable old-fashioned apartment, which was beautifully furnished with eighteenth-century antiques. The difference between Bertha and her old friend was that Bertha was living in the present and the friend preferred to live in the past. Stephanie found Bertha Viennese in the essence of her character; her humor, grace, and exuberant vitality proved fascinating and endearing to her new acquaintances and relatives.

In the late 1880s the population of Frankfurt was 185,000, of which ten percent were Jews. By the time Bertha and her mother took up residence in Frankfurt, twenty years after its annexation to Prussia, the city's importance in European affairs had declined substantially: once a capital and legislative seat, Frankfurt now was second place to Berlin, the new capital of the German Reich and seat of the Reichstag. Nevertheless, Frankfurt remained an important center for European commerce and in 1888 gained a new, imposing railroad station that securely placed it at the crossroads of European trading routes. As a center for chemical and electrical industries, Frankfurt provided industrial power as the "second industrial revolution" swept across Europe.

Bertha, as a Goldschmidt daughter, was warmly welcomed by and socialized within an elite Jewish society, as she had in Vienna. The Goldschmidts could trace their Frankfurt ancestry back several centuries. The number of Jewish families in the city had remained relatively constant since 1616, when Jewish immigration was forbidden. In 1812, empowered by Napoleon, the local authorities granted citizenship to the descendants of these families. The Frankfurt Jews were more thoroughly assimilated than their Viennese counterparts since they had been in place far longer. Although the Frankfurt Jewish community flourished, its members, like Jews elsewhere, tended to insulate themselves.

Benedikt Salomon Goldschmidt (1769–1826), Bertha's great-grandfather, a merchant in wool, wax, steel, bronze, and iron, married Bella Braunschweig (1772–1813), and after her death, her sister, Sprinze (Sabina) Braunschweig (1785–1855), descendants of Glückel von Hameln, who was to have an important impact on Bertha's adult image of herself. Bertha's grandmother on her father's side, Katharina Calman, née Wanefried, was also a descendant of Glückel von Hameln. Benedikt Salomon Goldschmidt's children became prominent members of the Frankfurt community. They founded important trading companies and banks, and influenced the establishment of various philanthropic institutions. Thus, both Bertha's inherited wealth and her entry into philanthropy were paved by the energy of her mother's forefathers.

Her trips to Karlsruhe notwithstanding, Bertha gradually grew close to her large Frankfurt family and their friends. Most of her relatives lived more ostentatiously than she and her mother did, residing in grand houses with luxurious gardens, well-stocked libraries, and collections of contemporary art. Bertha and her mother thought it both more prudent and more noble to maintain a simpler lifestyle.

Given the long and perilous path of Frankfurt Jewish history, the prominence of the Goldschmidt family was hard won. Frankfurt was the city where the Holy Roman Emperors had been crowned. In the eleventh century Heinrich IV granted Jewish settlers in his realm special privileges, such as the remission of customs duties. At the end of the twelfth century, Frankfurt boasted its first great rabbi, Simon Kara, better known as "Shimon Hadarshan" (the preacher). At the same time, in 1241, the Mongolian invasion of Europe gave rise to a general persecution of the Jews. After a quarrel in Frankfurt over the forced christening of a young Jew, there was a general massacre and devastation of the community, which numbered about 200 at the time. In the aftermath of the massacre the Jewish quarter reestablished itself near the Dom on the outskirts of town. The earliest tombstones in the Dom cemetery date from 1272 and are those of women.

In the fourteenth century the Jews were made scapegoats for the "Black Death," and the Jewish quarter was burned down, despite Emperor Karl IV's efforts to intervene. Bertha's ancestor, the famous poet Heinrich Heine (1797–1856), wrote piercingly of a legendary accusation against the Jews that persisted at the end of the fourteenth century. The enraged populace believed that at the feast of Passover "Jews slew Christian children to use their blood in the midnight service . . . the Jews entirely in the hands of their enemies . . . secretly put a bloody infant's corpse in the house of a Jew. Then there would be an attack by night on the Jews at their prayers, where there was murder, plunder, and baptism; and great miracles wrought by at least one dead child whom the Church eventually canonized." These two destructions of the Jewish community are paradigms of the Christian cruelty visited upon them. During the seventeenth century, tensions arose on the occasion of the election of Emperor Matthias. A riot was started by a shopkeeper named Vincenz Fettmilch, and the Jews once again became scapegoats. Although the Jews raised protective barricades around the ghetto walls, the ghetto was pillaged on August 22, 1612. The 1,400 Jews fled and sought refuge in their cemetery. Fettmilch was eventually hanged and the new emperor brought back the Jews under military escort.

As in other German ghettos, a vibrant cultural life flourished in spite of the tight restrictions on the inhabitants. The Judengasse went up in flames again during the Napoleonic War and the ghetto dwellers scattered to various districts of the city, in spite of efforts to reconfine them to a new ghetto. Bertha's ancestors lived in the Judengasse. Bettina von Arnim, an author born in 1785, describes the awakening of her social conscience in the old Judengasse.

> On hot summer days I often made my way through Judengasse to the greenhouse to see the flowers there. I no longer go past the brothers of Nathan the Wise with timidity and bashfulness, instead I see with astonishment the narrow, dark houses; the teeming people with no small place to be alone. The narrow window frames were filled with the beautiful eyes of children, with chiseled noses, with the pale cheeks of girls, all seeking a breath of air. . . .
>
> How odd that they all must wrangle and fight just for their place on the earth; yes, how dreadful it is! There in the greenhouse, where each tiny bloom was granted its own place, I felt my heart become very heavy; I was embarrassed by the Jewish children, who . . . drank up the tiniest breath of fresh air . . . in that moment I foreswore the fashionable world of those who place such store by their ancestors, merely to despise the common people. . . .
>
> On my way back from the greenhouse, I took a great bouquet of all variety of flowers, rosebuds and orange blossoms, carnations and myrtle . . . and passed them out to the Jewish children. Are these not the very children about whom Christ said "suffer them to come unto me"? . . . and the young girls said, as they pressed their bunches of flowers on their blouses, "oh, this really is something."

Bertha and her mother lived together in one of Frankfurt's most fashionable quarters, on Leerbachstrasse, near the elegant Rothschild gardens. To Bertha's delight her new apartment lay near the recently built, magnificent opera house. The buildings on the tree-lined street were stolid and comfortable. Frankfurt was a quaint, lively city, but to Bertha the people seemed restrained, staid, and provincial. Frankfurt burghers were hardworking, with little of the Viennese flair for playfulness and frivolity.

But Frankfurt still enjoyed a robust cultural life that pleased Bertha. In 1888 alone, Frankfurt premiered Richard Strauss's F-minor Symphony, Antonin Dvořák's Second Symphony, and Johannes Brahms's Double Concerto, each work conducted by its composer.

Frankfurt was also the home of a number of literary salons, which must have greatly expanded Bertha's literary curiosity and knowledge. The literary activity of Jewish women in Germany first took root in the famous salons of Berlin. From 1780 to 1806, when the French occupied Berlin, sixteen salons were created, nine of which were hosted by Jewish women. No fewer than ninety-eight princes, diplomats, and avant-garde intelligentsia frequented them. This tiny circle of Jewish women achieved stunning success as mediators of "high culture and pioneers in social assimilation." In their salons they held forth with dramatic flair their provocative, progressive ideas about women.

Bertha grew particularly close to her older cousin, Louise, who was also her aunt. Louise had married her uncle, Marcus Goldschmidt, who financed American railroads, while living in Prague with her mother. They had two sons, who died as infants, and two daughters. Although Louise gave generously to charities, she never became an active volunteer like Bertha and many of her other relatives. Bertha became involved with the wide variety of activities in which her female relations engaged, including politics, philanthropy, the arts, and feminism. The Goldschmidts also had a famous literary relative, the aforementioned Heinrich Heine, and one of Bertha's cousins studied the piano with Clara Schumann. Through her family, Bertha became involved with philanthropic politics and the arts. While she quickly adapted to Frankfurt, she remained homesick for Vienna for the rest of her life.

As part of the rich leisure class, Bertha and her mother could have devoted themselves to social life and travel. In Frankfurt she was able to follow at least one of her passionate hobbies: horseback riding. She rode in the Stadtwald which surrounded Frankfurt. Bertha and several of her cousins gathered at a riding academy early in the morning and galloped through the woods to an inn owned by a former forester.

In Frankfurt, Bertha was also able to pursue her obsessive collecting of antique laces, glass, and china. To this day one of the striking decorative aspects of Frankfurt are the lace curtains which grace the sills, as varied in design as snowflakes. Bertha organized a small sewing club to share this favored creative activity with her cousins.

There is little documented material about Bertha's first years in Frankfurt. Her activities are known, but not their specific dates nor details. The portrait of Bertha in Frankfurt is, however, directly opposed to the fragile Viennese woman of her years of illness.

In Frankfurt, Bertha began to blossom into an activist and author. One of her relatives introduced her to social work by asking her to work in a soup kitchen. Bertha was a member of the Israelite Women's Association and performed her first philanthropic work in their community house on Theobaldstrasse, which housed both a welfare center and an orphanage sheltering thirty little girls. Until the establishment of this orphanage, Jewish orphans were confined to Protestant or Catholic institutions. The Union of Protestant Women and the Union of Catholic Women were in the early stages of their organizations, whereas Jewish women's charities had been created in the early and mid-eighteenth century. Because of the historical persecution of Jews and the inferior position of women in the Jewish community, they had never formed or imagined their own "Union" until the Israelite Women's Association.

Just before Bertha and her mother moved to Frankfurt, a wave of violent anti-Jewish destruction spread through the Russian Empire, extending as far west as Warsaw. Hundreds of Jews were murdered, wounded, mutilated, and raped; thousands were made homeless; damage to property ran into the millions. An eyewitness to the devastation in Kiev describes "the crying, shouting, and despair on the one hand, and the terrible yelling and jeering on the other . . . [as] the destruction of Jewish homes began. The mob, having gained access to the houses and stores, threw everything that came into their hands out to the streets . . . The mob threw itself upon the Jewish synagogue, which despite solid bars, locks and shutters, was wrecked in a moment. One should have seen the fury with which the riffraff fell upon the scrolls. The scrolls were torn to shreds."

The ruination of property was mild compared to the physical assaults on the populace, especially the rape of women and girls, "some of them ten and eleven years old, and the murder of children, including infants who were often tossed out of windows to be crushed to death on the ground. The perpetrators of attacks on women were not loath to rape mothers and daughters in sight of each other."

In 1888, the plight of Eastern European Jews became a concern for the Frankfurt Jews. The city teemed with starving Russian and Polish Jews from the ghettos who were fleeing anarchy, despotism, and pogroms; they escaped with their lives, often leaving possessions and family behind. The acculturated German Jews were contemptuous of these "backward" refugees. Some turned their backs on them for fear of being identified with them; others embraced them as coreligionists in need.

While working in the soup kitchen Bertha became deeply moved by the terror and pathos of the children who had recently escaped pogroms. Soon after Bertha began her social work, she started spending every afternoon reading to the children at the Jewish Girls Orphanage.

Bertha began to devote more and more of her life to the orphans. They became the most important people in her life. Some of the children were literally orphans and others had been born to unwed mothers. Under Orthodox Jewish law an illegitimate child was not accepted by the Jewish community and was often turned over to state- or church-supported institutions, where the child would never be made aware of his Jewish identity.

Bertha's kindness to the poor and sick around her, Breuer had noted, was one of her salient traits since childhood. Her empathy with the suffering of others continued during her illness, even during her worst periods of intense suffering in Sanatorium Bellevue. Her generosity of spirit transcended the noblesse oblige charity of her privileged circle. Although "social motherhood" occupied many maiden ladies of her time, Bertha's capacity for deep involvement with those outside her own class and family proved extraordinary. Through her caring for the stigmatized, homeless Jewish children she began to widen her sphere of awareness with increasingly superpersonal love. In the orphanage Bertha cherished her spiritual bonding with scores of a wide variety of abandoned children whose gifts, flaws, moral character, hearts, and minds she began to know intimately. Her acceptance and protectiveness of all the children surpassed many mothers' possessive love for their natural children, whom they privately consider superior by reason of blood alone.

Bertha read both known fairy tales, such as those of Hans

Christian Andersen, as well as her own stories to the children. She had chosen the genre because the fairy tale held both cultural and personal significance for her. During the late eighteenth and early nineteenth centuries the fairy tale was acknowledged as the highest form of oral literature. It was through the enormous efforts of the brothers Grimm, who published their *Kinder und Hausmarchen* (Children and Household Tales) in 1812, that folk-tales were thought of as serious literature; and the extraordinary success of these collections of provincial Germanic stories became famous all over the world, re-viewed in universal and archetypal terms.

The literary fairy tale of German Romanticism elevated the folktale to a level of intellectual depth and stylistic brilliance without sacrificing its original sense of simplicity and wonder. The fairy tale became so prominent a form that the writer Novalis termed it the "paradigm of literature." The genre was particularly prized by the Romantics because it allowed the author access to the inner world of the imagination as it unfolded in images, symbols, and spiritual events.

In Bertha's early fairy tales there is a pendulum swing between existential poles of a sense of fulfillment and a sense of emptiness, between coupling and agonizing estrangement, between generosity of spirit and spiritual miserliness. Throughout these tales the reader encounters a hallucinated convergence of the commonplace and the surreal. In terms of its prominence in Bertha's childhood, illness, and her fanciful disposition, the fairy tale was thus her perfect form.

Bertha intuitively knew the value of telling fairy tales to the orphans. In *Uses of Enchantment,* Bruno Bettelheim documents the necessity of fairy tales in overcoming childhood traumas, such as those experienced by the orphans Bertha tended to. Although he charts how these tales of terror and redemption lead a child to sexual and moral maturity, he overlooks the gender bias implicit in the majority of the tales. In *Fairy Tales and the Female Imagination*, Jennifer Waelti-Walters finds that most fairy tales condemn girls, who are seen either committing a smiling, lifelong suicide, denying their own nature, or having no identity whatsoever. Waelti-Walters interprets most of the tales as representing the feminine as a "lifeless humanoid, malleable, decorative, and interchangeable . . . who is inherited, bartered or collected."

Bertha's fairy tales take on much of the tradition of her era. Her tales present courageous women who take risks but are conventional in their relationships to male authority, reinforcing the stereotypical views of female figures. From a feminist perspective, Bertha's writing, both in style and form, follows the male conventions of the time. In Bertha's early tales, an unmarried woman is stereotyped as a virgin, a hag, or an alien. The boys and men of her tales all have significant, active identities against which the "feminine" remains the passive "other."

Bertha's conscious use of the powerful force of the imagination in fairy tales helped her become a healer for her orphans, as she healed herself during her "talking cure." "Once upon a time," opens up worlds that suspend space and time, where playfulness is supreme and the possibilities are infinite. Bertha knew from experience that reading these wondrous fantasies with her dramatic flair would be an exhilarating diversion for the orphans. She also knew intuitively that through magical tales the trauma, fears, and social alienation of orphanhood might be in the same way alleviated as her own pains and anguish had been.

Bertha not only enchanted the orphans with her stories, she also took the children to her apartment and showed them her family's collection of antiques and works of art, for she was intensely concerned with aesthetics and beauty as a form of moral education. She introduced singing and Bible classes. On the Sabbath the older girls were taught Jewish history and religion.

In addition to working in the soup kitchen, Bertha organized a small Jewish nursery school, sewing classes, and a girls' club. During this time she wrote a collection of short stories entitled *In der Trödelbude* (In the Junk Shop) that she published in 1890 under the male pseudonym Paul Berthold. Since authorship continued to be a masculine province, women often adopted a man's name when publishing their creative works. Throughout her life Bertha obsessively haunted antique stores and junk shops, where she found rare laces and antique glass for her collections and as a stimulant for her vivid imagination. Bertha must have often imagined the strange and varied histories of the objects she bought at second-hand shops. She must have daydreamed for hours in such places and in her own home as she gazed upon these objects. The orphans, deeply moved by stories of the objects in the junk shop, were encouraged to tell their own tormented life stories. These children, like the objects, were castoffs who suddenly found themselves in a communal life in the orphanage.

In the Junk Shop is framed by a larger story, also a literary convention of the time. The "frame" story tells the melodramatic tale of Franz and his love for a young woman called Eva. In order to marry Eva and enter her father's business as a book dealer, Franz gives up his studies to become a professor. One day, while Franz is in Vienna on business, Eva leaves him for a French count. After Eva's departure, Franz allows his bookstore to deteriorate into a junk shop. Franz recounts his story to an old boyhood friend, who pities Franz because he is surrounded by dead objects. Franz responds that the stories of these objects around him reflect his own sadness, and that he finds solace in their collective melancholy.

Nine objects, primarily domestic articles, then tell their stories to the surrounding objects. The ambience is that of a transpersonal therapy session. In lieu of the wild adventures found in most fairy tales, Bertha feminized and domesticated the form. These stories of defective, rejected objects are stylistically much more evolved than Bertha's first stories. The flight of Eva from her true love to the illusion of a fairy-tale romance with a count is evidence of Bertha's early realization of the distorted fantasies of women's education. These stories are not only a meditation on her compassion for the poor and needy but also a vibrant projection of her own inner life. As the objects magically come alive they compete, chide, and provoke each other. Bertha's renowned dry sense of humor warms these tragic tales.

This collection also parallels Bertha and Breuer's experiences together. Each object—be it a piece of old lace, a coffee grinder, a doll, or a music box—is overwhelmed with memory and propelled toward a "catharsis" through a "talking cure." Each object tells its story to the others, who listen and respond; each came to the junk shop with a defect. In the process of deep pain, love, and loss, these disparate objects are bound to one another and each is transformed. They become more beautiful and more meaningful than their unblemished counterparts. Each story is unique, but the mark of suffering connects them.

The nocturnal emptiness of the junk shop becomes a "theatre," Bertha's "private theatre," where the human is less powerful than the unnatural, what Yeats termed the "rag and bone shop of the heart." Superficially, the tales are only tales of pathos, but the spiritual power attained by these objects as a result of their suffering often moves toward tragic insight, or liberation from fearful illusions.

At this time Bertha involved herself even more actively in the Israelite Women's Association and began contributing articles to the journal *Ethical Culture*. As an essayist, Bertha was outspoken. Her primary concerns were improving women's education and rights. But unlike Lange, she did not advocate granting women suffrage on principle. Stressing duty and practical self-improvement, Bertha believed that as the lot of women improved and as they improved themselves, suffrage would appropriately follow.

In 1895 the director of the orphanage fell ill and Bertha assumed her duties. The same year, Breuer and Freud published their *Studies on Hysteria*. For the first time Bertha appeared before the public in her pseudonymous identity as the patient "Anna O." Her treatment by Breuer was described in detail, but only the events from November 1880 to June 1882. Though they figured prominently in the case history, none of the fairy tales she told him were ever reproduced. That her hysteria had not been sexual in nature was noted prominently in the text. The book was a medical landmark and was written with such grace that news of it spread well beyond neurological circles.

In Vienna, though perhaps not in Frankfurt, those close to the Pappenheim family recognized her identity. It is not known if Bertha ever read the book or even took notice of it. Although Bertha loved talking about herself, her family, and her intellectual ideas, apparently she never spoke about her own creative ties with psychoanalysis. When she was approached about the value of psychoanalysis, which was then becoming popular, she said that "psychoanalysis is to the doctor, what confession is to a Catholic priest. Whether it is a good device or a double-edged

Bertha with girls at the Jewish Girls Orphanage, Frankfurt.
[Photo © Juedisches Museum, Frankfurt am Main]

sword depends on the user and how it is used." In later years, when someone suggested that one of her wards needed psychoanalytic treatment, she exclaimed vehemently, "As long as I live, psychoanalysis will never penetrate my establishments."

Taking on the position of housemother at the orphanage was the turning point in Bertha's adult life. At the age of thirty-eight, she decided to devote her life to altruistic work. She was proud of the generous monetary donations her relatives and other Jewish women gave to philanthropic causes, but considered this form of assistance a "negligent charity." Bertha felt that the aid was without method and that the donors did not understand either the reasons for giving or the persons to whom their money was given. By becoming a social reformer, Bertha was a pioneer, choosing to work out of conviction rather than need. At this time she not only changed her way of life, but also modified certain aspects of her self. Feeling that she must be a role model for her wards, she began to live in a more austere fashion, one with which she felt her "spiritual daughters" could identify. One of charges, Helene Krämer, wrote:

> This period meant a complete revolution in her life . . . with total renunciation of her former habits—she was very spoiled in Vienna and lived the life of a *höhere Tochter*—she did justice to the many demands which this new sphere of activity imposed on her. She increased her manual skills, mingled with the children . . . and participated in all kinds of housework.

In 1897, two years after she became director of the orphanage, Bertha published an article entitled "A Woman's Voice on Women's Suffrage." In the article, she wrote that women were not yet mature enough to have the vote or to be elected to office. She believed that women needed to undergo a process of education and intellectual development before undertaking such responsibilities. Not without irony she noted that even men have difficulty in understanding the "large complicated area" of politics. Her characteristic insistence on a woman's need for self-improvement angered some. By now Bertha's direct, readily controversial style had become her tradmemark. Frau Stritt of Dresden, a feminist leader, wrote of Bertha's "well-known method of overshooting the mark." The same year Bertha wrote an article on Mary Wollstonecraft, the well-known English feminist, under the pseudonym P. Berthold.

Bertha remained a housemother for twelve years. She walked to work every morning, a thirty-minute journey from her apartment, and very often worked late into the evening. In addition to dividing the household chores among the girls, Bertha invigorated the institution with kindergarten classes for the youngest and classes in history, geography, art appreciation, and music for the older girls. She taught the art appreciation class herself and often took the girls on trips to the museums.

Bertha developed a new character trait during her tenure at the orphanage, one that she was later to idealize in a prayer—the trait of severity:

> Wind blows over the graves,
> Sunlight lies on the stones.
> Drop by drop, remembrances trickle through my thoughts.
> I lay a small stone on the beloved spot and, childless,
> wish for myself a small memorial stone placed on the rim
> of the red stone, with the inscription:
> "She was very severe."

Her demeanor in the orphanage was one of professional distance. Her loving compassion toward the needy, which she had manifested from childhood, had become restrained in its expression; she showed no favoritism to her wards and was quite strict. A legend has been circulating, however, that at the turn of the century she once thought of adopting a poverty-stricken young girl. A gifted ten-year-old prodigy pianist named Manya gave a concert in Frankfurt to earn money for her parents, which Bertha considered child abuse. It has been said that Bertha paid for her education, furnished a home for the child's parents in Vienna, and introduced them to Viennese artistic circles. Ironically, the girl became a prostitute and ended up committed to an asylum as a hysteric. This incident may have led Bertha to keep a certain loving distance from her wards and to accept the blessings of "spiritual motherhood" of many, rather than devoting all her energy to one child. Helene Krämer described her goal:

> To protect young people and to bring them up as proper people and good Jews. For this purpose it seemed to her necessary to preserve the utmost simplicity, in contrast to what had been the custom until then. Thus, the food was often too Spartan and simple, and we would have been happy for her to soften the unflinching strictness which she showed in her demands on us. When we would talk about this later, and confess our feelings, she would often and proudly say that her system of education was not a bad one, for almost all the children of the Women's Association had been able to find and keep a position in life.

She took a continuing interest in many of her "daughters," as she called them after they left her care. Some of them became her co-workers and others, like Sophie Mamelok, were inspired by her. Bertha corresponded with Sophie, who became the director of a home for tubercular children, founded by the Jewish Women's Association in Wyk auf Föhr.

In 1907, when Bertha resigned as director, she was greatly praised:

> Her great gifts as an educator and her delicate feeling soon forged links to the heart of every child. With maternal solicitude she made use of this . . . sympathy to develop and raise their spiritual strength; and to form and strengthen the characters of those who were entrusted to her care. With grateful love, which often showed itself in touching ways, the inmates tried to return the happy influence of the protectress of their childhood and youth. This heartfelt, grateful feeling continued undiminished, even when the girls had been long out of the home and engaged in some profession. The revered housemother remained their deeply caring adviser in all the changes and chances of human life.

Chapter Six

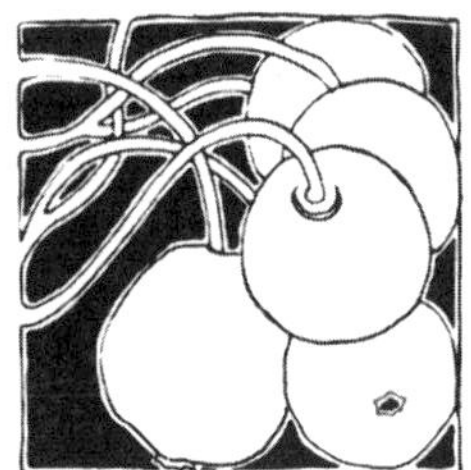

"THE COFFEE MILL'S STORY"*

"I'm sure that you all must be wondering how someone like myself ended up here?" the coffee mill asked, looking her neighbors over from the top to the bottom. Compared to the cigarette box without a lid or to the cracked lamp, she didn't really look so decrepit. After all, her brass bowl for holding coffee beans was polished to a mirror shine. It was only all of those dents and a missing knob on the drawer that bore witness to the fact that the inevitable passage of time had also taken its toll of this useful kitchen appliance. "Yes, ingratitude is all we can expect in this world. I could never in my wildest dreams have imagined . . ." With these words, the coffee mill choked with such heartfelt sobs that a guitar on the opposite wall, a truly sensitive and compassionate creature, sounded a soft whimper in accord. Heavy sighs caused the mill's crank to wobble so alarmingly that two old glue pots sharing the same shelf began to whisper between themselves that the newcomer must have some kind of terrible organic disorder. But a coffee mill who has been asked to speak and who has besides a deep need for self-expression knows how to get the better of such emotional mo-

*Text by Bertha Pappenheim. "The Coffee Mill's Story" first appeared in Bertha's collection of fairy tales entitled *In der Trödelbude* (*In the Junk Shop*), which was published under the pseudonym Paul Berthold in 1890.

ments of speechlessness, and so she raised her somewhat rusty voice and began to tell her life story.

"For years I led the most sheltered, enviable existence in the kitchen of one of the neighboring houses. I was under the scepter of an elderly cook who recognized my value. I was appreciated and that already says a lot about my life. I had a mighty feeling of being useful, even necessary, and that's the most heartwarming feeling anyone can have. Twice a day, with a smile, I was taken from my special place and later carefully put back. I was lovingly polished twice every week so it would have been base ingratitude on my part not to deliver those aromatic beans entrusted to me in the finest ground state. But I can tell you that it wasn't just my work which made my life so pleasant. My soul also . . ." The coffee mill halted for a moment and sighed so heavily that the guitar resounded.

"Go on, go on," breathed a perfume bottle, which had long ago lost its stopper. "The soul so fragile, so sweet, that's the interesting part. Who cares about ground coffee?" The coffee mill pretended not to hear this remark and continued her story. Her voice trembled self-consciously and she was secretly pleased that it had grown dark, for if she had continued her love confession in broad daylight, she would have turned red all over and there was no longer anyone to shine her clean again.

"Well, I think that I might already have mentioned that my place was in the kitchen cabinet. I stayed there whenever my old friend didn't need me, only I wasn't exactly all by myself—a mortar stood next to me. Believe me, none of you has ever seen such a mortar before: tall, slender, shining like gold! But what does a handsome appearance matter weighed against all the virtues I saw in him then, especially that voice of his! I once read the phrase, 'a divine tenor,' written on a tin of raisins the cook brought home. She had no idea what that meant, but believe me, I knew all about it! I experienced entire days of ecstasy, whenever sugar or pepper was pulverized. How I drank in those sounds and all the more eagerly one day, as if bumping into me by accident, he murmured, 'I love you!' Blissful day! From then on, I made sure that I positioned my handle on the right since his pestle stood on the left. And when he crooned softly during his tender rubbing—what bliss I felt during those sweet melodies!" The coffee mill again paused wistfully. Then an elderly horn, dangling from a nearby hook, stirred by a prophetic spirit, began the edifying hymn, "God Shield You from Danger," but since it wanted to give itself out as an antique, switched to the chorale, "Mysterious are the Ways of the Lord."

"Yes, you guessed correctly. I had to part from my beloved! Listen how it happened. One day, I'm not sure why, the old cook left and a young girl took over. I'd grown accustomed to gentle treatment, but my days of being spoiled were over. There were some days when not even the honeyed words of my dear mortar could allay my fear. This new cook was young and good-looking and, after a while, I found out that she had opened her heart just as I had; but the passion which ennobled my entire being had just the opposite effect on her crude nature. On a day when her fiancé didn't show up at the market or wherever it was that they managed to meet, the entire kitchenware had to suffer from her jealousy and distraction. Whatever she found in her hand, she slammed. Her hidden anger screamed out in the banging of metal pots; dishes went the way of all flesh; glasses clanked their death knell; and my mortar gave out such gnashing cries of pain that I trembled with pity and wonder. I myself still bear these dents and the loss for the knob on my drawer. I knew that this kind of housekeeping couldn't go on much longer. Soon a catastrophe struck, and I was the scapegoat. The cook received a postcard that made her as nervous as a cat. She took me down from my place a whole hour earlier than usual to grind the afternoon coffee. She sat on a chair and squeezed me with such colossal strength between her knees that I creaked in every single joint. With a grip of iron, she cranked away with her right hand, and held the postcard in her left in order to reassure herself about the time of her rendezvous. Then she heard footsteps. 'Good Lord, the missus is coming!' she exclaimed with terror, and before I knew what was happening, she crammed the stiff postcard down my throat and went on turning my handle, looking for all the world as if butter wouldn't melt in her mouth. You can imagine how sick I felt. I moaned and groaned in pain. I gave out the most horrible sounds until my insides were so jammed with shredded paper that I was struck dumb and motionless. That crude hand went on turning mercilessly and, crack, my handle broke, and I was useless. Then, that sneak of a woman stuck me back in the cabinet, so that my damage shouldn't be seen from below. I regained consciousness and only too soon became aware of my condition. At first, I consoled myself with thoughts of how the mortar was going to comfort me. I wasn't yet schooled in the deceitfulness of tenors. He was silent. He didn't dignify my suffering with even the slightest glance, and that very same evening, he began courting a voluptuous coffee pot. After that, I was numb to all pain. I didn't care what happened to me and I hardly minded when I was brought to live in this junk shop. My heart never could experience anything worse!"

"That's life," the old grandfather clock ticked away, and the guitar sounded.

Chapter Seven

FEMINISM AND WHITE SLAVERY (1899–1905)

Bertha's literary talent, feminism, and interest in theatre came together at the end of the 1890s, culminating in the 1899 publication of her German translation of Mary Wollstonecraft's polemic, *A Vindication of the Rights of Woman,* and her own play, *Frauenrecht* (Women's Right). Bertha's feminism had developed over the course of the decade, as she started to study feminist classics and assiduously read the periodical, *The Woman,* first published in 1893. She particularly admired its founder, Helene Lange, whom she had met in Karlsruhe. Lange was the president of the National Association of Women Teachers and the main theoretician of the German women's movement, which called for the right to work, the right to education, and the right to vote. To Lange women's exclusion from the existing educational structures and programs of study was doubly cruel because "These curricula themselves were male-created, the products of a one-sided male understanding of culture . . . irrelevant to the experience and concerns of female pupils." The idea of gender difference, or spiritual motherhood, remained the basis of her critique of male-dominated culture.

German feminist ideas struck intense chords in Bertha, yet her identity as a Jew created a distinct disparity between her world view and that of Christian German women. In time, she created her own campaign for the rights of Jewish women, transforming herself into the leader of what was to become the Jewish feminist movement. Her publications of 1899 reveal her initial exploration of this new feminist terrain, a reconnaissance preparatory to finding her own life mission.

It was probably in Lange's journal *The Woman* that Bertha first discovered Mary Wollstonecraft. In 1869, Jenny Hirsch had already translated John Stuart Mill's *On the Subjection of Women,* which provided a philosophical base for early feminist theory in Germany. In 1897, Bertha published an article about Wollstonecraft entitled "On the Women's Question a Hundred Years Ago." Bertha wrote that "with frequently recurring variations men and women have the same rights as human beings, and also the same duties: to teach women to be intelligent and to do their duty, then they will be also to share in rights to the benefit of mankind." In addition, Bertha writes that Wollstonecraft's emphasis on rights rather than duties "penetrated to the heart of the matter" of their disagreement; Bertha firmly believed that rights had to be earned.

Two years later Bertha followed up her article with a German translation of Wollstonecraft's book, *A Vindication of the Rights of Woman,* which she published at her own expense. Like Bertha, Wollstonecraft had been a rebel. The eldest daughter of an alcoholic father, Wollstonecraft earned her own living as a secretary, then a writer. While in Paris reporting on the French Revolution, she fell in love with an American and had an illegitimate child. The father offered financial support, but she refused it. She later married the philosopher William Godwin, with whom she had her second child; five months after the delivery, she died. Her first child, Fanny, committed suicide. Her second child, Mary, married the poet Shelley and was herself the author of *Frankenstein*. As historian Marion Kaplan intuits, Bertha would have recoiled from Wollstonecraft's radical lifestyle, but in admiration Bertha hung a picture of Wollstonecraft on her living room wall.

Wollstonecraft's book became the manifesto of both the English and American feminist movements of the nineteenth century. Her work was an avant-garde response to Rousseau's program for training women. She objected to his assumptions that man's nature and virtues were different from woman's. Rousseau identified man with reason and woman with passivity and sensitivity; for Wollstonecraft, denying women rationality meant denying their full humanity. Wollstonecraft argued that traditional training for girls left them empty-headed, frivolous, selfish—instead of good and noble—and barely rendered them competent to raise children. She believed that "it is vain to expect virtue from women until they are independent from men. While they are dependent on their husbands they will be cunning, mean, and selfish and men gratified by the fawning fondness of spaniel-like affect have not much delicacy, for love is not to be bought." Ultimately, she argued that this was damaging not just to women, but to society as a whole. Unlike Bertha's concern for the lower-class Ostjuden, Wollstonecraft did not address the plight of lower-class women, only the problems of middle-class and aristrocratic women. That difference aside, Wollstonecraft's critique resonated deeply with Bertha's own experience. Wollstonecraft wrote that the "most respectable women are the most oppressed. . . . How many women waste life away . . . who might have practiced as physicians, regulated a farm, managed a shop and stood erect, supported by their own industry. . . . How much more respectable is the type of woman who earns her own bread by fulfilling any duty, than the most accomplished beauty!"

The same year she published her translation of Wollstonecraft's book, Bertha also published her first play, a feminist drama entitled *Women's Right.* Both works were radical developments in her literary career. In the nine years since the appearance of *Short Stories* and *In the Junk Shop*, Bertha had transformed her "private theatre" into a "theatre of public events." In England, short plays were written by some of the suffragettes, but *Women's Right* is the only German feminist play written during the first wave of feminism. It serves as a fascinating counterpart to both Hauptmann's *The Weavers* and Ibsen's *A Doll's House*, popular monuments to the revolutionary birth of "realism" and "naturalism" in the theatre. As an inveterate theatregoer, Bertha may have seen or read both of these plays.

Hauptmann's *The Weavers* (1892) was one of the first plays to depict the anguished plight of the German working class and his detailed focus on their lives riveted public attention. Hauptmann became Germany's leading playwright and won the Nobel Prize. *The Weavers* continues to be thought of as the finest naturalistic play. Working conditions in the 1890s were so poor that Wilhelm II, Emperor of Germany, considered this play to be highly provocative. In Hauptmann's *The Weavers* there are no protagonists; all the workers have the same importance. The crises in the play are not due to individual character flaws, but to the cruel social forces that overwhelm the lives of the poor.

The merits and defects of Ibsen's *A Doll's House* (1879) continue to be debated by contemporary critics in the second wave of feminism. Ibsen's play focuses on the hypocrisies of bourgeois life and explores the suppression of women. Nora, the protagonist, discovers that her husband has always treated her as a plaything rather than a partner. As the play progresses she is forced to forge her father's signature so she can borrow the money to take her husband to Italy so he can recuperate from a critical illness. Because of her forgery and lying, she believes that she is ethically unsuited to rear her own children, and eventually she leaves her husband and her children for an unknown future.

Bertha's play *Women's Right* moves back and forth between the bourgeoisie and the working class, combining the individualistic critique of Ibsen with the social critique of Hauptmann. The play stresses the political and economic exploitation of women who, unlike their male counterparts, must also confront sexual exploitation.

The first act of the play takes place in an unheated attic, where Susanne, a poverty-stricken working woman, is unable to feed her starving child. Other working women meet with her to organize a protest; among them are two prostitutes who inform the police of the clandestine meeting, and as a result Susanne is arrested.

In the second act, Alice Scholl, the wife of an editor, tries to use her own money to help a poor, sick woman she has befriended, but her husband, Martin, who has control over his wife's property, won't give her the money. In the meantime, Weidman, a gambler and family friend, asks Martin for a loan. When he refuses, Weidman tries to arouse Martin's suspicions that his wife is unfaithful. Meanwhile Alice, to justify her request, persuades her husband to visit the poor woman.

Susanne's attic room is the setting of the third act. She has returned from jail and is fatally ill. When Martin appears, she recognizes him as the former lover who abandoned her when she became pregnant.

The middle-class men in the piece are irresponsible seducers of working-class women. Weidman spends his time as a reckless dandy, bribing poor women into meaningless sexual liaisons.

Martin, the seemingly responsible husband, is exposed as having fathered and abandoned an illegitimate child. Alice, the protagonist, fails in her attempt to use her dowry to help a working woman who was arrested for trying to organize others to fight for improved conditions. However, Alice decides to take responsibility for the child. Unlike Ibsen's Nora, Alice does not leave; she remains in the marriage but refuses to engage in sexual relations with her husband, proclaiming as Martin tries to touch her:

> I am supposed to go with you, Martin, and you can believe, after what I've now found out, that everything can remain the way it was between us? No! I'll go with you, but only as far as duty requires as the mother of our child and for the purpose of sparing my daughter my fate. I am no longer your wife. This is my right as a woman.

Alice's individual solution is balanced by the collectivist vision of Susanne, the leader of the working women, who declares early in the play:

> We have to help ourselves. One lone person can't do it, of course, not even twenty people, and not even the workers from one factory or a town. Everywhere in the whole world—in England, in Switzerland, here, and in Berlin—it has to start. The manufacturers have to be shown that they're nothing without us.

Moreover, Susanne despises the easy charity of the rich, asserting:

> We want our rights . . . when we're working ourselves half to death and the children go around in rags . . . then the ladies come with their pity and charity and ask us a thousand questions before they grant us a half-pound of potatoes. We don't need anything for free if we're paid for our work as is right. I demand my rights and the

> rights for my child—and for all children whose fathers forget and disown them.

German liberalism provided German feminism with its basic ideology. Resonating with the thrust of the male-dominated liberal movement, feminists emphasized the necessity of earning their equality, rather than viewing equality as something to be accorded them as a natural right. They stressed duties rather than liberties. In stark contrast to English and American feminists, who focused on the struggle for universal suffrage, German feminists concentrated on educational and social reforms.

Women's Right also exposes the discriminatory German laws. Until 1908 women were legally forbidden to assemble, participate in political organizations, or engage in any form of politics. Bertha's play intertwines themes that were to motivate her for the rest of her life. Her concern about the effects of poverty on women and how they are inexorably passed from generation to generation; the position of women as male property; the exploitation of women as prostitutes; and the agony of illegitimate children, her particular preoccupation, are all dramatized. The biting scenes, though sentimental and melodramatic, evoke the feminization of poverty. As a work of art, Bertha's play cannot compete with the technical skill of Hauptmann and Ibsen. It is not known whether it was performed or widely read. Like Wollstonecraft she published her work at her own expense. Still, *Women's Right* remains unique in German theatrical history as the first feminist play.

It is of great import that Bertha first received recognition as an author, not as a philanthropist. In 1901 she had already established herself as a writer. In a report in *Israelitischer Hilfsverein* she is referred to as a well-known author (*bekannte Schriftstellerin*).

While her literary career went forward, however, Bertha found herself increasingly active in another arena—social work. At the turn of the century social work was not yet a profession, nor were its institutional foundations set. Instead, a potpourri of private charities and municipal agencies, the latter as much concerned with maintaining order as with rendering service, co-existed with numerous overlaps in both personnel and responsibilities.

Bertha had decided to devote her life to social work in the late 1890s after a revelatory conversation with the deaconess of a home for young prostitutes. She asked the deaconess if there were any Jewish girls under her protection. "No, very seldom," the deaconess answered, "for the most part, the Jewish communities take care for their own people. Previously it never occurred to us that Jewish girls should be counted among the fallen, but now it is more common. And when we receive a Jewish girl, she is worse than the others, for it is as though she is possessed directly by the devil." Bertha was so shaken that she resolved to commit herself to the protection of Jewish girls and not leave them dependent on Christian aid.

Jewish women were not yet as well organized in their welfare work as their gentile counterparts. In a 1901 adddress before the Israelite Women's Association, Bertha stated, "In non-Jewish society, Catholic as well as Protestant, one already finds women of the highest standing from the preëminent circles of society engaged in these efforts with a degree of true sacrifice. It is greatly to be hoped that our Jewish women . . . might want to learn something from their non-Jewish sisters." Striking a new note, Bertha went on to observe that a "decline in piety increases delinquency." Constantly aware of the judgment of gentiles and of her proud ethical history, she lamented that "the growing immorality is bemoaned from all sides, and as Jews we have greater cause than most for despair, because a greater and deeper morality has long ruled in our circles."

In 1902, while Bertha was still director of the orphanage, she founded Weibliche Fürsorge (Care By Women), expanding her commitment to the welfare of women and Jews. She stressed that social work was the "duty" of the donor, rather than a "right" of the recipient. She turned exclusively to women because she felt that "men always and in every situation follow their private interests." She taught her followers new casework techniques, methods of child care, ways of finding foster homes, and methods of helping traveling immigrants. She instituted "Monday Meetings" where, as chairwoman, she would present a single case, followed by a lengthy discussion of methods and solutions. Bertha's methods were of her own creation and they quickly became a model for others. "Weibliche Fürsorge," Bertha wrote in an annual report, "has become a good school of Jewish social thought and practice and has attained a spiritual importance which far exceeds what bureaucratic routine can accomplish . . . and gives its members . . . a powerful rootedness in the interest of the Jewish and the political community." Bertha continued that "if one were to seek an artistic representation for this work, then it could be Jewish woman as the maternal guardian of the vital treasures of the Jewish community, braced by the rock of the commandments, and tradition, and listening into the distance in order not to miss anything in the great world." Johanna Stahl, one of Bertha's "daughters," writes of this period, "It was a long rich, and often not easy path that I was allowed to walk with Bertha Pappenheim . . . the sparkle of her personality permeated everything." Bertha told Johanna, "You shall learn to give your life a meaningful content, to stand alone with your own strength.

Early group portrait of Weibliche Fürsorge (Care By Women), 1904. [Photo © Leo Baeck]

And when you marry, keep a corner of your heart free, apart from your husband and child, that can be filled outside the family." In later years, when she had a truly illustrious career to look back on, Bertha considered the founding of Weibliche Fürsorge to be one of her greatest achievements.

It was as a representative of Weibliche Fürsorge that Bertha attended her first congress on the white slave trade. The year 1902 saw numerous public discussions on this issue in Frankfurt, which as a major railroad center was a gateway for immigration and thus a focal point for the uncovering of new social ills. In July, Frankfurt hosted a conference of rabbis on the issue of white slavery. And in October, the German National Conference on the Struggle Against the White Slave Trade was held in Frankfurt. Bertha attended along with another delegate from the Israelite Women's Association. Bertha's outrage upon learning that numerous young Eastern European Jewish women were becoming prostitutes was superseded only by her wrath over the discovery that Jewish traders were centrally implicated in white slavery. She later recalled the time when,

> although I had already been active for some years in social work—the word "white slave trade" first sounded upon my ear. I did not know what it meant, and could not at all grasp that there were people who would buy and sell human beings, girls, and children, for purposes which lay as far from the range of my experience as perhaps it lies from that of many of you.
>
> And the frightful fact of the white slave trade has oppressed and persecuted me. I did research, listened, and was told things, and learned something which added deep shame to the frightfulness: many Jews are dealers; many Jewish girls are sold. It was whispered both by Jews and by Christians. Jews at the head of philanthropic organizations did not believe what was said and spoke of slander! Among our people whose family life is considered a model of purity, could Jews be dealers, goods for sale, consumers?

Although there are biblical and Talmudic references to prostitution among the ancient Jews, the practice was insignificant compared to other Near Eastern peoples. The most heinous form of humiliation the Romans could perform was to force Jewish women into brothels, where many committed suicide. The "moral purity" of Judaism, which proscribed religious prostitution and devalued secular prostitution, is testified to by the lack of Jewish brothels in Europe until the fourteenth century. Jews, who lived in small, isolated communities in Eastern Europe, were relatively free from this "sin" until the nineteenth century.

Jewish involvement in both prostitution and trafficking in the white slave trade has its roots in the Russian pogroms of 1881 and the endemic anti-Semitism of Eastern Europe, which caused displacement and poverty. Edward Bristow, the major historian of the German Jewish white slave trade, reveals how through the invention and efficacy of the telegraph and steamships, numerous Jewish profiteering procurers went to Eastern Europe to take advantage of Jewish girls, who were anxious for a new life, having been abandoned by their husbands or drifted into prostitution, often because they had been lured into an illegal marriage. The victims of white slavery were taken to brothels in Alexandria, Constantinople, New York, Chicago, and Buenos Aires by men who claimed that they had voluntarily chosen this life. Bertha equated the voluntary nature of this choice to that of a "young foreign legionnaire, who had no idea of what he was getting into."

Bristow recounts a typical victim's story. Tauba Schiwek left home to work as a kitchen maid in an inn in Galicia. One day Israel Londoner, whom she knew from her hometown, offered her a trip to visit her sister. They took a wagon and stopped at the Hotel Rumania in Vienna. Tauba describes:

> As I was falling asleep Londoner knocked on the door and wanted to come in. I was only in a slip; I unlocked the door and he came in. I asked him where he expected to sleep since there was no second bed. . . . "With you," he said. "What's the matter?" He was very loving to me and said he would be as good to me as a father or brother. He lay with me in bed—and I was so frightened and so stupid, that I cannot say what he did with me.

Another typical victim, Feige Goldschmidt, a domestic servant in Kovno, was approached by a Mrs. Zipper to take a trip to London. Mrs. Zipper's husband was a notorious trafficker in Buenos Aires. Feige vanished. When the local Jewish Community tried to trace her, some people in Kovno were so afraid of the underworld's revenge that they refused to help.

Another problem for young girls who feared spinsterhood was the *stille chuppah*, a symbolic religious marriage performed without a rabbi. Procurers were able to court girls, marry them, and then coerce them into prostitution at home or abroad.

The appearance of numerous Jewish prostitutes in the larger cities of London, Vienna, and Berlin fueled the anti-Semites, who made a connection between Jewish immigration and white slavery. Enormous publicity was given to this apparent phenomenon in newspapers, and also in a massive body of films, plays, novels, and tracts. The image of Jewish white slavery was used not only to debase the Jews but also to argue against the emancipation of women. The "unclean" ones, as respectable Argentinean Jews called the white slaves, were so numerous in Buenos Aires that they formed a second Jewish "world" where they had their own synagogue and cemetery.

Arthur Moro, an officer in the Jewish anti-white slavery protest movement, wrote in 1903:

> We have positive evidence that to almost all parts of North and South Africa, to India, to China, Japan, North and South America, and many countries in Europe, Yiddish-speaking Jews are maintaining a regular flow of Jewesses. . . . This horrible blot on the reputation of our race, exists in most places of the world.

The association of Jews with white slavery was used as propaganda by the new anti-Semites. In the early 1890s the image of the alien Jewish trafficker contaminating Christian flesh was a stereotype of German anti-Semites. Yiddish writers themselves wrote of the subject, which was eventually used against them. Sholem Asch's *The God of Vengeance* (1907) was the most frequently produced play in Yiddish repertory. After it opened in New York, it was booed and closed shortly thereafter. In 1909 it was performed in Berlin; Bertha attended one of the performances.

The most painful portraits of Jewish prostitution were by Peretz Hirschbein in *Miriam* (1907) and Moshe Richter in *Sklaven Hendler* (1910).

As Bristow notes, however, the shame of the participation of Jewish men in the demeaning double standard was perhaps most skillfully captured by Jean-Paul Sartre in *The Anti-Semite and the Jew:*

> A Jew goes to a house of prostitution, chooses one of the women, and goes upstairs with her. She tells him she is a Jew. He finds himself impotent, and very soon is overcome with an intolerable sense of humiliation that expresses itself in spasms of vomiting . . . the sense that he is contributing personally to the humiliation of the Jewish race . . . in the last analysis, it is he who is prostituted . . . he and the whole Jewish people.

The Jewish response was to work on publicly combating white salvery. Bertha, along with many other Jewish leaders, wrongly assumed that openly fighting against a minority of coreligionists would keep the gentiles from racist stereotyping.

The October 1902 National Conference on White Slavery focused on the special problems of Jewish women in Galicia. The conference decided to send two women to investigate local conditions—Bertha Pappenheim, "a lady of sharp powers of observation and thorough training in social problems," and Dr. Sara Rabinowitsch, "a lady of great economic knowledge." Bertha and her colleague spent five weeks in Galicia. Upon their return each wrote up her findings and the two reports were combined in a monograph, *On the Position of the Jewish Population in Galicia: Impressions and Suggestions*. Bertha's half of the book, the descriptions of her travels in the late fall of 1902, are her earliest extant diaries.

Until Poland became a unified sovereign state in 1918, the lands that had once constituted the Polish state belonged to the Prussian (German), Russian, and Austro-Hungarian Empires. By the end of the nineteenth century, the Poles, along with the Germans and Hungarians, had been given the power of home rule in Galicia, which they shared with large Jewish and Ukrainian populations. From the beginning of their history the presence of Jews was an important "physical and spiritual component of the Polish landscape." Difference, alienation, and isolation are "linked to another problem of cardinal importance in the psychological climate of the . . . Jewish question in Poland." There were several strains of Jewish culture in Galicia. In religious terms, on the one hand were the assimilated Jews, who admired Germanic culture and language. In the middle were the Orthodox Jews, who represented the majority of the Jews in Poland. At the other extreme were the Hasidic Jews, who were totally insular, mystical, and intolerant of secular education or any departure from their strict and restrictive traditions, language (Yiddish), and customs. They did, however, accept their isolation within the Diaspora. Toward the end of the nineteenth century these groups divided into two opposing political parties, the Bundists and the Zionists. The Bundists, who were socialists and eventually communists, advocated a Jewish renaissance. They believed that Jews were not only a religious group but also a national community with its own language and culture. While the Bundists wished for a Jewish renaissance within the countries they had settled in, the Zionists longed to create a homeland in Palestine. The Zionist movement was pioneered by Theodor Herzl, who was himself a product of assimilation in Budapest and Vienna. In 1896 Herzl published *Der Judenstaat* in Vienna and in 1897 he organized the German Zionist Union, which was antagonistic both to liberal assimilationists and Orthodoxy's resigned acceptance of the Diaspora.

Throughout the thousand years of Polish Jewry, the anti-Semitism of non-Jews grew increasingly hostile. When Bertha traveled to Poland in 1902, there were three million Jews living there. It would have been impossible for her to imagine a Poland without Jews. Unconsciously, though, her writings reveal her fear of impending tragedy.

Bertha's report is also notable for its clear understanding of how social conditions were promoting the white slave trade and for the practicality of her suggestions on how to combat it. The journal *Ethical Culture,* to which she had so often contributed, took explicit notice of the report and congratulated the authors for preferring practical solutions over utopian ones.

In 1903, Bertha attended her second conference on white slavery in Lemberg, this time as a representative of the Frankfurt Committee for Eastern European Jews. This conference was the first meeting of Jews held on this issue and it solicited the participation of Jewish organizations thoughout Germany. As a woman, Bertha was becoming increasingly aware of the male domination of charitable and social work organizations. She was outraged by the lack of women leaders at a time when traditional Jewish charities were being overwhelmed by Russian immigration. She attacked the Jewish establishment for "underestimating the value of women's work and trifling with their interest by refusing to admit them as equal partners." In an effort to combat this domination, Bertha started a new women's section at the Lemberg conference.

She also became increasingly concerned with the rising numbers of Jewish conversions to Christianity. Her anxiety over this issue is illustrated in "The Weakling," a short story she wrote for a Jewish literary publication. The story's main character is a Jewish boy who is rejected by his father because he wants to become an artist. In an act of defiance, he converts to Christianity. However, he soon begins to miss his people and his heritage. One day he meets a Jewish woman who despises converts and berates him, saying, "Today, when we Jews are constantly under attack, Jews must stick together. . . . It is cowardly and dishonorable to defect to the side of the attacker."

"The Weakling" is Bertha's first specifically Jewish work. The story is far removed from "The Pond Sprite" and "In the Junk Shop." Bertha believed that the older generation of Jews who had been ghettoized were preventing their children from entering the secular world now open to them. She also laments the inferior position of Jewish women. The woman in her states, "I would have been interested in and enjoyed learning about art and politics if I had been educated and understood them. I believe Christian girls know much more about these things."

In 1903, Bertha's brother Wilhelm, forty-two, now a prominent lawyer in Vienna, married Ida von Herzberg, a widow who had a daughter, Marianne. The more intellectually gifted of the two siblings, Bertha always envied her brother's higher education. As Breuer had noted in his case history, one of the reasons for her illness was her lack of meaty intellectual challenge and education.

It is no small accomplishment that Bertha continued to educate herself throughout her life in spite of her continual self-doubts. Her inner strength and willpower, as well as her charm and charisma, propelled her into roles of leadership for which she had shown no ambition. Breuer had described her as "energetic, tenacious, and persistent; sometimes it reached the pitch of an obstinacy which only gave way out of kindness and regard for other people."

The year 1903 was Bertha's eighth as director of the orphanage. Many of her "daughters" left the orphanage and went into the world to earn a living. She organized a club for them and other working Jewish girls called the Girl's Club. It occupied several rooms at Fahrgasse 146. One room served as a library and another as a dining room, where meals were prepared according to Orthodox Jewish dietary law. The club sponsored evening lectures by prominent speakers on world events, art, literature, and social problems. Bertha did not think of the club as a welfare project but rather as a social group supported by its members. The small fees which the girls paid entitled them to express themselves freely and to send representatives to the board meetings.

Because of the enormous success of Weibliche Fürsorge, B'nai B'rith asked Bertha to form a women's auxiliary. She demurred, refusing to be a mere adjunct to a male organization. The demand for a separate women's organization was certainly there: the immigrants from the czarist pogroms were now so numerous that expanded services were urgently needed. Bertha was also concerned that some of the best of the Jewish women were being lost to the mainstream German feminist movement. Bertha now made a decision that was to affect the direction of her life in ways she hadn't imagined. She decided to create a

Bertha Pappenheim c. 1904. [Photo © Leo Baeck Institute]

national organization for Jewish women that would be equal to and independent of the men's organization.

In 1904, with several other Jewish activists she founded Jüdischer Frauenbund (JFB). This was the first national organization of Jewish women in the world. She envisioned an organization that would protect Jewish girls, extend modern social work techniques, and represent all Jewish women. She wrote of the meeting at which the JFB was formed, "The German feminist movement gave impetus and direction to those uncertain women who did not know which path to take. For the Jewish women most closely connected with social work, this meeting was one of the highlights of their life." Bertha's belief in the primacy of spirit over politics formed the basis of JFB. She wrote, "From the moment of the idea's conception, JFB was not intended to be a mere unifying of clubs and national associations; it was intended as a mission for Jewish womanhood in which every Jewish woman is to attain consciousness of her sphere of duty and to attain the spiritualization of the same." Bertha was proud of her leadership of the organization, which from the beginning had so many devoted followers. JFB was accepted as a member of the German Federation of Women's Organizations (GDF), which Bertha saw as an awakening of German Jewish women to the higher meaning of German acculturation. "The German women's movement brought the shy, insecure progress of the Jewish woman's will to sureness in its methods and objectives," she lauded. "From German, as well as from Jewish, women's lives, this confluence of two cultures cannot ever be imagined away or extinguished . . . for those immediately involved in social progress, consciously practicing Jewish women, the experience of this coming together was a high point of their existence, and was the psychological victory of JFB." A woman could become a member of the Federation by joining a local volunteer group. In Frankfurt, Bertha's Weibliche Fürsorge became the representative organization.

With the foundation of JFB, formally chartered in 1905 with Bertha as its president, Jewish women finally found their own institutional voice. The German feminist movement was mostly comprised of moderates led by Helene Lange and Gertrude Baumer. Small groups of radicals supported the newly founded *Bund für Mutterschütz*, which advocated homes for unwed mothers, contraception, legalized abortions, and state regulation of prostitution. These radicals wanted to launch political campaigns and propaganda that moderates like Lange opposed. Socialist feminists emphasized radical reforms for all of society, not just reforms based on gender. Lange argued that working women's clubs could join the essentially bourgeois movement, but not socialist organizations, which were barred by Prussian law.

The moderation of the German movement, in its attempt to gain power through accepted channels, was in part a legacy from its Jewish sisters. Jewish women like Bertha experienced a double inequality. They suffered from German patriarchal oppression as well as Judaism's cultural and religious prejudices against women. The highly esteemed practices of prayer, study, and leadership of the Jewish community were male monopolies. Most Jewish women accepted the dictates of the patriarchal culture and confined themselves to the moral upbringing of their children within the home. Historically, one of the only forms of outside activity available to them was religious charity work. In the nineteenth century Jewish women were involved with poverty relief and participation in burial societies. They provided the needy with rent money; bought coal, bread, potatoes, and milk; provided dowries for brides; donated old clothing and sewed new garments for the poor. Many societies maintained holiday funds for Passover or Purim. By the end of the nineteenth century, however, Jewish women began to demand greater control over their own lives. Many resented male-led women's charities. One Frauenbund member recollects: "The women sat quietly, while the male chairman read the annual report. Then they were able to nod their approval."

For twenty years, until 1924, Bertha acted as the president of JFB and she stayed on the board of directors. Her esteem grew at the helm of this organization. The members of JFB stood in Bertha's shadow; many were more timid and cautious than she. An energetic, battling, impetuous, and often belligerent leader, Bertha was the driving spirit and the dominant personality in this organization. Ottilie Schönewald, the last elected member of JFB, wrote, "In the hearts of thousands of Jewish women Bertha Pappenheim fanned the buried and often already extinguished divine spark of maternal responsibility, eagerness to sacrifice, and willingness to struggle for the highest spiritual goals. These sparks are united in our JFB . . . a flame we will pass on to coming generations with which we forge the invisible chain that fastens a life's work to eternity."

During Bertha's first fifteen years in Frankfurt, she transformed her sense of "double inferiority"—of being a woman and Jew—into a double creativity. In the theatre of public events she went beyond Germany's borders; she empathized with her sisters at the desperate margins of society and created social havens for the Ostjuden, whose crudeness and illiteracy embarrassed most assimilated German Jews. She embraced them with loving-kindness and sought to integrate them into German culture. In her private theatre she was not cured by either Breuer or the sanatoria but by her own relentless determination to heal herself. Through acts of the imagination, she shaped her inner pain and struggles into art. Her storytelling continued to be her "catharsis," a purification of her pain. Her art also provided a "catharsis" for her young, displaced orphans, who could identify with her images and replace their feelings of abandonment, alienation, and loss with thoughts of redemption. Finally, her art allowed her to take the pulse of feminism and combine it with her own increased recognition of social distress. Her play *Women's Right,* at once private and public theatre, prepared the inner space where she forged a great and lasting commitment to others.

Bertha's great creativity was her response to a patriarchal culture that left most women of her class with vacuous lives. The two major responses to the misogyny and patriarchy of her times were the flight into hysteria or the fight for feminist rights. Bertha is unique, for she embodies both responses. She made a momentous change from a bedridden, paralyzed hysteric to a powerful active feminist author and social leader.

The evolution of Bertha's life began to closely resemble the pattern of what the famous psychologist Erik Erikson has identified as "the great man theory." He shows that recovery from an early crisis and breakdown may give men of genius the strength to fight often futile battles in their later life. Although Erikson never alluded to greatness in women, Bertha's life seems to fit seamlessly into this pattern. His catalogue of the common characteristics of geniuses—a secret foreboding that a curse lies upon them; a tie to the father, which makes open rebellion impossible; a sense of being chosen and carrying a superior destiny; "a feeling of weakness and shyness and unworthiness . . . and a final settling into the conviction that they have a responsibility for a segment of mankind" are strikingly characteristic of Bertha.

Erikson's work focuses not only on the life histories of the great men, but also on the interaction of the individual with the overriding social themes of his historical era. The social work that Bertha originally started as a "dutiful daughter" was soon to make her one of the most prominent Jewish women in Germany and renowned throughout the Jewish communities in Europe.

The year 1905 saw one phase of Bertha's new life begin with the founding of Jüdischer Frauenbund. It also saw another phase of her life close: in May 1905 her mother died.

Chapter Eight

EXCERPTS FROM *ON THE CONDITION OF THE JEWISH POPULATION IN GALICIA: IMPRESSIONS OF A VOYAGE**

I know that what I say in the following will displease many; the Orthodox will find it too modern, the modern too old-fashioned, the philanthropists too socialist, the socialists to philanthropic, the educated too amateurish, the indolent too discomfiting, the cautious too incautious, and the adventurous too tame. To all their objections, I have a single response: I am representing things as I saw them, as I understood them. I could not come to terms with the idea of appearing to be objective at the expense of the subjective truth. . . .

In order to keep track of the order of my impressions, I kept a diary that allows me at any time to account for details that are easily lost from memory. What I will present today is neither a chronological listing nor a geographical accounting; rather, I have tried to group my impressions by content so that there is a clear relationship between the trip and my intentions regarding the same.

I hope that the act of writing down what I saw has brought me some peace. I hope that the agitation which often seized me so forcefully in the face of such misery, apathy, and neglect has

*Text by Bertha Pappenheim. Bertha and Dr. Sara Rabinowitsch wrote about their 1902 five-week trip to Galicia in *Zur Lage der jüdischen Bevölkerung in Galizien: Reise-Eindrüche* (On the Condition of the Jewish Population in Galicia: Impressions of a Voyage), which was published in 1904.

left me sufficient warmth to inspire the zeal of those who live in spiritual prosperity and have been born and raised according to commonly held moral precepts to essential and, I believe, fruitful action. I think that I will best fulfill my intention of remaining clear and synoptical if I organize the material in such a way that I first share what we found and observed, and then develop my suggestions. Above all, I must take care not to seem like an expert on Galicia after a mere five-week sojourn there.

My Austrian citizenship, my Orthodox Jewish upbringing, and not least, the profession that has provided me with ten years of experience in caring for the poor, were all a certain justification for my offering to make this trip which will not, I hope, remain without practical results.

Not everything in Galicia that appears strange or alienating to the non-Austrian or non-Orthodox Jew can simply be added to the list of things that are to be leveled by the West European cultural plane. One must take care not to expect things which are too contradictory to the individuality of a country that has distinct character in its mixture of German-Austrian, Polish, and Jewish elements. New demands can and should only be made where one is dealing with neglect or ignorance of civilizing factors equally indispensable to all peoples. . . .

When, for example, my companion and I are sitting in the parlor of a wonder-rabbi and as he is arguing against the necessity of schools for boys, a rather large insect falls from the ceiling and lands in the lap of my companion, I do not need to eat a bucket of salt in that house to form a fairly accurate picture of the spirit of its occupants, man and woman. The same is true with regard to the conspicuous characteristics of the country and its Jewish population, which we were able to observe for only a relatively short period of time.

I may add that we took our assignment seriously, that we observed eagerly and never lost sight of our purpose. As women, we were not only able to associate with the intelligentsia, but we sought and found opportunities to speak with men and women, teenage girls, and children among the populace. Many of their words and perspectives gave us insight into areas which would not have been accessible to a man and were essential to our understanding of the circumstances.

Nevertheless, I would like to claim for my part that I consider this report neither an exhaustive nor a scientific work, as I am in the position of being able to furnish neither. I can only say how I saw these things as a woman and, according to my impressions and personal interpretation, draw conclusions and make suggestions.

As concerns the physical circumstances of traveling, I must say that the great dangers which friends feared we might encounter never arose.

The journey was, nevertheless, accompanied by strain, discomfort, and sanitary inconveniences of all kinds. We suffered less from the uncleanliness of some of the hotels in the smaller locales because I always made special arrangements for each night's rest and energetically demanded what I considered indispensable. Male travelers probably suffered a great deal more as they lack practice in self-help. . . .

Naturally, I did find myself exposed to many things I was unaccustomed to. As a result, I learned to sharply curb my water consumption and became accustomed to seeing (Jewish) chamberboys carrying out the duties of chambermaids!

Rides on the local trains seemed endless. If our observation of fellow third-class passengers had not shortened the time on stretches, this dawdling with stopovers of anywhere from ten minutes to an hour would have become an unbearable test of our patience.

The carriage rides in cold wind and rain are not particularly comfortable because even the good carriages and good roads are bad by central European standards. But many a ride was beautiful as it led through newly green beech and birch forests under a purifying May sun or, as once happened, over charming moonlit hillsides.

The small villages along the main roads are a considerable distance from one another. The Ruthenian churches, crowned by three gray cupolas in the indigenous style, are almost the only masonry structures that one sees. Because their bells, usually four, hang in a separate, low, roofed structure, they lack a far-reaching resonance. The homes are usually low huts with thatched roofs that hang low over the small windows and doorways and are in constant danger from the flickering fires of every open hearth within.

Everywhere one finds standing wells from which one gets water only slowly—and certainly, for dousing fires it must be terribly slow. Their location near garbage dumps of all kinds sufficiently explains the constant presence of typhus in the country.

In the windows of the peasant houses one usually sees flowers, but I cannot remember having ever seen flowers in the windows of the Jewish houses which were either pointed out to us by our coachman or which we recognized for other reasons.

In general, it seems that the sensibility for beauty among the Jews seems to have withered under the spiritual oppression and the awful poverty of their daily life. The women adorn themselves with garish trinkets, but they do not make themselves beautiful. And to have any aesthetic expectations of living quarters which are so hygienically deficient would seem like mockery.

But even the synagogues, despite what is permitted by law, are devoid of ornament although one finds the occasional brass candlestick. In Brody, a veritable treasure of magnificent, old silver Torah crowns are testament to past, more prosperous times.

Scenically, the largest part of Galicia with which we became acquainted in our travels by rail or carriage was flat, monotonous, and relatively charmless. We frequently comforted ourselves with the knowledge that those were fruitful fields and good pastures that presented themselves to eyes seeking diversion.

The layout of villages and towns seemed to consistently repeat itself. A large square ringed by low houses in the center, market square with an open market. Often in the center there is some kind of public building or a small complex of vendors' stalls.

It is typical among the generally illiterate population that merchants' signs not only carry their name and the nature of their trade in both Hebrew and Polish, but also that, much in the way a children's primer does, they use pictographs to communicate it as well. Typically, a number of these images consistently recur and one finds scissors and a twisted tape measure symbolizing the men's tailor or a tightly swaddled child, looking much like an insect larva, announcing midwives, and so on.

The markets offer a very lively, bright picture with the farmers and their wives in the garishly colored jackets and scarves, the Jews in their traditional garb shouting and gesticulating. They conduct their business often in a rather questionable manner, so-called "pleasure deals," brokerage, transference of obligations, etc. . . . But we also saw many Jews performing hard work, as load-bearers or draymen, though only for a few hours at a time, and generally sporadically. As far as I could observe, they avoid systematic, consistent, physical labor although on the other hand they are the masters in starving. Their earnings are paltry, while the prices of foodstuff in comparison are relatively high. . . .

A number of women complained to me that there was simply no better child care or service personnel to be had in Galicia. But I think that if they were really convinced of the importance of these positions, they would be able to investigate the reasons for the inadequacy of the available material and to remedy them.

As most people do, the Galician housewives always seek the origin of the evils that torment them in others and never in themselves. In all the cities and villages I asked why the girls seemed so reluctant to take on domestic positions. Everywhere I was told firstly, that women treat the girls badly and pay them just as badly, and secondly, that serving girls are frequently subjected to seduction by the Jewish heads of the households or their sons. Consequently, a tremendous contempt has arisen for the serving classes—those individuals who expose themselves to such treatment or tolerate it. I, myself, could only observe that women load the word "servant" with a degree of contempt that is really outrageous. In addition, the living conditions and the standards of cleanliness in the country are such that housework actually has become a Herculean task, so that the girls' disinclination toward domestic work does have a certain validity.

The inadequate understanding of child care and the neglect of one's own household are regrettable enough where they involve the bourgeois population, but for the masses of the Jewish population who live in deepest poverty, they must be seen as the root of much sorrow, sickness, degeneracy, and depravity. . . .

But this so-called "usurpation of trade by the Jews" is so frequently pointed out by anti-Semites that an outsider might reach the erroneous conclusion that a large part of the Jewish population is able to acquire great wealth in luxury.

Aside from a very small number of affluent merchants, the Jewish petty-tradesmen in Galicia rank among the poorest people in the world.

The weekly wages of some fathers are just sufficient to buy the Sabbath bread and candles. The whole lifestyle of these Jews, who are referred to in the jargon of anti-Semites as "vampires that suck the blood of the Christian population," is such that no Christian peasant or tradesman who sees it could possibly feel the slightest sensation of envy.

"The stomach has no window," they say, and where all energy hasn't yet expired, memories of better times and of good family background (*yichus*) intertwine with hopes of better days to come, like two threads from which life hangs. The precious link which they twine are the children. If only these people understood how to make this, their only wealth, valuable for the family and for the state.

The craving for luxury among the girls is, when one considers the poverty of living conditions in general, possibly to be viewed as a misguided kind of regenerative urge. One of the most noble assignments of the future educators of the people should be to positively rechannel this energy and through education, to exploit and transform it. . . .

If people live worse than cattle (whose owner at least takes an interest in their well-being and flourishing, which cannot be said of anyone in relation to the Galician Jews) is it any wonder if the desire to earn money overshadows all other considerations until it becomes so powerful that it results in criminal abuse of usury?! . . .

Though the Jewish faith permits no dogma and no priest to

mediate between God and the individual, the importance of the interpretation of the laws among the Galician Jews, which could not possibly be understood by anyone who is unfamiliar with the Talmud, has allowed for the development of a kind of priestly caste which takes the most dangerous and thorough advantage of its influence over the people. This is terrible, not only because it cripples any stirring of advancing prosperity, but because it deadens the spirit of Jewish teachings. In Galicia, there are dynasties of these "wonder-rabbis" whose "enlightenment," influence, and livelihood are handed down from father to son and, when necessary, to the son-in-law. It would probably be an injustice, with respect to certain of the men, to represent all of them as swindlers, for we did have the opportunity to have an "audience" with one or another who did not seem all that bad.

We found all the rabbis' wives, the "Rebbetzen," to be far more intelligent than the men in their Talmudic wisdom. Their interaction with the public in their husbands' anterooms seems to have made them smarter and more worldly. This was evident particularly in their understanding of our mission's importance to the country and the people. A number of the women, in the characteristic headdress that covers the hair and crowns the forehead with a pearl tiara, look quite distinguished.

The miracles the rabbis perform usually consist of providing medical, business, or legal advice which, if effective, is simply the product of a routine familiarity with affairs or psychological or suggestive clues. That some of these wonder-rabbis have agents who go about promoting their miracles on the trains, in restaurants, and in the marketplace is a business trick that arises from competition and has a counterpart in modern advertising.

However, not all of them are as successful at acquiring riches as the result of the superstition and the limitations of their followers as the gentlemen of Chortkov, Sadogora, Belzhetz and others are. They also allow their influence to come into play in the political arena by influencing elections. Many of the wonder-rabbis are poor and remain so, forced to carry their wisdom to market in exchange for a scrawny stewing chicken.

When one considers the bleakness of the Galician Jews' lives, their physical and spiritual privation, and how embittered or closed off they are from all that which gives human beings hope and causes them to strive and enjoy—God, fatherland, science, art, prosperity—is it surprising if they greedily seize cheer on an idea that promises them freedom? Freedom to live in a country of their own as citizens, no longer to have to be stepped on and despised, and to enjoy life as other people do?

Zionism provides such an idea. Added to its freeing and invigorating aspects is the greatness and power of the idea. If the Zionists truly honored what Zionism promises, then it would be a blessing for the Jewish people.

Naturally, it would be wonderful to give Jews a land of their own. But with conditions among the people what they are today, these people cannot as yet live as a nation. They cannot work and lack even sufficient maturity to understand what they have yet to learn. The individual must not only learn how to perform physical labor, he must learn to accommodate himself to progress. . . .

The position of the woman in a culture can explain the position of a people among other people. I think it is no coincidence that in America, that land of advanced freedom for women, Jewish men have found the courage to intervene on behalf of their fellow-believers in Russia.

Zionist women should not be satisfied with invoking the spirit of ancient, historical Jewish heroines and attempting to revive it. The modern age demands modern women with abilities and power to accommodate themselves to the current state of social development and to follow the forward surge of progress.

It would be a thankful task for women's organizations in Galicia to make it their goal to teach the country's daughters through actions, and not to flatter and deceive them about important facts. There are a few organizations, like the "Rachela" in Stanislaw, which take care of a small number of children but only for the Zionist ends. In addition to those, there are some Reform Cheders, or Hebrew schools operated by Zionists, which compared to the other Cheders, promote good things and deserve to be recognized and supported as schools.

Maybe history will recognize Zionism as the fanfare that awakened their sleeping spirits and caused the Jews to unite and to fall in step with other peoples in doing their duty and claiming their rights. If so, Zionism will have fulfilled a great purpose, even if the founding of a Jewish state remains a utopia.

I hope that the Jewish Zweigkommittee zur Bekämpfung des Mädchenhandels (Branch Committee to Combat the White Slave Trade) will understand why I have arrived at a subject so late in my report that I, as a delegate of this organization, perhaps should have discussed in the first place.

Since it is not possible to fairly address the question of a country's morality if one is unfamiliar with the conditions and prevailing circumstances there, it was necessary to first describe the soil in which such sad moral conditions can take root. Lack of education, income opportunities, poverty, frightening living conditions, laxity or dishonesty in religious matters; once these are understood, one can only conclude that they are the cause of the morality question.

Anyone who expects, however, that I will flavor this most

important part of my report with spicy tidbits, will be disappointed.

Not even my short visit to a number of public houses in Cracow provided anything that could be considered sensational in this regard. But it is precisely the matter-of-factness with which all classes of the population speak of the presence and the "necessary" expansion of this immoral profession, and their thoughtless and uncritical judgment of the same, that poses a terrible danger for society.

The number of public houses is very large; that their owners and inhabitants are usually Jewish, i.e. Jewesses, is widely known. . . .

In Galicia one thing is obvious: neither the brothels nor the while slave trade will have the same kind of corrupting influence on the population as the widespread secret prostitution that contaminates this country. In evaluating the situation, it is important to note that it is not just poverty and seduction that push girls to sell their bodies. I was repeatedly told, especially by medical sources, that a frighteningly high number of women and girls from "better" families—those who have no need of an income, not to mention an additional income—have access to secret, extramarital intercourse. These are not women and girls who have been somehow "infected" by modern and emancipated ideas. They are women and girls who live ultra-orthodox lives, who keep the Sabbath, who observe the food laws and other ritual commandments with great fear, but are completely unprincipled in regard to morality.

This contradiction can only be explained by the fact that the rituals become useless as soon as their spiritual meaning is lost and that clinging to empty rituals leads directly to lies and hypocrisy. Regrettably, this contradiction has frequently led to the assumption that there are certain passages in the exposition of Jewish law which endorse a casual view of sexual intercourse. In response, it must be emphatically stated that the laws of the Halachah as well as the Kabbala strictly condemn any intercourse that does not lead directly to procreation.

For millennia Jews viewed the woman solely as a sexual object. As there has never been any value attached to mutual affection or the wife's spiritual inclusion in her husband's life, devotion has never had a truly sensual or spiritual appeal. Consequently, a certain apathy in sexual matters has taken root among Jewish women.

Further, because Jewish women are uneducated, their spirit and often lively imagination are cut off from all healthful nourishment, hence they have no room to grow outside the physical self. As a result one sees their fantasy literally forced onto paths that eventually lead to corruption.

The final and certainly most important factor that explains this condition is, in my opinion, boredom, which cannot be adequately explained by social or religious causes.

The lives of women and teenage girls in Galicia who do not have to earn a living in the most oppressive and shameful ways are bleak. They are devoid of stimulation or any kind of interest. The complete devotion to domestic affairs, which was once and still frequently is common among German housewives, has disappeared in the Polish households, both Christian and Jewish. And there are no other financial, philanthropic, scientific, or political interests that might take its place.

This lot of physically and intellectually lazy women, who are chattel in the lowest sense of the word—girls who only wait to "make a good match" and succumb to sexual devaluation—have their counterpart in another lot of idlers: the soldiers, the small-town bureaucrats, and the youth, zealous in Talmudic studies.

Both sides need and seek amusement and diversion. They find it, too, to their own detriment as well as to the detriment of the commonweal. An example of the influence education and work can have, as opposed to ignorance and idleness, can be seen in Borislaw.

There are no groups of women standing around there gossiping while men lounge about doing nothing. Everyone works: Christians and Jews, men and women, belowground and aboveground.

There are things for which, in individual cases, there theoretically should be no excuse. But if they recur and become increasingly common, one comes to see that they are symptoms of a larger condition and then their causes can to a degree excuse them.

Besides boredom, a kind of excuse for this mass of morally misguided individuals is their total ignorance of the physical consequences of these moral transgressions. During our trip, we frequently sought to discover how widespread this ignorance was in certain circles. Often, we discovered, it was total.

Instructive in this regard was the agitated reaction of a group of women in a small town upon hearing what information we provided regarding the moral and physical consequences of certain behavior. That is not to say that professional procurers, pimps, dealers, and brothel owners are unaware of these factors when they exploit the women. But the girls do not know what lies ahead of them, and even those parents who have a lax interpretation of morality have no idea of the extent of the physical damage (which often reaches into the third and fourth generation) that can ensue when they allow their daughters to make themselves up and "walk the streets."

Just how much of a distance there is between an amusing affair, whose charm quickly becomes indispensable, and a second one that will be followed by any number of other transgressions, is only a matter of circumstance.

In some cases it is the fear of parents or employers, in others an unwanted pregnancy, fear of abandonment and injured pride, or an inability to find an inner strength to enable them to leave the trodden path, that causes women to move from secret into open prostitution. Usually they go away, as far as possible from home.

It is precisely these girls who are the most likely victims of the white slave trade in its various forms.

The assumption that the white slave trade is popularly sanctioned is false, even if there are instances where parents and procurers collude. It is just that there are innumerable factors which conspire in this unhappy country to create all manner of corrupt institutions.

In the wonder-rabbis' "antechambers," under the gateways, at the bread seller's, and other places where the gossipmongers gather, stories of the white slave trade are exchanged with horror. Unfortunately, the horror usually comes too late and people lack the clarity to abstract certain truths from these stories and apply them to themselves.

The existence of the white slave trade is directly related to emigration that, in Galicia, is impossible to prevent. When a country can no longer feed its people, massive emigration is inevitable. The Jewish intelligentsia, helpless in the face of a steadily growing population and increasing misery, supports this "evacuation of the country."

The people have no concept of geography. Since she does not know whether America is a city in the vicinity of London or how long it will take to reach a certain destination, and since, not being able to read or write, she cannot depend on letters or news to ascertain whether something is actually true or not, every girl who emigrates, i.e., leaves her hometown, is a potential victim of all sorts of unfortunate circumstances or evils.

The girls' unwillingness to engage in consistent labor and their ignorance of any languages other than a jargon [Yiddish] and bad Polish, directly prevent them from getting good jobs. They are most attracted by positions as waitresses, peddlers, and minor sales clerks, which allow them to retain certain irregular lifestyle habits and remove them from any direct supervision and decent familial connection.

I have never seen drunken Jews in the streets, with the exception of a beggar who lurched along the street in Dukla, primarily because his robe was made up of so many tattered rags that the original fabric was no longer distinguishable. This man was one of those many apparitions that made me regret that I had neither a pencil nor a Kodak at hand. . . .

But the country is not weak, it is only weakened and cannot pull itself up alone. Help has to come from outside. And the first step has already been taken: more people have begun to take an interest in Galicia.

Whether their interest is egoistic or altruistic is, objectively speaking, irrelevant. Attitudes can change with the passage of time. Whoever takes an egoistic interest in Galicia today out of fear that the dreaded Polacks might leave their country in ever greater numbers and make him uncomfortable by settling in a place that is clean and dear to his heart, can do as much to prevent this calamity as another who, inspired by altruism, desires to provide some assistance to this suffering mass of sinking, but intelligent people. And it is not inconceivable that the work itself might transform egoists into altruists.

I think the decision to contract Dr. Rabinowitsch and myself to undertake this investigative journey resulted from a combination of such views and feelings.

Chapter Nine

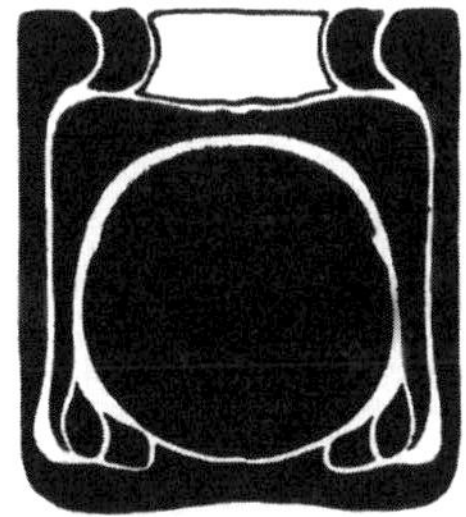

FROM SPIRITUAL MOTHERHOOD TO MATRIARCH (1905–1910)

Bertha's mother died in 1905 at the age of seventy-five, when Bertha was forty-six. Recha's health had been failing for several years, and since Bertha was now spending much of her time at the orphanage, she had hired Selma Flies as a live-in companion to care for her mother. Recha was "a Goldschmidt in every way," Selma commented. There was a confusing mixture in Recha's personality: she could be both subtly dominating as a grande dame and matriarch and also warm and charming. At times she would retreat into a restrained sadness and withdraw from all contact. Although Breuer noted young Bertha's "disturbed relationship" with her mother and Ernest Jones later described Recha as a "dragon lady," mother and daughter had lived peacefully together for seventeen years. Since Bertha never married or had her own children, she remained at home with her mother, as was customary for maiden women.

Recha's funeral was simple, attended mostly by relatives. Bertha buried her mother in the Old Jewish Cemetery in Frankfurt. The tombstones surrounding her mother's grave are those of their relatives and friends: the Warburgs, the Rothschilds, the Goldschmidt-Rothschilds. Bertha arranged for a simple marble headstone engraved with the years 1830–1905. Bertha's father was buried in faraway Pressburg and Bertha's two sisters were

Bertha's parents' Biedermeyer chest c. 1905.
[Photo © Leo Baeck Institute)

buried in Vienna. The family was strangely scattered in death. On March 7, 1933, at the age of seventy-six and slowly nearing her own death, Bertha wrote a prayer for her mother:

> Next to your grave, Mother, lies the piece of earth Which is unconditionally mine. My right to this piece of earth goes back for generations. Purely, I shall preserve my claim upon it, with peace and silence each at its own time in the service of the community.
>
> That I may retain the strength to make this honest claim upon this little piece of earth beside your grave, Mother, in peace and silence and action as long as I breathe.

After her mother's death Bertha grew depressed, but there are no accounts indicating that she regressed into the hysterical pain

Bertha's parents' bed c. 1905. [Photo © Leo Baeck Institute]

of her young womanhood. In fact, she began to function with a new, deeper, and greater vision of her social mission.

Finding herself alone, Bertha moved from Leerbachstrasse to a smaller apartment on Feldbergstrasse, closer to her beloved cousin Louise. Every time she moved, Bertha took all of her treasured family antiques with her. She was especially attached to a black Biedermeier chest that displayed her father's gold-and-silver wine goblets. She also greatly treasured her parents' antique canopied bed, in which she slept. The headboard of the bed was carved with the year 1705, a Christian cross, the sun, and the Latin letters I.H.S., representing Jesus. In contrast to the Spartan tastes so evident in the decor of the orphanage, her own environment was resplendent with beautiful objets d'art. Her quarters were filled with her collections of delicate wrought iron, famous lace, and antique glass. Bertha's refined aesthetic sensibility permeated every aspect of her being. Her love of natural and artistic beauty was so passionate that it calls to mind Plotinus' doctrine that beauty is the earthly emanation of divine good. She found evenings at the opera and musical concerts to be transcendent experiences. She took almost obsessive care of her decor, just as she prided herself on her graceful gestures and majestic politesse. Even her outbursts of righteous anger were framed by an acerbic wit.

Free to travel without worries about her dying mother, Bertha courageously set off by herself. She went to Russia in 1905 and 1906 in search of destitute and abandoned women and children. The worst pogroms of this era occurred in Kishinev, in Bessarabia, in 1903 and 1905. The unspeakable viciousness of these pogroms foreshadows the atrocities of the Holocaust. An eyewitness recounts:

> In the course of the entire day of April 7 . . . Kishinev was the scene of bestialities such as find few parallels even in the history of the most barbarous ages. . . . Many Jewish families hid themselves in their cellars, or in their garrets . . . but the murderers succeeded in hunting down their unfortunate victims. The Jews were slain in the most barbarous fashion. Many of them were not killed at once, but were left writhing in pre-mortal agonies. Some had nails driven into their heads or had their eyes put out. Little children were thrown from garrets to the pavement, and their brains dashed out upon the stones. Women had their stomachs ripped open or their breasts cut off. Many of them became victims of rape. One . . . pupil . . . threw himself upon them. He himself was slain, and his mother's eyes were put out.

This barbarous behavior was condoned by the majority of Russians, who made no attempt to defend the Jews. In fact, the "enlightened" public—officials with their wives and children, students, lawyers, and physicians—strolled leisurely through the streets, "while the terrible 'work' was going on." Although the majority of German Jews turned their backs on the Ostjuden émigrés, protecting their own tenuous assimilation, or helped them from a safe distance with financial aid, Bertha opened her heart and intimately embraced the shattered children of her Eastern Jewish sisters. In Kiev, after a barbarous massacre, she wrote a poem expressing her desire to awaken the consciousness of Jewish mothers:

Cruel mothers!
Do you see the shadows which gather round your house?
They are not men, though they look like men,
They are full of envy,
For you are of the tribe who believed
In one God, when they knew only idols
They despoiled us of our wisdom
And called us despoilers.
Mothers, the shadows are gathering fast.
They are taking the bestial form of barbarism,
They murder, they burn with savage joy.
Mothers, they will kill your children at your breasts,
Do not be cruel to them, poor mothers,
Do not give what is dearest to you over to death,
If you want it to bloom in the fullness of life,
Do not give what is dearest to you over to death,
Tear yourselves away, and take them with you
to a distant land!

In 1906, during her Russian sojourn, Bertha rescued 120 children, victims of the pogroms, and brought them back to Frankfurt to be relocated in various Western European cities. She published a thinly veiled fictionalized account of one of her travels to Yekaterinoslav entitled "Igren—a Leaf from a Diary." This story describes Bertha's unflagging persistence in trying to save Jewish children, taking hazardous travels to remote Jewish villages. As the story opens a guide asks her if she wants to go to a remote village where four families had been victimized—three men were killed, one beaten, and one woman was widowed with six children. The end of this story describes the culmination of her mission:

> When we entered, a pale, blond girl, perhaps eight years old, stood up from a bench, quickly sprang to a water bucket, washed her face with her hands, dried off with a piece of cloth, wound a scarf around her head like an old woman, and sat down again on the bench next to an equally pale, very handsome little boy, about two years old, who sat unmoving. We were met with the hostile gaze of two pairs of big, blue, dark-circled children's eyes. . . . I explained the purpose of my visit and asked if the woman would give up one or both of the children to be educated abroad. The craftsman's wife said: "I will not." The husband said: "Why shouldn't she, she has nothing to feed the children with." The wife said excitedly: "But I'm the mother!"
>
> I then explained to her that no pressure would be put on her, that all she was being offered was a relief, and that she need not renounce her rights as their mother.
>
> The man told me, "Madame, you are doing a very noble deed if you give the children a good education somewhere and make normal people out of them. You know, there are mothers who can bring up children, and there are mothers who can earn money. This is a mother who can't provide for herself, much less for her children, and she can't earn a kopeck. Write down the children's names."
>
> I noted the names of the children. . . . Both of them

looked at me with such inexpressible sadness, and both children sighed heavily and deeply, oppressed by the burden which they had to carry, with their whole people.

The author Ellen Jensen describes a photograph depicting Bertha and other members of the Jewish Relief Committee standing in the emigration hall of the Hamburg-American Line in 1906. They are surrounded by throngs of children, orphaned in the bloodbath of the pogroms, on their way to countries that would accept them. Bertha accompanied nineteen of the children to London and stayed until they were safely settled.

Beginning in 1907, JFB began meeting trains and boats in an effort to protect unaccompanied young girls fleeing Eastern Europe from the white slave traffickers. According to historian Marion Kaplan, the Frauenbund members furnished these young women with job counseling and placement services. By 1908, JFB's placard hung with those of the Catholic and Protestant Associations. The placard showed a Star of David with the initials J.F., the slogan "Combat White Slavery," and a list of contacts. The Frauenbund volunteers wore yellow armbands with the motto, "Help by Women for Women." This work continued and expanded until 1936, when the Nazis forbade JFB from continuing with their railroad station assistance.

Through Bertha's travels and social work, she became increasingly obsessed with the plight of unwed Jewish mothers, often children themselves, impoverished, uneducated, and born out of wedlock. Jewish agencies did not accept the idea that illegitimate children required protection under Jewish law. The unwed mothers and the "agunah" obsessed Bertha. The agunah were wives whose husbands had left them, often destitute, for the promise of a better life in America. Left at the margins of Jewish life, not able to remarry without a *get* (a religious divorce, granted only with their husband's agreement), these women were often able to survive only by selling themselves or being sold into white slavery. At a meeting of JFB in 1906 Bertha protested that to the Jewish charities, and even to the women's organizations that were officially sympathetic to orphans, an unmarried mother simply did not exist. She believed that the timely intervention of a Jewish social organization could "extricate a young, unmarried mother from the filthy corner to which her needs have chased her, and prevent her from becoming saleable market goods."

Bertha felt that with her experience at the orphanage she was prepared to start a new organization. To reduce the number of orphans, she wanted to educate unsupported young mothers and young women who were in danger of becoming victims. She knew that she would miss her little girls and wrote to a co-worker: "Who does not want children, dries up the fountain; who educates his children badly, pollutes the fountain." Bertha did not leave the orphanage without finding a proper replacement. On November 21 she wrote to Sophie Rosenthal, who had been one of her orphanage "daughters" and was now a kindergarten teacher in Cologne:

> A lady from Vienna, who may be my successor, arrived yesterday. You understand how difficult it is to give up my beloved work when I am still at the peak of my ability. Come whatever may, it is a good-bye, and all the old furniture and laces will not help.
>
> I am glad you graduates know how much I am one with you, which makes me very happy indeed. Life lies before you, it will bring you much. You can hope for everything, for the most beautiful things we women may experience. But for me my work and you children are my entire life, a life I had to conquer.

Bertha had decided to build a home for unwed Jewish mothers and their babies. She envisioned a revolutionary refuge not only for unwed or abandoned Jewish mothers and their children but also for pregnant girls, young prostitutes, youths at risk, and the "morally ill." She described her vision in a lecture, "On Welfare for Female Youth at Risk," given at the Academy for Trade and Social Sciences:

> What I have in mind is something near a mid-size community, two houses with bedrooms of 10 to 15 beds.
>
> One building will take older youths, young prostitutes, pregnant girls, or those who have given birth in prison—the children will remain [with them], too.
>
> The other building will hold youths at risk, childish, morally inferior youths in whose life all is still undecided, who have a great tendency for what is called "moral insanity." . . . Both buildings should be furnished in a simple manner, but with a homey and friendly touch, so that the residents should not feel they are incarcerated; the clothing should also be simple but not ugly or disfiguring. The building should be of a half-urban, half-rural simple style.
>
> No resident would be kept by force. Corporal punishment would be out of order. Free hours should be spent reading books and newspapers.
>
> The directors of the home should share the work and leisure time with their fellow inhabitants and speak in a friendly tone that excludes the possibility of authoritarian pretension and disrespect for the "morally sick." . . .
>
> What I can give you today is only a list of indications that will not be enough for you to form a picture of the education and healing through living a life that should be in every way a healthy contrast to that which brought these women to risk and to "fall." . . .
>
> Men should not take over the care of youths at

> risk. . . . The women shall not be those with haughtiness in their cloistered and otherworldly, religiously ascetic world-view.
>
> The care of the "morally sick" shall be led by those who are in the prime of life or know life well and have gained their experiences from the real world.
>
> The majority (should be) married women, who know about sexual relations and are therefore neither excessively strict nor permissive, and as often happens with the one-eyed stance of the spinster. . . .
>
> It may be possible that the next time we meet, we shall be able to tour a newly founded home for the healing of the "morally sick."

Bertha's emphasis on the education and spiritual healing of the "morally sick" introduced a profound loving dimension to the then common institutional social work practices. Aid to delinquents and prostitutes was often punitive and involved prison-like incarceration, with only superficial instruction in menial work. It was said that Bertha Pappenheim was rounding up prostitutes to start a house of immorality.

In spite of the controversial nature of Bertha's project, she was quickly able to fund it. Bertha's cousin Louise Goldschmidt donated a double house and property in nearby Neu Isenburg (also referred to simply as Isenburg). Charles Hallgarten, a famous Jewish philanthropist and an adviser and mentor of Bertha's, donated 5,000 marks. Baroness Edmond de Rothschild, born in Frankfurt, sent 2,000 marks from Paris. Her mother, Baroness Willy von Rothschild, president of the steering committee for the Israelite Orphanage in Frankfurt, also donated 2,000 marks. Mrs. Max von Goldschmidt-Rothschild gave 2,000 marks; Mrs. Rudolf von Goldschmidt-Rothschild gave 500 marks; and Mrs.

Adolf Stern gave 1,000 marks. All were members of Bertha's influential circle of friends.

Bertha's innovative Home for Wayward Girls was the first of its kind on the continent. During the first year of the Home's existence, Bertha herself paid for the housemother, Clara Schloss. She became its president, and termed it the "first property and favorite child" of the Frauenbund.

While the establishment of the Home was the cause of some alarm in Frankfurt's Jewish community, Bertha's "social feminist" speech "On the Morality Question" at the Second Congress of the Frauenbund created a scandal. In this speech, which Bertha considered a "milestone in the history of the Jewish women's movement," she insisted that the murkiness of current morality resulted from the abnegation of women's rights in Orthodox Judaism.

Bertha asserted that although the Jewish morality question had heretofore been associated solely with sexual relations, it should really be seen as a result of the interconnected issues of housing, wages, and working conditions. She noted that Jews tend to cram themselves in the center of cities, "as though unconscious ghetto memories make living in unpleasant, narrow streets seem more comfortable than living in the open countryside." She denounced the Jews in England, Rumania, and Russia as more adept at starving than working, and thus encouraging the excesses of hatred against them. More generally, she found that the decline in piety and the immorality weighed "like a growing cloud on the horizon of cultural life." She insisted, however, that the rich were no more moral than the poor, and that "one must ultimately recognize in this, gratefully, a kind of divine justice." Still, even in the more worldly assimilated Jewish circles, the "echo of the ghetto" could be heard. Parents who protected and isolated their daughters were merely raising them "behind bars" for marriage, without giving them knowledge of the sacredness of marriage and motherhood. She argued that these sheltered young women ought to be encouraged to join women's organizations and experience reality. Centuries of women's oppression explained the contradiction between the ancient ethic of Judaism and the moral decay "which shames and debases us in the eyes of the world community." Jewish women had to demand of themselves honesty and introspection, wisdom and clarity in raising their daughters; and the same virtues should characterize their public activism. She had found that the "new ethic" proposed by the militants of the women's movement was the same as the "old ethic," except for the masses to be educated, mobilized, and organized so that their own ideals would now become law. Women's voting rights would make the "new ethic" obsolete.

Bertha's central point was that the source of moral evil was the denial of women's rights within the Jewish family. She characterized the traditional poetic exaltation of Jewish women as hypocritical and bearing no relationship to the actual rights a Jewish woman was able to exercise in daily life: "Under Jewish law, a woman is not an individual, she has no personality; she is only valued as a wife and mother. . . . Under the law only married women receive any kind of acknowledgment. Women and girls who do not marry are objects of contemptuous pity." Bertha illustrated that the devaluation of the Jewish woman occurred in both affluent and poor circumstances, while claiming that Jewish prostitution and the white slave market were the result of legal oppression that did not allow women to defend themselves. The Jewish woman "does not count, she is unimportant, she learns nothing, her spirit needs no strength or grace. . . . Even when nature lay beauty as a present into her crib—she must mutilate or uglify herself. Under Jewish law, women are not individuals or personalities, just sexual beings."

Bertha's speech outraged the rabbis and male leaders of Frankfurt's Jewish organizations. One of her sharpest critics, Dr. Isaak Unna, Rabbi of Mannheim, wrote a protest in the *Frankfurter Israelitischer Familienblatt* on October 18, 1907. He questioned whether "the moral damage that these philanthropic ladies do to the Jewish people with such statements greatly outweighs the improvements in the material life of the Jews. That the Galician girls' trade has nothing to do with the Jews as such . . . should be evident to anyone who thinks objectively. But when the view of women as sexual objects is set up as a Jewish conception and this sorry view is connected to the essence of Jewishness, we need not elaborate on the extent to which this gives cannon fodder to the anti-Semites. We always will appreciate the practical work of helpful women; but they should leave theoretical explorations of the views of the Jewish people to those who know more about what it means to be Jewish." Bertha's remarks at the Congress caused such a scandal that the Orthodox rabbi Horovitz publicly denounced her, accusing her of besmirching the Jewish people. Bertha fiercely denied this accusation and invoked her pride in her Jewish heritage.

This encounter, in which Bertha was virtually accused of heresy, was one of the many situations when her feminism clashed with her Judaism, and one of the many public events when she vehemently tried to reconcile the emancipation of Jewish women with her deeply felt religious piety. The repressed rage that had made her ill in her twenties had turned into a social rage by her forties, transforming her into a warrior and a matriarch.

The Home continued to evolve as Bertha had envisioned.

Every day Bertha took a twenty-minute tram ride from her home through the Frankfurt forest to Isenburg, six miles southeast of the city. She then walked down lovely, shaded woodland paths from the town square along a tranquil street to the house on Taunusstrasse 9, whose two acres bloomed with fruit trees and wild flowers and provided a visual metaphor for Bertha's own flowering. Isenburg is a small, quaint provincial town over the Prussian border in Hesse, a separate state of the German Reich that had a more liberal policy toward stateless girls and aliens than Prussian Frankfurt. The small Jewish community there, in contrast to the elite circle of international bankers and businessmen surrounding Bertha in Frankfurt, was mostly composed of petit bourgeois shopkeepers. Before the Home could be officially founded, Bertha had to formally agree that its graduates would not become a burden on the town. In 1908, the public school agreed to accept the children of the Home and an Isenburg doctor promised to make regular visits to examine and treat the residents. In 1909, there were nine wards in the Home; and in 1910, a neighboring property was donated by Baroness Edmond de Rothschild.

The rules Bertha instituted for the running of the Home were at once high-minded and shrewdly practical. She did not underestimate the difficulties facing her charges as they struggled to right their lives, but neither did she underestimate their capacity to respond to humane care. The girls did not wear uniforms. There was no mention of their past. Residence in the home was strictly voluntary. Everyone ate together and helped in both the preparations and the cleanup of the meals. Bertha chose not to install running water in the rooms, lest the girls develop unrealistically high expectations that might cause them heartbreak later in life. Heating was provided by gathering fuel. Both furnishings and clothing were to be simple and tasteful, not ostentatious. Expectant mothers were given time off to prepare for and recover from childbirth. If they could not be persuaded to give up their babies for adoption, then the children were cared for inside the Home.

To staff the Home, Bertha chiefly recruited married women with life experience. She insisted that the staff always treat the girls with courtesy, kindness, and respect. All forms of institutional punishment—corporal punishment, deprivation of nourishment, or restriction of freedom—were forbidden. The prohibition against corporal punishment was written into every worker's letter of employment. No one was to be put in isolation and Bertha refused to create a room for private reflection. She was as wary of her co-workers' sentimentality as she was of their severity, so she also prohibited any form of coddling and baby talk. All forms of self-medication were also banned, both to spare the expense and to discourage self-absorption. The severest punishment a girl could suffer was to be refused the chance to participate in the work of maintaining the Home.

Education and religion were at the center of Bertha's program. The girls were encouraged to become involved in the affairs of the outside world by reading newspapers, listening to the radio, and engaging in discussion. The older girls were taught home economics and encouraged to take pride in their growing expertise. The staff created games that taught young children to make their beds and clean their drawers. Jewish education consisted of bi-weekly religious instruction and the communal observance of Friday evenings and holidays.

The Home gave the former prostitutes and unwed mothers a realistic preparation for life and a grounding in the skills they needed, all in the context of a community. Bertha's keen eye for detail and concern about the relations between staff and residents no doubt reflected the lessons she first learned during her stays at Inzersdorf and Kreuzlingen. She also had an intuitive and profound understanding that the heart of any organization was its sense of purpose and morale. Jewish tradition and Jewish piety were essential to the property functioning of the Home: "What matters, above all, is that we Jews know how to do things that are necessary from the great Jewish perspective, which is greater than political parties, greater than time, and greater than man." This same intuitive sense about the importance of an overriding purpose was embodied in the three fundamental tenets on which she first founded the Home:

1. Every idea must be thought through to its conclusion.

2. Nothing is an isolated entity, but has to be accommodated to the peculiarities of educational work.

3. In every action one must try to recognize the larger perspective into which each task fits.

Bertha's character as a "spiritual mother" and matriarch was lovingly described by Dr. Bertha Badt-Strauss. She recalled one of Bertha's favorite sayings, "Motherliness is the primal emotion, which even an untouched can feel." Sensitive to Bertha's ever deepening spiritual life and devotion to God, Badt-Strauss noted that the childless often have the largest number of children. "In the Bible it is always the childless women who are finally rewarded by the Lord in the greatest way [and are] most blessed with the power of prayer. . . . Thus, Pappenheim has received a real Jewish primal motherly fate. Life did not allow her to raise and take care of her own child: but in its place, God made her the mother of many children—and he gave her the power of prayer which could uplift others along with her."

By 1909, the structure of the Home was successfully in place and Bertha felt free to make several voyages. She received word that English and American Jewish women's organizations had expressed interest in working with JFB on the question of unwed Jewish mothers. She traveled as an emissary of JFB to London, Toronto, New York, and Washington, D.C.

Bertha was dismayed at the moral degeneration of the Jews who emigrated to London and Paris. She visited London several times for conferences on white slavery and was shocked by the presence of Jewish prostitution and the prevalence of Jewish conversions to Christianity, an issue which continued to plague her throughout her life with a pain almost equal to that caused by the profound ignorance and illiteracy she discovered in Galicia. Later, in a short story written in 1916 entitled "The Redeemer," she would use London as the point of departure for a bitterly ironic tale of the fate of converted and assimilated Jews.

By contrast, she saw the English suffragettes as "heroines," although she often disapproved of their tactics.

> London, May 1909
>
> Miss P. notified us that the next morning at 6:15 the imprisoned suffragettes were to be released from prison and would be received by their female comrades, literally, with drums and trumpets at the prison gate. Wanting to participate in this historic moment, we actually got up before 6 o'clock. In London this means about 4 o'clock—and after suffering all sorts of discomfiture, under which I consider "no breakfast" the most serious for myself, we arrived at the jail at the very second the women came through the gates onto the street. They all looked very well, despite having been outrageously treated like dangerous criminals. The 16 or 19 heroines were packed into six waiting Landaus. There were sixteen women riders at the head of the parade with sashes

> in the Vote for Women colors, the carriage horses wore green blankets with purple ribbons and white letters reading: "Vote for Women." Leading them was a young lady wearing green gaiters, a green skirt, a white wool jacket, and a purple hat, with a banner "Vote for Women." Behind her marched a band of musicians, then the heroines with bouquets, then about one hundred excited suffragettes, two motor-cars with international delegates, a little pony cart, and then a cab with Miss K. and myself, because having risen so early, I naturally insisted upon following the procession. We proceeded to the criterion where there was a breakfast for about two hundred people. A white tablecloth with green garlands and purple. Very lovely. Then enthusiastic speeches, three prisoners spoke too, and if Mrs. Asquith had arrived at that moment and had brought the vote for women, it would have been a terrible disappointment because what would these suffragettes have left to do today? I really did ask the woman in the office what they would do if they had the right to vote, and she said to me very pointedly, "educate women to use it." In this sense the entire movement is very imposing and useful, even if for me personally the form it takes is very disagreeable.

In preparation for the first International Conference on White Slavery, Bertha twice carried petitions to Queen Marie of Rumania, who granted her audiences in 1908 and 1909. Her efforts were in vain, for Rumania was a country in which endemic race hatred outweighed woman-to-woman sympathy. According to Marion Kaplan, Bertha was impressed by the Queen's concern but realized that "one stroke of the Queen's pen" would not solve the Jewish problem, since neither the Queen nor other Rumanian women had any influence in politics. Only ten percent of the nation's Jews were admitted to schools, and they were almost completely restricted from practicing either agriculture or liberal professions.

As a result of her trips abroad, Bertha was invited by the Americans to lecture on white slavery at the 1909 Canadian International Women's Conference. That same year, she lectured in Chicago and New York, quoting surveys to show that eighty percent of Jewish prostitutes in those cities were victims, not sinners. In New York, Bertha was particularly interested in the social work of the Henry Street Settlement. She also visited Washington, D.C., though her activities there are unknown. In Washington she did find time to write the following letter, which displays her sense of aesthetic superiority:

Washington, June 4, 1909

> . . . the famous White House seemed almost funny to me, although it is beautifully situated, with its row of columns—in Washington there are columns everywhere and on some buildings they seem to me utterly ridiculous—at the end of a lovely park. But of the reception hall and the rooms leading off of it . . . I can only say rubbish. Of course, if one remembers that the emperors' and kings' palaces were built by their subjects' sweat and blood, then this democratic tendency, which is elevated to tastelessness, is better and more healthful—but one shouldn't pretend as if the White House were anything special. Wonderful in contrast, is the Capitol where the Senate and the Congress meet. A lofty, powerful, and yet unimpressive dome divides the building into two parts. We sat in for a few minutes at a meeting that seemed to bore everyone else too, but there were a large number of women in the gallery. . . . In the rotunda stand a large number of marble statues (among them a woman) of people who rendered service to their country, and in the hallway a row of paintings. Beautiful heads, strong and

> intelligent, so distinct and imposing in their expression, that one understands that they had to ascend from the masses to lead the people, and that the people entrusted themselves to their leadership because they would not submit: That is a triumphal avenue which represents the best victory.

In April 1910, Bertha was the emissary of JFB at the first Jewish International Conference Against the White Slave Trade in London. Delegates from England, Austria, Belgium, France, Galicia, Holland, Hungary, Rumania, Russia, and the United States attended the conference. Although the sessions were held in private and the press reports were censored, the conference was considered controversial and was protested by many Jews. *Der Israelit* reported, "Over the suitability of the Conference, opinion in Jewish circles was strongly divergent." A British paper, *Jewish World*, vehemently wrote, "Unhesitatingly, we are of the opinion that such a gathering ought not to have been held."

Bertha again delivered an eloquent speech. Public speaking was yet another form of her "talking cure," through which her "private theatre" became increasingly integrated with her public personae. In her speech, Bertha presented a long, personal account, describing what she called, "the saddest chapter of Jewish moral history." She recalled the time when, after many years of social work, she first heard the term "white slave trade." It was a foreign idea to her. "The horrible existence of the white slave trade pressured and haunted me. I did some research, listened . . . and I learned something not only terrible, but also something shameful: many Jews are traders, many Jewish girls are goods." She was greatly angered that the Jews themselves had turned "a blind eye." She could excuse the poor Jews of Eastern Europe because of their struggle for mere survival, but she excoriated the

Bertha's passport photo wearing JFB brooch. [Photo © Leo Baeck Institute]

"so-called Jewish intelligentsia in Galicia and Rumania" as accomplices who, by virtue of their wealth, were marked by "indifference and a frivolous philosophy of life that only recognizes acquisition and pleasure as worthwhile goals." She noted that only a small number of Jewish women were aware of the exploitation of their own kind. Bertha blamed this on Jewish men, who wished to keep women ignorant, holding on to "an antiquated ideal of the innocent woman." She condemned Jewish men for destroying the purity of family life, which for thousands of years was the "bulwark" of Judaism. "No matter whether it is a rich man who has one mistress or several; whether a husband who, under the guise of 'polygamous male tendencies,' unscrupulously goes outside of the marriage to look for a victim; or whether young boys and students who only want 'a taste of life' or to 'live it up'—these men are still 'prostitution consumers' of the basest morality."

In closing, Bertha invoked the primary ethic of Judaism, "Love thy neighbor as thyself," as the only solution. At the very end of her speech, Bertha, the warrior, intoned, "I would like to leave you with a battle cry. 'It isn't enough to do no wrong, one also cannot tolerate any injustice'."

Bertha's ethic reflects her ties to her familial history, and evinces the inspiration of her revered ancestor, Glückel von Hameln, who wrote in the beginning of her memoir, "The kernel of the Torah is, Thou shall love thy neighbor as thyself." As Bertha was delivering her public exhortations, she was privately translating these very memoirs. The year 1910 marked the sprouting of a new kind of literary activity for Bertha as she began the first of many translations from Yiddish to German. In an essay on "The Jewish Woman" (1934), Bertha later wrote that she believed Yiddish is the Jewish woman's special language. She translated and privately published the *Memoirs of Glückel von Hameln*. This archaic German edition was consciously created for her family members. Few copies were printed and most were distributed to her relatives, although several books were also made available to Jewish libraries. At the age of fifty-one, Bertha, like the Goldschmidt women before her, became a powerful matriarch. She traced this identity back to Glückel, who had become her role model.

Glückel's book is the first autobiographical work of a German Jewish woman ever published. Glückel was born in Hamburg in 1645 and died in Metz on September 19, 1724. In the introduction to her translation, Bertha stated that she hoped to "breathe new life into the image of a woman who though deeply rooted in her time, stood out because of her unusual mental gifts, was true to her faith, to her people, to her family, and to herself." According to Bertha, Glückel embodied "the toughness and *joie-de-vivre* of the Jews of her time" and her story "belongs to those who humbly and unconsciously embody the best and most valuable qualities of womanhood." During the Thirty Years' War, Glückel's mother and grandmother had earned their living making fine lace with gold and silver thread. Bertha's own obsession with tatting and collecting lace thus followed an ancient family tradition. In fact, lace-making because Bertha's primary metaphor for describing life. Glückel, who was betrothed at age twelve and married at fourteen, had twelve children. Her memoirs describe the weddings and funerals, the details of her financial successes and failures, and the tenuous situation of Jews. Her personal anecdotes are interwoven with folktales, parables, stories, and passages from the Torah, which, with unusual scholarship for a woman, she had translated from the Hebrew. After her husband's death in 1689, she successfully took over her husband's far-flung business. She arranged dowries and important matches for her children while traveling throughout Germany, France, Denmark, Holland, Austria, and Poland buying and selling "goods," precious jewels, seed pearls, and coins. At the heart of Glückel's life, however, and at the heart of Bertha's life, was a joyous devotion to the service of God and the truth. Glückel opens her memoirs with instructions to her children:

> The best thing for you, my children, is to serve God from your heart, without falsehood or shame, not giving out to people that you are one thing, while God forbid, in your heart you are another. Say your prayers with awe and devotion. During the time for prayers, do not stand about and talk of other things.

Bertha identified so deeply with Glückel that she commissioned a dramatic portrait of herself as Glückel von Hameln. She wore a bonnet, white lace cuffs, and a fur coat borrowed from her friend Clem Cramer. The portrait was done by Leopold Pilichowski (1869–1933), a well-known painter who danced around her as he painted.

Chapter Ten

SISYPHUS-ARBEIT*

Neu-Isenburg
September 1924

By way of apologizing for the publication of these travel notes, I would like to mention that after a chance perusal of them some twelve years after they were written, I was totally shocked to realize how little was accomplished of the work I then attempted to initiate with hopeful confidence: a novel understanding of questions of social ethics also in those countries which were not perceptibly touched by various reform movements, and whose improvement still lags far behind.

I then reported in my letters, as I had also done in earlier travels undertaken to study Jewish suffering and in the service of protecting women, girls, and children, to a select circle of women in Frankfurt, the "subscribers," in the hope that somehow my notes might spark a movement. Nothing of the sort ever happened, not with us, nor elsewhere. All I discovered was that a *single* voice, the voice of an unknown woman, produced no effect.

---

*Text by Bertha Pappenheim. In the spring of 1911 and the spring of 1912, Bertha Pappenheim went abroad to investigate white slavery. Her circular letters were collected in a volume entitled *Sisyphus-Arbeit* and published in 1912. These excerpts are taken from a 1924 reissue of that volume.

Today, I believe I have not yet fulfilled my duty. No one who knows that an injustice takes place somewhere may remain silent—neither gender, age, religious creed, nor political affiliation can serve as a ground for silence. To be aware of injustice, yet remain silent, equals complicity.

Budapest
March 9, 1911

An acquaintance from the congress at London deserves mention. Dr. M.F., of Laudongasse 3. He is the secretary of the Burial Society, one of the wealthiest of the local associations. I asked him about his budget of "one million crowns." "How do you spend it?" "On everything. We have the best, the most splendid organization, with just a little hitch: all we do is spend money (600–800 crowns a day!), for funerals and other occasions." "Do you have a Women's Committee for your investigations?" "God may protect me. As long as I have MY say, no woman will walk in here." (Are you getting the picture?) Yet, I felt obliged to talk to him about the white slave traffic and women's care. "This is completely outside MY realm. . . ."

In the office of the feminists I met a Mrs. Von S., a Jewish woman who is on the way to forgetting her background. She is very involved in the protection of mothers, a movement which here does only practical work [birth control]. In no time I was in a deep conversation with her, and she quickly understood what I wanted, what made me tick: and I believe I too understood her. She took me to her home where I met her mother, who is on the board of the Jewish Women's Society. We went to Rabbi Dr. H.A., . . . a tall, dapper gentleman in Hungarian clerical garb. He let us wait for a long time. Without a word, stonelike, he then let me look at his nondistinguished profile, and talk. When I had finished and asked him for collaboration, in the interest of both individuals and of the entire Jewish community, he said, without batting his eyelids, "The issue doesn't interest me." Mrs. Von S. reminded him that he was Chairman of the Society for the Protection of Children. "Yes, but only of children up to 12 or 13 years of age. The older ones are not my business." Well-mannered, quiet and restrained as I am(!), I wanted to utter a "But . . . ," when the dapper spiritual leader of the Jewish congregation of Budapest raised his hand forbiddingly and said, "I shall not be converted."

Budapest
March 12, 1911

Fräulein A. has been taking very good care of me since yesterday. I know her from various white slavery congresses and thought that she was a converted Jew. But she is a born Catholic and, therefore, has every right to be on such good terms with the Catholic clergy. She pretends not to be an anti-Semite, even gives out that she was a philo-Semite before, but now that the Jews have done so much harm in Hungary (so she claims), she can no longer be partial to Jews!!! Yesterday, I went with her to the little Rochus Hospital which has 140 beds for female venereal patients—nothing but prostitutes running around the wards half nude and without any supervision at all. Only one nurse, and uneducated female, in a room of 30 patients. I had the feeling that I had wandered into an insane asylum.

There was one in the courtyard wearing silver shoes, torn stockings, a chemise and open hospital smock, in a familiar embrace with another, wearing a pink-flowered silk slip, a scarf twisted around her tangled hair. Seated at a table in the ward, a girl with hair piled high, wearing nothing but a low-cut chemise, writing a letter; another one lying in bed wearing a yellow silk chemise with lace, wiping away tears—yes, tears of laughter; a dark-haired tubercular-looking Jewish girl tugging at her chemise because it keeps slipping from her shoulders, etc. A complete picture of moral and physical depravity in human beings between the ages of 16 and 30, about whom no one in the world cares, except the police—and they in their fashion. A third of these girls are Jewish. I think that yesterday I must have been the first Jewish woman ever to cross the threshold into these rooms of horror out of concern for social welfare. . . .

As a matter of fact, lectures on the social obligations of the community should be held in every single rabbinical seminary so that all of these rabbis, grand rabbis, and chief rabbis and wonder-rabbis might know what is really going on among their flock. I would like to scream in their ears that they have other obligations besides raking in their fees and letting the Jewish people go downhill. . . .

Saloniki
April 2, 1911

The best part of my trip consists in the innumerable times daily that I am reminded of the remarks and opinions of my parents and my governess, Miss Hoffmann. I am reminded of those to whom I not only owe my life, my father and my mother, but also those who gave it a precious content. . . . It has been said, "Blessed is he who loves to remember his forebears." The Jewish women of Saloniki are said to be especially beautiful. The most beautiful one I saw here, maybe the most beautiful Jewish woman I ever saw, perhaps the most beautiful alive, I found today in a brothel. What a pity, such a hearty human flower, born in that environment to such a fate. I understand that a man will risk everything for such a woman, yet I can't understand how this twenty-year-old can sell the best, the most beautiful thing she owns—her body—in this way. Does she not have a soul? . . . It's ten o'clock; I'll stop for today. I'll go to sleep. Maybe I'll dream of beautiful Yolanthe; I can't forget her since I saw her today. . . .

Saloniki
April 3, 1911

Of course I did not dream of Yolanthe. I wanted my shoes to be lighter. They felt too heavy. "Dreams," my father would have said reprovingly.

Constantinople
April 8, 1911

There was a service in the Mosque of the Doves; the melodies reminded me of the Schiffschul in Vienna; my father was its co-founder. Now his daughter is not "happy" (married), as our old guest at the Seder used to say, but busy with pursuits my parents would not even have known to name. Sometimes this worries me; yet they could not have foreseen my development.

The chief rabbi knows a little, certainly not enough. I also believe he does not have the power to accomplish anything. He knows for instance that there is a synagogue of white slavers in Constantinople. He has enough power to close this "House of God," but does not do so. His reasons are nonexistent. . . .

It is commonly known that 90 percent of the girls on the slave market are Jewish, and that nearly all the dealers are Jews, too. I told him what I thought of the congregation of white slavers—everybody here is afraid of them.

Constantinople
April 14, 1911

What happened yesterday was deeply embarrassing. Countess R. proclaimed that even if the Turks had no share in prostitution and white slavery, simply by tolerating the traffic through their government as if they had no knowledge of it, and by protecting the dealers, Turkey was fully an accomplice. Every decent person would agree, and this is true of the Jews, too. I remember the synagogue of the white slave dealers, and the knowledge Jews have of the goings-on. To prove their good intentions, and their own decency, Jewish organizations should engage an agent.

April 23, 1911
On board the *Tsarevich* en route to Jaffa

My neighbor at the dinner table is a doctor and orientalist on a mission for the German government to Aleppo to establish some sort of a German institute there. I've never before met a man of such deep-seated immorality, which he hides beneath a scientific veneer. Of course, I can't be expected to remember all of his words of wisdom, but perhaps the following will suffice: "I've never dismissed a prostitute whom I've kept overnight without first elevating her morals in the morning. Since I'm a doctor, I can warn her and explain what she should know. I uniformly make them a present of just what they need in order to amuse themselves without coming to harm." You can imagine how I told him that he was abusing his medical knowledge, but, of course, that didn't make any impression on him whatsoever. I'm quite sure that he is capable of committing any act of depravity that he can get away with, that is, without damaging his position as a German or Prussian official. Naturally, he comes from Berlin and is only a "political" anti-Semite. He likes the whole idea of Zionism because it means a mass exodus of all Jews from the great German nation. "They're finally admitting what they've wanted all along—to become a national power," etc.

On board of the *Tsarevich* (Smyrna–Jaffa)
April 25, 1911

It is a dear thought to believe that, as you say, I mean "something" to the young people in Frankfurt. The very best a woman can do is to mean something to someone and I am happy if I feel sometimes that I will not die without having warmed someone at my small fire. I am pleased that you are enjoying my letters, for actually they are written but for myself, so that later on I could look up where I've been and whom I've met. The *practical* result of my trip is nothing but demonstrating to myself and others that I am expendable in Frankfurt, where I'm so unpopular in the "influential circles."

Aboard the *Tsarevich* (Tripolis–Jaffa)
April 26, 1911

I really must tell you about a dream. I dreamed that I was telling my mother that I had tamed two jackals. Mama didn't want to believe me so I brought them out and, even though I was sure beforehand that they were jackals, I now saw for myself that I was leading two cats on a leash. I got irritated, tugged on the leash, and lo and behold, there were Herr H. and Herr S., whom Mother politely invited to take their places in the dining room in the house on Leerbachstrasse. Be it as it may, it definitely reeked of jackals in my cabin. . . .

The day did, however, bring a pleasant surprise. I came to shore in Beirut two hours ago, and it was summer! Masses of pink and yellow roses in the gardens, fig trees, all of it just taken for granted. I was wearing my gray knit jacket—on the 26th of April—and had to take it off. Nothing to snap up in the bazaar, a few stalls to trap the tourists, but nothing reasonable, nothing for the heart.

On the other hand, I was confronted with two dreadful sights. A youth, perhaps 13 years old, brown, practically naked, was lying in the midst of a very busy street, a cloth bound around his face like a compress and moaning. My dragoman—I had taken one in order to return punctually to the ship—told me that he wasn't sick. In a more secluded street, I saw a woman lying under the shade of an overhanging rock, clearly wrestling with serious illness or even death. The guide said in English, "When she is dead, she will be taken away."

Jerusalem
May 4, 1911

Things here are so complicated, and what usually comes to mind when one hears the words Jerusalem and Palestine is so different from the actual reality that the brainwork here is twice or three times as hard. . . . I spent yesterday again in the company of Mrs. T., a good, intelligent and socially active woman, who certainly takes also her Zionism seriously, but the discussions about Zionism are bringing me to the brink of despair. Is there nothing else, nothing wider, nothing bigger in the entire world?

In addition, I feel the more I understand this material, the more I see the mistakes, the dangers of the movement and the more sure of myself I am in discussing it, though I am not enjoying it any longer. I would rather find somebody who might bridge the gap in my knowledge and give me a sort of introduction into history, but I found no one. . . .

Yesterday morning, I was with Mrs. T. in the Home for Girls, which is financed by Zionists and by the Hilfsverein der deutschen Juden and is very good. Then we went to the girls' orphanage. It has seventy-two wards, no funds, and it exists only through begging, through the well-known kind of propaganda fund-raising in Europe—I'm told that seventy percent is kept by the agents. It's, of course, important to keep the children off the streets, where they would be victims of Christian missionaries, physical or moral exploitation, but the management is just incredible. A Women's Committee has been making plans for the last three months to educate girls, but the girls don't go to school and barely learn a thing. Sewing has been taught for several months. Yet, in spite of incredible poverty, the main impression of the institution is favorable, especially since the building is a good one, everything is kept clean. I could not help telling Mrs. T., a Galician constantly pointing out the poverty, that everything in Jerusalem is better than in Galicia and that I thought she would have plenty to do in her own country.

First, the buildings here are all much better. Also, the climate makes poverty less painful than in Galicia and Russia and Rumania. I advised the Women's Committee of the girls' orphanage to get in contact with Weibliche Fürsorge to get a headmistress, if the Board allowed a European-style bookkeeping and control. I later saw the Diskin orphanage where 300 boys live off a "propaganda factor" [charity]. This house, with its large, beautiful rooms could be good, if it were not miserable and dirty. The children, who are taken in already at the age of 2–3, look poorly fed and learn nothing but Yiddish and Talmud. . . . A young man led us through the building, and I liked him quite well. He defended with sincere eagerness the worldwide begging as an unfortunate necessity, and felt very hurt by my outspoken questioning of this method. To prove how unselfishly he was working, he told me that for months he has had two French books (or a German and a French one) and though he would have loved to read them, he could not find time to do so. He made some additional remarks which impressed me very much, and to make good for my offense I will give him a nice edition of *Nathan the Wise*. The bookstores here do not carry it. Then I saw the Eveline de Rothschild School. The head, Miss L., is at present in London. Here the lace technique started, which Mrs. T. took up as an industry. Miss L. had learned it from Arab women.

Then I had coffee with Mrs. M. Her husband owns the leading bookstore in Jerusalem. She is a young woman whom I had met as Miss L. in Hamburg, a passionate Zionist, and she immediately turned the talk to this topic. I noticed that people are enormously interested in what I will have to report, but I believe it will be for the best if I give my information to a small circle only; otherwise, I will be wildly attacked. I have already made it clear I wasn't going to be pulled into any polemic. . . .

Yesterday morning I saw the Church of the Holy Sepulchre

and the Omar Mosque; later, I learned that neither Jews nor Christians should enter it. If I had been asked at the entrance about my religion, race, or congregation, I would not have denied any, but nobody asked me; thus I walked through, incognito, and hence without any difficulty. I saw many interesting and beautiful things, but the most fascinating, the underground buildings, allegedly from the days of King Solomon, have been closed off for the last three weeks because Englishmen supposedly are doing "scientific research"; in other words, they have been stealing.

In the afternoon I saw the Leimel School, which is now helped financially by the Hilfsverein der deutschen Juden, and actually run by them. I could not visit the school, but it seems to be the best place of the quiet German culture, though much Hebrew is also being taught.

Later I went to the German Consulate where I heard that with the advent of Jews from abroad "all sorts of questionable things," previously unknown, have moved Jerusalem. I heard about a "hotel" which belongs to one A. L. and is not supposed to be "clean." No German girls in Jerusalem are involved in prostitution.

In Sha'are Zedek Hospital Dr. W. told me about the moral purity among the Jews here. It is a fact that true piety as well as early marriages are a great protection. Dr. W., who has been here over 20 years, has yet to bring to the world a child born out of the wedlock. . . .

I am glad that I stayed for one and a half days longer than planned, for that enabled me once more to go to the Wailing Wall. To go there on Friday afternoon, one is cured forever. What I saw was neither prayer nor devotion. Professional beggars fighting among themselves; professional worshipers I found, but nobody—just as on my first visit—who was truly mourning the past. I saw anti-Semitic Germans with spiteful faces, Englishmen with Kodak cameras. And I wished that around this single authentic Jewish holy place there would be a wide safety screen! I then saw the Ecce Homo Church, a gift of a baptized Jew, Ratisdonne; the tombs of the kings; David's tomb, for which I had to dole out an extra tip, for since the theft in the Omar Mosque, this monument isn't to be shown to tourists either. It is most interesting to have been in Jerusalem for a short time, particularly because of its landscape, which is wild and barren, but I would not want to live here permanently, even as a social worker. If Frankfurt is the German Jerusalem, it seems to me that Jerusalem is the Oriental Frankfurt. There are so many movements and antimovements here, so much gossip and hate. Here one could have success only as a new Christ or Moses or Croesus, but if a Moses would come who could bring water from a rock, then he would become a Croesus.

Even concerning poverty, Jerusalem is unique, as poverty here does not lead to general depravity. Great piety outweighs it, as I have been told by everyone. This fact remains relevant also as far as the education of the local youth is concerned, and schools, hospitals, and orphanages ought to be run in the spirit of the absolute majority—against the Zionists. . . .

Jerusalem
May 6, 1911

You can't imagine how overjoyed I am to have been here, because now I know what it is like. Unless you're interested in the beauty of a landscape, which can be found elsewhere as well, there is really no reason to travel all the way to Jerusalem.

Poverty and suffering are infinitely greater in Eastern Europe; and the huge ghettos of London and New York are also larger heaps of destitution and as such most important for the Jew, who is either a social worker or has a social conscience that seeks to expose corruption and vice. Concerning questions of morality, the Jewish population of Jerusalem is as unscathed as it was centuries ago. . . . Bright and early tomorrow morning, I'll take my leave of the Holy City without shedding a tear and without ensuring my return by hammering a nail into a crack in the Wailing Wall.

Jaffa
May 7, 1911

There really are strange coincidences! Only recently there were several cases of white slavery here. When I arrived today, Frau T. gave me a scandalized account of everything that has happened and told me that there was an assembly of Jewish workers yesterday, which would like to form a defense committee against the slave trade. This committee plans to set forth the necessary measures and I came just in time to give them advice. Naturally, I recommended that their group should be as international and ecumenical as possible, and that they should eventually join with a league in Constantinople. One of the gentlemen present had already worked with a league in Alexandria, so all the suggestions were quite reasonably accepted. I hope that all of their good intentions will be realized. I promised to hold a little lecture for a large assembly of men and women next Saturday evening and, since I can't get a decent ship to Port Said before

Monday (perhaps another Russian ship on Saturday), everything is working out fine. I sent my little piece of Arabian lace to Frau T. for a touch-up. . . .

Alexandria–Ramlah
May 23, 1911

At six o'clock, I met with an employee of Mr. H., who was to show me the brothel quarter, etc. At first, Mr. V., an Englishman, didn't seem very pleased with his mission, but slowly and surely, he became visibly interested in my way of going through the bordellos. If I may say so, the houses here make a better, less vicious and disgusting impression than they do, for example, in Belgrade or Budapest. From the point of view of hygiene, nothing really is being done.

I could only speak with those girls who understood German, French, English, or my most insufficient Italian, but my guide was a very good interpreter indeed and the more interested he became, the better it all went. A Jewish girl from Czernowitz, an Italian, a twenty-two-year-old married woman with a 3-year-old child, and a young Arab girl proved themselves to be worthy of social concern, and will accept it as well—but who will finally provide it for them? I could be very useful here.

The most moving of all was a tall, strange Arab girl who didn't speak a word and only listened to what I was discussing with another by means of the interpreter. Once we were out in the street, my companion told me that, just as we were leaving, he heard her tell her girlfriend in Arabic, "She (meaning me) should be healthy and blessed, and her entire family as well, because she is the first such woman who has ever spoken with us."

Lodz (Poland)
May 6, 1912

I am glad to hear that L.C. helps in the library of the club, a good and healthy beginning in social work for her. Good that Mrs. C. trains her in this way. How happy are present-day girls! When I remember how it was with me at this age and how difficult people make it for me to keep from the way that's right for me, forget it!

Lodz (Poland)
May 6, 1912

Yesterday I was with Mrs. B. in Alexandrow at the wonder-rabbi's; a visit most interesting in thousands of details. Frau B. is German, from Silesia, highly respected all over, especially since she still leads a strictly Orthodox lifestyle. It was quite doubtful whether the rabbi would receive us at all, but a Frau D. who lives in Frau B.'s house is the rabbi's sister and she offered to introduce us.

This woman is a true living Glückel von Hameln. It's just wonderful of what and how she talks, her faith, her healthy common sense, her naiveté. I hope I remember the story she told me as a parallel to the exposure of Moses. But since it took at least half an hour to tell, I cannot possibly write it down. She asked about my business, of course, and after I had told her what I intended to do on my travels, she grasped all very quickly and with doubtfully raised eyebrows said, "Does a swallow want to drain the sea? The Lord, blessed be He, may help, but since it is done in purity to the glory of the Lord, the rabbi, my brother, may he live a long life, will also help." Isn't that true Glückel?

And how she introduced us to her dear sister-in-law, the "reb-betzin." I explained to her about the women's movement, and she told me right away how she, in her way, talks to young wives, and even to their husbands.

We spoke about the out-of-wedlock children, the mamserim, and much more. She just could not finish spitting [to ward off evil]. Finally, after we had waited for two hours, the rabbi received us. Piously he turned his back on me. I gave an animated talk. He called my endeavor a great mitzvah; he will warn people in his own circle. I am to write down all I told him. . . . The respect for the rabbi is such that there is complete silence in his house. Only he who knows the Hasidic Jews, can understand what this means!

Warsaw
May 10, 1912

I feel entitled to be absent from Frankfurt for such a long time because I am convinced, now that I think it over, that I've not become necessary or rooted in my work, my character, or my class. Not needed by anything or anyone. This is not meant as a reproach—it is most probably the fault of my own personality—but simply a statement of fact. It makes my nomadic life easier for me. I do sometimes feel homesick, but that is only a longing for my home, for my desk with its petroleum lamp, for my amusing silhouettes, for my colorful glasses, and above all, for my lace, those miraculously varied patterns, all based on a fine, straight linen thread. If I were not an enemy of poetic comparisons, and if all metaphors weren't so lame, I might claim that our very life must be formed from such fine, strong, genuine material, straight and even with interlacing and interweaving, which whether simple or complicated, represent ethical or aesthetic values. I also long to live such a life and I loathe the clumsy fingers which destroy the beautiful design and rip or confuse the threads.

I have often thought that when you have nothing at all to love, hatred is a fine surrogate. That must be why I so greatly enjoy reading the *Arbeiterzeitung* [workers' paper], because it expresses the feelings of large masses, or, at least, of their leaders, in such strongly incendiary language, with hatred, but also with love for an ideal. . . .

Moscow
May 24, 1912

If it was irreparably stupid to stop working for the Frauenverein, my trip here was most certainly one of the smartest things I have ever done. Moscow, as it is, is one of the most interesting places. It has 40 times 40 churches, with cupolas of gold, silver, and brilliant colors; the Kremlin and some streets are so beautiful that one is glad to find a reason to go strolling in the bright sunshine over and over again.

Yesterday I had a most interesting encounter with a Countess, Barbara B. A manservant opened after I rang a bell at a house slightly set back from the street. I climbed wooden stairs with somewhat disheveled rugs to a narrow hall, which alluded to a great length of the house, crowded with many trunks. I was led to a large room. It betrayed a cultured milieu with cabinets of china, pictures, and furniture of good, old, and bad days. Unfortunately, there were also framed photographs. A definitely modern large desk with a phone. There is no better sign of the victory of the feminist movement than the disappearance of the lady's desk. Wherever and if I have to wait (and I always have to), and I see a lady's desk and furniture in slipcovers, I always find undeveloped female brains.

But yesterday I found a big, solid desk, well placed toward the light for writing. Countess Barbara B. did not let me wait long. She does not speak German, but speaks English and French, dresses very simply, has a softer face than Countess P. at Petersburg.

She told me very clearly that she had no time for women's problems, protection of girls, prostitution, etc., because her energies were taken up with the night shelters in Moscow. The city grants her two million rubles yearly. Should I be interested, she would show me tonight the shelters she runs as well as those she wants abolished.

You can well imagine how anxious I am to see Moscow's Whitechapel. I will call tonight for Countess Barbara B. All that's needed is an old short skirt because of vermin, and strong nerves, besides.

Moscow
May 26, 1912

Yesterday evening was one of the most important for me, and if I may draw the conclusion, it was equally important for all of us, for all Jews in the service of social work.

I arrived at 7 o'clock sharp at the house of Countess B., who saw fit to repeatedly explain to me that she didn't "sympathize" with either the feminist movement or the Society for the Protection of Girls, neither with the causes nor with the women who worked for them whose "standpoint" was so different from her own. . . . We got into her automobile. Then I finally told her what I really should have made clear right away—that I am a

Jewish woman. She had known it days before, because the woman who telephoned her about me had that unmistakable, dreadful Jewish accent. She literally screwed up her face as if in memory of something truly disgusting. And then she explained that it was absolutely impossible for Russians to accept Jews in their midst; they could never mingle; they were too different. During a pause in her vehement speech, I interjected that it wasn't a question of mixing, but simply of toleration . . . "I don't know a single wealthy Jew who is taken with an ideal, of whatever sort, for which he would live and die and make any sacrifice whatsoever. Every Jew thinks first and foremost of his own personal gain. We Russians, we have our ideal, the people, the *muzhik* [peasant] . . . *nous faisons tout pour le relêvement de notre peuple* [we do all to elevate our people]."

"Mais à nous juifs, on ne permet pas de faire la même chose, pour nos correligionaires. [But we, Jews, are not permitted to do the same for our coreligionists.]" She wouldn't hear any objection. She spoke with great anger and fanaticism which was devastating—for Countess B. represents a type; she is one of thousands who think in exactly the same way. . . .

She added that in dealing between Jews and Christians, no matter if Russian Orthodox, Catholic or Protestant, one always reached a point beyond which one could go no further, since the Jews have an entirely different ethics and aesthetics. I tried to say that the Christian ethics was actually borrowed from the Jews. *"Ce n'a jamais été, jamais, jamais.* [No, that never happened, never, never.]" Here we were, two women, both of us worked up and if we hadn't been held in check by the restraints of our upbringing and culture, if we had found ourselves not inside of a rushing automobile, somewhere in the steppes or desert, the "interchange" of Christian and Jewish women might have taken a completely different turn. Physically, I think that she would have been the victor. She'll probably be the winner anyway, for the enemy is right—they work *pour le relêvement du peuple*, and we Jews stand by and watch the demoralization of our people, its ruin and dissolution.

Countess B. brought me first to her own asylum . . . which she had established with public funds. . . . The Moscow Night Community is a large three story building, which accommodates 1,500 people a night in its heated rooms—some 300 women and girls, the rest men. The aim is to protect the good element . . . to keep them apart from the rough element in other asylums, the out-and-out hooligans. But nothing is done to educate the people or to influence them in any way. . . .

The women seem to be by far the worst of the visitors, living depraved existences, casual rather than professional prostitutes. No one is looked after, not even children or minors! That would be the duty of other societies, for individual social welfare, which Countess B. doesn't take into account, just as she disdains work for women, the women's movement, congresses, the right to vote, etc. . . .

We drove to one of the night shelters which Countess B. is attempting to combat. . . . I will spare you all the grim details of what I saw. I need only refer you to [Maxim] Gorky, a name which my guide pretended not to hear when I mentioned it to her. Of course, the scenes which Gorky presents have to do with individuals, but to actually see the masses of drunken men and women thrown together, to hear the screaming and laughing and howling from the windows, to feel those insolent figures pressing against you, to breathe that air, to see that hole of a cellar where they throw the bodies of those who die in the nightly brawls, to know that 4,000 people are crammed together at a given moment in a relatively small room, ready to turn into pogrom beasts in the blink of an eye—my breast felt suffocated in terror.

Countess B. was kind enough to bring me back to my hotel in her car . . . I thanked her. . . . My thanks were meant sincerely, even though I felt that I was politely and conventionally shaking hands with an enemy.

The dreadful thought of those 4,000 hooligans, sleeping in one mass in a single night, but still representing only a fraction of the latent criminal force in Moscow, was made bearable during this long, restless night only by weighing it against a Tolstoy. . . . It was clear to me that evil is finite and ephemeral and that the beautiful and good endures. If we didn't have this consolation, the insight into the night side of existence would crush us.

Chapter Eleven

STRUGGLES (1911-1918)

> The use of technology to enlarge the spheres of strength and power has devalued mankind, has driven the spirit out of man and nearly extinguished it.
>
> In war and in the experience of war technology has been rendered ethically inferior by its very ubiquity, and has therefore renewed the achievement of the individual, which is attained through one's own power, will, skill, and dexterity, and elevated it to an exquisite, priceless significance.
>
> Bertha Pappenheim

As the second decade of the twentieth century began, Bertha achieved an international reputation as a feminist and opponent of white slavery. Her perspective was unique, combining aspects of traditional Jewish piety, keen insight into relations between the sexes both in the Jewish and gentile spheres, and a firm understanding of the causal role of social factors in personal vice. Her recommendations were at once practical and inspired. The same balance could be seen in her activities, which were divided between the Home at Isenburg and her writing and public speaking. She had the time, energy, money, passion, and insight to occupy herself in several spheres at once.

Yet there was a gap between the public and the private person. When Bertha founded Weibliche Fürsorge—Care By Women, in Frankfurt, she could enjoy the fruits of her labor twice over, taking pride in what was being accomplished while simultaneously taking solace in the companionship of her colleagues. Similarly, at her writing table she could give voice to her deeper feelings yet be secure that her books, articles, plays, and translations would find an audience, at least locally among her circle in Frankfurt. As an international figure, Bertha seemed to be needed everywhere at once. She pitted herself against a tidal wave of social forces whose dimensions dwarfed the power of any individual. At the same time her own prominence was itself a product of other social forces, of the increasing concern for social order and social welfare and the rise of feminism. She straddled forces whose homogeneity was suspect, whose inner cohesion might splinter like a giant ice floe breaking up at sea.

The struggle against prostitution and white slavery was neither a popular nor a respectable issue for a Jewish woman to take on. As often as not, Bertha encountered hostility and little support. She often compared herself to Sisyphus. Like Sisyphus, every time she apparently made any headway, her appeals for help would go unanswered and again she had to push the rock of her appeals up the mountain of indifference, all the while knowing that it would once more fall back down. As Albert Camus has written in his essay on the myth, it is precisely the conscious knowledge that makes Sisyphus's predicament both terrible and tragic: "There is no more dreadful punishment than futile and hopeless labor. . . . If this tale is tragic, that is because its hero is conscious. . . . If the descent is thus sometimes performed in sorrow, it can also take place in joy." Camus's vision is existential, but his words well capture Bertha's sense of religious fulfillment: "The struggle toward the heights is enough to fill a man's heart." No matter how often she failed to gain support, particularly from male Jewish organizations, she continued in her passionate mission.

In Frankfurt, Bertha could immerse herself in her collaboration with her sisters in JFB and in the care of her "children" at the Home. Still, she suffered from bouts of loneliness and a sense of isolation. In the spring of 1911, she embarked on a long voyage to investigate conditions in far-flung cities from Eastern Europe to the Middle East. She went as her own emissary and she allowed herself to be absent for several months because she believed, *au fond*, as she wrote in *Sisyphus-Arbeit,* that she was needed "for nothing and to no one." From the Middle East she wrote of her fatigue and of her duty. Yet the letter hints at more, for Bertha says that without her sense of duty, her "fancies" would take flight and be her undoing. Duty was thus a sacrifice that she enjoyed and needed.

In her letter-writing Bertha reveals an inner tension between the personal and the public. Her letters from her trips of 1911 and 1912 were not personal but circular letters meant to be distributed by subscription to her friends in Frankfurt. The goal on both occasions was a public one, to inform colleagues about moral degeneracy in cities like Jerusalem, Alexandria, and Moscow. Her letters were sufficiently informative—and shocking—that she elected to publish them unedited in a volume. The title, appropriately, was *Sisyphus-Arbeit* (Sisyphus Work). At the same time, the letters are also personal. They recount her dreams, note when she needs to take a nap, and record personal encounters that lay outside her mission. Taken as a witting study of her character, *Sisyphus-Arbeit* is an idiosyncratic masterpiece. The letters reveal the complexity of their author, casting light on her compassion, her ferocity, her moral rage, her pride and sorrows as a Jewish woman, her obsession with beauty, and her persisting, scathing sense of humor.

Besides her travels, Bertha exercised her loneliness in private reflection. A poem, written in 1911, captures her intermittent despair:

Love was not for me,
So I live like a plant
In a cellar without light.

Love was not for me,
So I sound like a violin
Played with a broken bow.

Love was not for me,
So I bury myself in work,
And make myself sore with duty.

Love was not for me,
So I try to look upon death,
A friendly face.

As the decade progressed, the inner tensions informing the various movements Bertha pioneered exploded. At the Fifth International Jewish Conference on White Slavery in 1913 in London, periodic friction erupted between Jewish and Christian delegates. The hundreds of delegates from more than two dozen countries engaged in a bitter debate over the repatriation of prostitutes. Bertha was bitterly opposed to sending young women back to the same oppressive circumstances that lured or forced them into prostitution.

In 1912, with modest means Bertha attempted to found a Jewish hospital in Przemyśl and ended up risking her life in the process. To initiate nurses' education among the local Jewish girls, two nurses from Frankfurt accompanied her, and she prescribed the commonly worn long hospital gowns also for the Przemyśl girls. Their mothers threw stones at Bertha for fear their daughters would be turned into nuns.

In response to these and other incidents Bertha again took to her writing table to purify her vision. Her constant concerns with the interdependent consequences of pogroms, prostitution, and Zionism inspired a new dramatic work, *Tragic Moments: Three Images of Life,* published in 1913. The first scene takes place after a pogrom in a Russian village in 1904. The play's protagonist, student Uri Gurewitsch, has suffered through the unexpected rampage along with her fellow villagers. Uri's mother has been killed, as have eighteen other Jews; after being raped, his sister, Esther, commits suicide by slashing her wrists. Uri and his fiancée Fella are married by a rabbi in a cellar and forced to flee. The rabbi gives them a false passport and an ornate Torah scroll and instructs the couple to protect the holy book.

The second scene takes place in a shabby room in Frankfurt in 1908, where Uri, Fella, and their baby son, Shiri, are living. As immigrant Jewish students, the only work Uri and his wife can find is addressing envelopes. A businessman named Rosenberg approaches Fella and tries to lure her into prostitution and make her husband her procurer. Uri strikes Rosenberg, who reports him to the police. In desperation they give their precious Torah to an unsavory usurer named Goldschmidt, who arranges for them to flee once again, this time to Palestine.

In scene three Uri, whose wife has died of the hardships in building a Jewish colony in Palestine, awaits the return of his son, Shiri. Shiri, whose name in Hebrew means "my song," has been completing his studies in Europe. Uri's life at fifty is still not peaceful. He is constantly fending off Arab attacks on his land.

Before his son's arrival Uri leaves to fight a massive attack by the bedouins, who destroy the work of a whole generation, including Uri's orange grove, which he planted with the hope that Shiri would reap the harvest. However, when Uri, bloodied from fighting, and his son finally meet, he discovers that Shiri has changed his name to Jerome. Jerome gives his father the holy Torah, which he has retrieved in Frankfurt. When Jerome asks Uri if he remembers his son's bar mitzvah, Uri replies: "In my mind's eye I saw the colony prospering and spreading, and people with our children and our children's children, who with all the fibers of their soul—the liberated, strong, Jewish soul—would again have taken root in their old homeland, the homeland of our fathers. And on that day, when you came of age, I asked you to remain faithful to the land of your fathers. Do you still remember it, Shiri?" "I can't remain, Father," Jerome replies. "By a thousand ties I feel myself connected to the civilization that's been developing for centuries in Western Europe. Through the contribution of Jews and Christians, it has become the possession of all. I need the books, the paintings, the stage, the newspapers, the battle about issues and interests, the commotion of the city—I can no longer play at being a peasant. And as a Jew I also cannot respond to the Zionist appeal. It's cowardly to leave the battlefield with a few thousand and settle in a protected corner, to found a new language ghetto, knowing well that never will all Jews, particularly the poorest and weakest, find a homestead there. It's unjust to carry unrest and duplicity into the Jewish communities instead of telling them: Be patient with one another, live uprightly, and be faithful to our Judaism—adhere to the content of the teaching—don't let it be presented to you in alien form—for ours is the teaching of the One God and the commandment of loving one's neighbor!" Uri responds by putting a revolver to his head and killing himself.

Bertha's play about a twentieth-century "displaced Jew" explores her conflict of how to respond to the evil of ever-changing persecutors, and the degeneracy of some of her own people. Bertha, the epitome of a cultured woman, obviously identifies with the assimilated son. She also clearly perceives that with the increased prosperity in Palestine, Arabs will replace Christians in the unending chain of threats to the Jewish people. Although the work is melodramatic and poorly structured, and its characters are intellectual props, Bertha's theme, that the Jewish homeland resides within the spiritual life of the individual, vividly captures her own hope for salvation.

In 1914, World War I began. Although Bertha, at fifty-five, had been suffering from rheumatism, gallbladder trouble, and a weak heart, as the leader of JFB, she joined the BDF (Bund deutscher Frauenvereine) in support of the fatherland during the war. At the beginning of the war Bertha made one of her houses available to the city of Neu-Isenburg as a military hospital, but the city gave it back after several months when it was no longer needed. The wards contributed to the Isenburg war effort with 25 pairs of socks, 122 bandages, and 66 breast protectors. For the Frankfurt war effort, they produced 100 military coats and 100 helmet protectors.

World War I was a catastrophe for the seven million Jews in the east who were caught among the Russian, German, Austrian, and Rumanian armies. Edward Bristow justly remarks that the dimensions of this disaster tend to be forgotten. During the ten-month Russian occupation of Galicia there were murderous expulsions of 600,000 Jews from Poland and the Russian border regions. By 1916, relief workers estimated that nearly half of the six million Russian and Polish Jews were without means of support.

While the war quickly disrupted international white slavery, it caused increases in Jewish prostitution in the eastern and southern war zones, where women were desperate to avoid starvation. The Germans regularly forced Jewish women into prostitution and dispatched mobile brothels to the front. Of the 2,689 women prostitutes registered with the police in Warsaw, 24 percent were Jewish. Some of the more notorious Jewish traffickers in Warsaw became major war profiteers and probably agents for the Germans.

From 1914 to 1918, most of Bertha's normal activities and extensive travels were frozen. Only Vienna remained more or less accessible to her. Few of Bertha's letters from this period remain. Although the most important letters are addressed to the philosopher Martin Buber, the earliest ones are addressed to Sophie Mamelok, one of her "daughters" from the orphanage, whose career as a nurse and director of an orphanage in Galicia and whose plans for marriage and family Bertha attempted to control from afar, in much the same manner Bertha had been controlled by her own mother. In her letter to Sophie on February 28, 1914, Bertha is mildly depressed that she can't make definite, long-range plans for travel, but she still intends to go to Munich, Berlin, and Copenhagen. On September 12, 1914, Bertha writes, "Relief work for the Jews and some sections of War Welfare Department take all my time, and I forget my somewhat wretched body. Today, I ordered myself to bed because it is Saturday, but I'm not very happy about it. I am thinking of the myriad soldiers in the field, of the seriously wounded who may have to forgo the bare necessities. . . . As long as there is no peace, it goes without saying that you must stay on as a nurse in the Berlin organization. Nobody will insist that you go to Galicia while there is still war. Helene Krämer returned about a week ago, since her institution had been closed. First she stayed with me, and now she is with her married sister whose husband is a soldier. . . . All individual stories are of no importance in the great overall events." On December 8, 1914, Bertha again writes with magisterial directness: "First of all, about the important question of your offering your services to the Red Cross. Obviously, I cannot forbid you to do it, but I believe that since you have been trained by the Berlin Organization of Jewish Nurses you ought to stay with it. . . . You know that you are prone to asthma attacks and will be no good in a field hospital."

In 1915, Helene Lange, who had so deeply inspired Bertha's early feminism, betrayed her. In a speech, Helene mentioned the Catholic and Protestant women's associations that belonged to BDF, but neglected to mention JFB. Bertha demanded that Gertrude Baumer, the president of BDF, censure Helene Lange. Baumer refused, and Bertha withdrew from the National Women's Service (a wartime volunteer service), accusing both of them of "hatefulness towards Jewish women and Judaism." The problem of anti-Semitism in BDF was not thereby solved, but Bertha found personal vindication when she received a letter of apology from Gertrude Baumer.

Two issues that were anathema to Bertha were embodied in the person of the feminist Alice Salomon. Salomon was born Jewish, but converted to Protestantism and became a member of the Christian branch of BDF. In 1914, Salomon founded the first school for professional social work in Berlin. Bertha was still vehemently opposed to those who worked for money and not from altruism, but Salomon's school was the wave of the future.

In her own career Bertha essentially represented a unique

hybrid of two distinct kinds of social worker, the old evangelical crusader and the new modern social worker armed with statistics. In both England and America toward the end of the nineteenth century, there had existed evangelical maternity homes for "wayward" and "fallen" girls. Women who worked in these homes did so out of Christian duty, not for money. Referrals to these homes came not from social agencies or municipal bureaus, but through active recruitment of prostitutes and homeless women directly off the street.

In some respects Bertha represented a Jewish version of this evangelical style of social worker. In her twenty-nine years as the director of the Home in Isenburg, she never accepted a salary. She believed social work was a vocation and moral duty that should not be monetarily rewarded. In other respects Bertha already belonged to the first generation of the modern social workers. Referrals to the Home came from Jewish welfare agencies, not from workers roaming the streets at night. She kept meticulous files and statistics, following the newly conceived idea of "case work." Like most records from this early period Bertha's files contained essential data and notes; the voice of the ward was muted. In 1912, she allowed a psychiatrist to begin examining her charges, which was itself highly innovative. Max Sichel, the Home consultant, had been trained in the treatment of abnormal children. By 1914, Bertha was willing to specifically acknowledge his observations as valuable. In fact, by that time he had diagnosed five cases of mental illness. After the outbreak of World War I, Sichel was called to active duty, and Bertha then retained a Dr. Mannheimer to help with urgent cases.

Bertha drew the line when it came to establishing social work as a paid profession. Nor was she willing to substitute a scientific or sociological rationale for her own brand of moral duty-cum-piety as a treatment philosophy. As the status of professional social worker in Germany began to rise, Bertha's power struggle with its leading adherents mirrored the clashes between the new professionals, contemptuous of their evangelical predecessors, and the adherents of the old school. Further, this struggle reflected a still larger shift in contemporary public opinion as the traditional understanding of the "fallen" woman gradually gave way to a new "scientific" understanding of prostitution.

In the nineteenth century, prostitutes and homeless women, as well as unwed mothers, were universally considered by reformers to be in need of protection. Nineteenth-century reformers believed in the redemptive potential of white middle-class models of domesticity and desired to translate "feminine" virtue into social policy. According to social historian Regina Kunzel, social reformers turned the dominant ideology of gender difference to their advantage, using the rhetoric of domesticity to stake claims for social change and public policy. She notes that in the "multiple and changing understanding of the unmarried mother—as innocent victim, sex delinquent, unadjusted neurotic . . . both evangelical women and professional social workers inscribed their own anxieties . . . in the narratives of the out-of-wedlock pregnancy."

In 1916, Bertha attempted to organize an International Jewish Welfare Organization, bemoaning that Jewish communal life was so internally divided that it was bleeding to death and "weakens Jewry . . . and makes us long for a "Nathan the Wise," who will remind us of our worth and dignity as bearers of our ethical mission among the people. . . . Every Jewish man and every Jewish woman can perform an interesting, important, and sympathetic deed, even if they recognize their Judaism as little more than their 'origin'." Because of the war, the project had to be disbanded.

In 1916, Bertha initiated a correspondence with the philosopher Martin Buber, which would continue until her death. With the exception of her relationship with Breuer, most of which we know about from Breuer's own accounts, this relationship, along with brief close relations with her cousin Fritz Homburger, is the only other long relationship she had with a man. Although theirs remained a formal relationship, the correspondence reveals a deeper, unspoken bond. Unfortunately, Martin Buber's replies to Bertha do not seem to be extant. Of Bertha's twenty-year-long correspondence with Buber, only a score of letters remain. Bertha was acutely aware of Buber's major work, his mysticism and social activism. His masterpiece, *Ich und Du* (I and Thou), was published in 1923, but its early structure dates from 1919 and may have influenced Bertha's "Mystic Activism."

Martin Buber was born in Vienna twenty-one years after Bertha, on February 8, 1878. His parents separated and he was raised by his grandparents in Lemberg (today Lvov) in Galicia. Buber's mother tongue and culture, however, were German. In contrast to Bertha, Buber was able to reconcile his intense Jewish spirituality with Zionism. At the time she first wrote to him Buber had begun publication of his celebrated monthly journal, *Der Jude* (The Jew). In *Der Jude* Buber attempted to combine a wide spectrum of Jewish spiritual thought as well as politics, economics, and literature. Buber sought to unify the Jewish people with this journal, which, although Zionist in spirit, accepted articles by non-Zionists and writers in German, Yiddish, and Hebrew.

When Bertha first wrote to Buber in 1916, she ironically referred to herself as old. The war had increased her tendency toward self-battery. In the manipulative and controlling manner she used on both devotees and enemies, she forced her attention upon Buber and was elated when he responded. Her letters reveal the extent to which she had continued to internalize anti-Semitic Germans' perception of the inferiority and crudeness of Ostjuden—Eastern Jews—while alternately embracing them to the extent of calling them her "daughters" in her Home. Bertha's smugness in her superiority and education, and her idealized concept of the nuclear family, including the ethical position of the role of the mother within the family, was in direct contrast to Buber, who tended to shift easily among German high culture, socialism, and Zionism. Bertha's noblesse oblige attitude toward Eastern European peasant women reflects her sporadic desire to cleanse them of their own Jewish ghetto culture and to Westernize them. With even greater contempt and hatred Bertha rejected Zionism, which threatened her Western European identity. She perceived Palestine as a ghetto settlement where socialist ideals threatened to obliterate her upper-class identity with an artificial "equality" among all Jews that did not include women. She was also threatened by the concept of the collective rearing of children, which remained an unbearable thought to her. Bertha's compassion and identification with Eastern Jewish women's suffering was undercut by her desire that the Ostjuden be willing to give up their own "inferior" identities in favor of the intricately constructed image and values of the "civilized" Western Jewess.

Bertha first wrote to Buber with false modesty:

> Frankfurt A. M.
> May 28, 1916
>
> Dear Sir,
>
> I do not know if you recognize my name. I am a Jewess, an old woman with experience in social work who, by belonging to Jewry . . . upholds all the obligations and rights such responsibility calls for.

> Yesterday, I read with interest the 1st issue of the monthly journal you publish. I was . . . enormously appalled by the publication of little Dana's mother's letter. It has been clear to me for a long time that the life of an East-European Jewess is to be blamed largely on East-European culture, a blame shared by men who are believed to be cultivated and civilized. The ideals of child rearing and parenting are the most important criteria for a cultural aim of a nation. If Dana's mother's letter from the Front had been more than a release of a foolish woman . . . then it is but a tragic proof of an unstoppable decline among the widest multitudes in whom we have placed all our hopes, to whom all the rest of the western communities . . . have nothing to offer.
>
> These "Danas" are the ruin of our people. Just read the letter from which feebleness, blind devotion and superficiality scream out. The father is on the Front, but the chubby girl (how good of her!) doesn't bum about (not yet), doesn't obey her mother, and doesn't look like a soldier's daughter. The father is on the Front, the world is shaken by the events, but little Dana is only complaining that she would have a birthday party, and the grandmother in Israel gives her dresses, gloves, shoes, cakes, and barely gets by with 30 rubles from the Town Council (charity). There is no doubt that the girl is lazy. . . .
>
> I have given up a long time ago the attempt of letting the Eastern-European Jews and the Zionists know what it is they suffer from . . . they ought to bear the consequences of their weakness. . . . I hope the article won't attract the attention of the experts, for that would be grist to the mill of the malicious.

Bertha was delighted to receive an immediate response from Buber, who, by asking her to submit an article to *Der Jude,* obviously recognized her as one of the most famous Jewish women in Europe. They began a correspondence that included an exchange of ideas, texts, and collaboration on projects of mutual interest, although they disagreed on most political issues.

May 30, 1916
Heppenheim a.d.

Bergstrasse

Dear Sir,

I have enjoyed your letter very much. I was not sure I would receive an answer and thought you either would keep silent or, with a great gesture give a familiar speech to parry. Naturally, I am pleased to know that there exists someone like you seem to be from your letter. It has been gracious of you to have put me on the list of collaborators to your journal. I would write an article on the subject, whose effective transformation has become a part of my life's meaning. Do not worry that I would hold anything back where the truth is called for, for it is of essence everywhere. I have but one tongue and one pen. But I do dislike the profusion of Jewish publications, and before I am ready to give of myself in a literary form, e.g. before I would be willing to submit an article, I want to better acquaint myself with your journal. The first issue, as I have told you, confounded me. Now, if you agree that your article 'From the Front' did more harm than good, and if you uphold the principle of unreserved rectification, then in your next issue you will publish my letter, without cuts or revisions—that goes without saying. Under those conditions, I would grant you the right. I would be pleased if a working relationship were to develop between you and me, at least in the areas where our conscience would allow it. I am an opponent of Zionism and even more so of the Zionists.

Respectfully
Bertha Pappenheim

Buber and Bertha both supported the German Fatherland during the war in spite of protests by left-wing political leaders and ideologists like Gustav Landau who condemned the "war-Buber," writing "to speak of the Jewish stake in German victory was to ignore all the Jewish blood spilled by the murder of Germans, Slavs, Rumanians, Italians, Austrians, and Russians . . . a pity for the Jewish blood . . . a pity that you have gone astray in this war!"

The title of Bertha's 1916 collection of short stories, *Kämpfe* (Struggles), refers to the conflicts of the external war, which mirror Bertha's internal conflicts: the opposing forces of Jews and gentiles; of German Jews and the Ostjuden; of Jews and converts; of feminism and Judaism; of Jewish feminism and German feminism; and of feminism and patriarchy. Bertha's stories are investigations into the Jewish struggle for existence, which dramatize many of these themes. Bertha's style moves toward the literary conventions of "realism," although the plots remain melodramatic. Melodrama as a descriptive term has always been pejorative. However, as a genre, Eric Bentley argues for its importance against "realism" and "naturalism," because of its expression of emotion in the pure histrionic form of dreams and its representation of the quintessentially dramatic, the embodiment of the root impulse of drama. According to Peter Brook in *The Melodramatic Imagination,* the melodramatic mode of conception is the "very process of reaching a fundamental drama of the moral life and finding the terms to express it." Brook finds melodrama the only term which applies to a mode of "high emotionalism and stark ethical conflict" that is neither comic nor tragic. Brook notes that the "bearer of the sign of innocent may be lost, pursued, disguised, but must be brought into the sphere of public recognition and celebration. Opposed to virtue and innocence states the active, denial of them in the "person of evil, known traditionally as *le traître* . . . betrayal is a personal vision of evil . . . and undoes the moral order."

Of the five stories that comprise *Kämpfe,* four of them take place in Galicia and are almost long enough to be called novellas. In each story loyalty to Judaism is under siege; the central character betrays or revolts against Jewish ideals and tradition either through relationships with gentiles, conversion, or immoral behavior. Each story describes a generational struggle in which a parent terminates what he/she considers the immoral behavior, yet a catastrophe still results.

"The Redeemer" is the only story that does not take place in Galicia, but in London, although the protagonists are East European Jews. A young boy, in his attempt to prevent the religious conversion of an immigrant Jewish girl, promises to protect her for life. The two children, Reisle and Wolf, are separated for many years, but eventually meet again in Paris. Wolf is infatuated with Reisle, but discovers that she has not only converted, she has become a prostitute. Wolf murders Reisle, paradoxically, to "redeem" her. Again, the denouement reflects Bertha's conviction that justice has primacy over love.

In "The Weakling," a son defies his rabbi father and his traditional upbringing in order to study art in Vienna. He converts to Catholicism and marries a Christian, having "never before known a Jewish girl." Through his extramarital contact with a Jewish woman, he realizes that his father's teachings were morally right and that he has permanently lost his identity through his denial of Judaism. In utter despair and guilt he commits suicide, a Christian's ultimate sin.

Similarly, in "Incident in a Hungarian Village," chronicling the attraction between a Jewish merchant's daughter and a

Catholic miller, the final result is the Jew's suicide. As in "The Weakling," a devout parent foresees an impending disaster and attempts to intervene, but is unable to avert it. In this case, the father is murdered by a gentile, again illustrating the rift between gentiles and Jews.

In "The Commemoration," Bertha tells the story of Pinkas, a fence guard, who places his hedonism over the commandment "thou shalt not steal." During a fire in a synagogue, Pinkas steals silver in order to buy a violin. He is plagued with guilt and incapable of giving voice to the music locked within him, perhaps paralleling the author's own loss of voice during her hysteria: "And in his madness and his pain the old man turned around in a circle, scratched on the instrument, listened to an inner melody, hummed confused notes and then standing in front of Benjamin [the son of the man killed in the synagogue fire]," he was unable to play and became mute. Once again, religious treachery is punished, and the memory of the goodness of the parental figure, Benjamin's deceased father, sparks a moral conversion.

In "The Miracle Rabbi," the story of a dynasty of mystical rabbis who serve their community as theistic psychologists, solving the practical problems and moral dilemmas of their congregation, the illness of the Reb Wolf's son, Arieh, is attributed to his reading of the Romantics and other Western literature rather than the Torah. Arieh's illness leads to Reb Wolf's unwilling return to his obligation as a "receiver" and paternal figure. Again, a child raised in an Orthodox household feels that his religious upbringing is confining, and wreaks hardship upon his family.

In "Friday Evenings," perhaps the most optimistic story of the collection, Bertha introduces a young girl whose family has sent her to work away from her poverty-stricken home. On Christmas Eve she is plagued by a desire to share in the exchange of gifts with her landlord's family, against parental admonitions: "She even knew that this was against the principles of her father, who always warned his children against becoming intimate with Christians. 'Seen up close, every goy is a devil,' he used to say." On her way outside, she inadvertently overhears threatening, anti-Semitic remarks and is evicted by the gentile landlord. Her redeemer becomes "one of her people, who stick together like tar and sulfur," a Jewish boy with whom she has attended lectures.

In all of the stories the gentile protagonist is cast as a betrayer. The Jewish characters, as a result of their artlessness and their trusting nature, bring clearly preventable disasters upon themselves. In Bertha's estimation the love between a Christian and a Jew is dislocating for both, and therefore a potential source for a disaster.

Throughout the terrible years of 1914–1918, when civilized Europe lay frozen under the ice of war, Bertha continued to support Germany's cause. On August 18, 1917, she asked Sophie Mamelok to come to Isenburg to help with 200 to 300 Jewish-Russian girls who were expected to work there as munitions workers. She suggested that Weibliche Fürsorge look after these girls in a friendly but strict manner and she needed someone who understood Yiddish and Jewish customs. Bertha knew that Sophie would supervise the girls without attacking their self-respect. In 1917 Bertha received the Cross of Merit for her aid in the war effort.

In June 1918, Bertha was familiar enough with Buber to invite him and his wife to visit her at the Home for Wayward Girls, which she humorously calls a "settlement," gently mocking Buber's Zionism. On June 17, she felt comfortable enough with him to rather viciously attack both his philosophical writing and his Zionism:

> I took time to read a small volume [Drei Reden über das Judentum (Three Speeches about Judaism)] . . . which I wanted to read with my young employees. . . . Now, despite my lack of knowledge of history and philosophy . . . I believe I partially understand your book, perhaps the fundamental thoughts: a paraphrase of "Jewish social policy" as I would like to live it and see Jews live it, too. . . . Does one really need for this, which is obvious, such a large scientific apparatus, so many things and words a woman—and there are among Jewesses thousands like me—does not know. . . .
>
> The mystery of Judaism which binds us Jews so strongly beyond time and place . . . this I feel is not explained in your book. . . . I believe that for many the thought of Zion in practice is a mendacity . . . for he who knows that the Ten Commandments and Love Thy Neighbor are Jewish . . . lives in this spirit—You may have a condescending smile of rejection for my explanations.
>
> In the next few days I'll send you the 3 speeches back again and will ask you for a book that I would be able to read with my employees.

According to Maurice Friedman, the revolutionary element in Buber's "Three Speeches" is existential. Buber transforms the "Jewish Question" from an abstract question of social identity to a deeply personal look at the meaning of Judaism to the Jew himself. Buber describes the Western Jew as divided because his culture is different from his community of blood. He calls for radical Jewish Renewal, not gradual evolution or liberal Reform. He proclaims that "My soul is not by the side of my people; my people is my soul. . . . I want my future—a new, total life. . . . Judaism has not yet done its work, and the great forces active in this most tragic and incomprehensible of people have not yet written their very own word into the history of the world." Buber called for the realization of three tendencies—unity, the deed, and the future. He called for messianism in which the Absolute is lived in the everyday. "All men, somewhere, in some loneliness of their pain or of their thought come close to God. . . . But the Jew, bound up with the world, immured in the world, dares to relate himself to God in the immediacy of the I and Thou—as a Jew. This is Judaism's primary reality."

Despite Bertha's attacks on Buber, an exchange she obviously enjoyed, her own relationship to the immanence of the Jewish God deepened and moved toward the mystic.

After the war, the JFB became a pacifist institution.

Chapter Twelve

TUESDAY AND FRIDAY EVENINGS (1919-1929)

If after hours of loneliness I find myself overwhelmed by the painful and melancholy thought that I live as the last one of my line, that no one will say Kaddish for me, then I am comforted by the thought that I could have had a stupid husband or a wayward child! (February 28, 1919)

• • •

Men are so vain and over time so indulged in their self-evaluation, that they consider a factual criticism of their behavior and attitude by a woman merely as a general "antagonism toward men." Women, on the other hand, have so little self-confidence that they believe "the man" to be always a support, helper and rescuer, even if he is obviously inferior and, in a specific situation, useless. (September 5, 1919)

• • •

If I may be permitted to criticize the Bible, I would say that from the unjust position the Bible assigns to the woman it is clear that it is the writing of a brilliant but masculine human being, not a divine dictation. In other words, there is no logical, necessary consequence of the differences between the sexes that is ordained by God. (December 5, 1923)

• • •

The difference between the professional social worker and the voluntary caregiver is like that between a craftsman and an artist. . . . The artist works (and starves if necessary) for the sake of art, the voluntary social worker, for the sake of love—both driven by an irresistible urge to perfection that liberates the soul. (January 6, 1927)

Bertha Pappenheim

Following the fall of the German Empire and the establishment of the Weimar Republic, in 1919 German women gained political equality and the right to vote. Political leaders now had to concern themselves with "The Woman Question." Although women won the vote, they did not organize a women's caucus in the Reichstag, nor did they form a national women's political lobby. Having obtained the right to vote, the primary goal of the BDF, the largely middle-class members became more conservative and the organization stopped attracting new young members. Women between twenty and thirty believed the new constitution had solved the "Woman Question," and the word "feminist" became a shrill, doughty anathema to them. Claudia Koonz cites a young law student's explanation of her indifference to feminism: "We are neither blue stocking nor crusader, nor rich or idle. The New Woman can be a genuine, one-hundred-percent woman now that women's rights have been won." The icon of the "Womanly Woman" gradually took hold in Germany. This movement revived Romantic ideas of selflessness, loyalty, and maternal love and fought against the "masculinization" of women. Jewish women, however, still did not have suffrage in the Jewish community. It wasn't until the end of the 1920s that they forced male leaders in six out of seven major German cities to give them suffrage under Jewish law.

Bertha, at the age of sixty, continued her exhaustive work at the Home and as the president of JFB. By 1919, JFB had 44,000 members in 215 branches, comprising twenty percent of all Jewish women in Germany. In the early 1920s, the women who had been or became Bertha's closest friends and associates took on leadership positions in JFB. In 1924, Hannah Karminski, a professional social worker who had become Bertha's best friend, began the JFB's monthly journal in Berlin. Ottilie Schönewald, a wealthy feminist who had been elected a municipal councilor of the German Democratic Party, was voted to the executive board of JFB in 1925. In her memoirs she recalled how an earlier encounter with Bertha at a German Women's Conference in 1912 had "determined my fate." At this meeting of BDF, which dealt with the position of women in the three major religions, Bertha was the clear victor. "With superb rhetoric," Bertha had forcefully forged the connection between women's rights and public duty, using as her leitmotif Lessing's parable of the three rings. This parable, the focal point of *Nathan the Wise,* propagating religious tolerance, became an increasingly important symbol for Bertha. Ottilie also describes the spiritual strength she gained from Hannah Karminski and Cora Berliner, her closest co-workers in the JFB. Ottilie resigned from the Parliament in 1926 when several Nazis were elected to it. Bertha's vision of the broad mission of JFB made it easier for Ottilie to quit German national politics in favor of Jewish feminist politics. She envisioned herself as an exemplar of Bertha's maxim "that the Jewish community had forfeited the interest and the cooperation of the Jewish woman by refusing her the full joint responsibility that alone leads to the fulfillment of duty." Helene Krämer, one of the many "daughters" whom Bertha had guided from the Frankfurt orphanage into social work, returned from Poland, where she had been a director of an orphanage, to Isenburg, to be the headmistress of the Home under Bertha's directorship.

The financing of the Home became a major problem. The wealthy circle of Bertha's Frankfurt supporters were ruined by the postwar inflation, which reached its peak in 1923, the same year that Adolf Hitler wrote *Mein Kampf.* For financial help Bertha increasingly had to rely on the American Joint Distribution Committee and food shipments from Switzerland, the Netherlands,

Denmark, and England. Bertha assumed that the Joint Committee would fund her because her cousin Felix Warburg was a rich American. Felix spent enormous energy reigning over a maze of time-consuming charities and, along with his wife Frieda, held court as the King and Queen of American Jewry. The Joint Distribution Committee's executive branch met at Felix's office or in the "Rembrandt Room of his mansion, named for the etchings on display."

Felix had given money to Bertha in 1920 when the postwar inflation started to threaten the financing of the Home. In her shame over not being able to repay him, she wrote with ironic wit:

> Dear Mr. Warburg, June 9, 1920
>
> The spirits I summoned. . . . Now Mrs. Levy-Heinemann from Rockaway sends constantly wonderful things to me, unfortunately not only necessities, but luxuries like sardines, even chocolate, and my debt with you must grow immeasurably. This depresses me greatly. Now I want to tell you that—because of currency problems—I can't pay right away or even soon, but I'll see to it that you, my creditor, will be paid according to my testament. Please help me only to have Mrs. Levy stop sending everything except flour, sugar, oil, and corned beef. I do it, too. In my disquiet toward you because of the repayment, I have spoken with Mrs. Louise Goldschmidt, if it was proper, because I could possibly pay only after my death. She didn't think this plan was not correct, and because I am quite shaky—maybe because Mrs. Levy wants to take care of me since such a short time ago—your chances are increasing accordingly. Maybe you will become my sole inheritor through this unusual way! In reality, I am not in a jocular mood.
>
> A great, great joy for me to see your mother during

her transit to Switzerland. I can only say "unberufen [touch wood]." She said that you have the intention to come to Europe again. That would be very nice. Please keep Mrs. Levy from being so zealous, and be assured that I am mindful of my obligations and remain so, even when the circumstances are uncomfortable.

With best regards,
Bertha Pappenheim

By 1924 conditions at the Home had deteriorated to such an extent that Bertha again sought the assistance of her cousin, this time in a desperate panic:

Dear Mr. Warburg, March 28, 1924

Not because of lack of respect for the sanctity of the organization, but to avoid the long painful red tape, am I approaching you directly because you are the head of the powerful Joint [Distribution Committee]. I am pleading for financial help for the Youth home of the Jewish Women's Organization in Isenburg. We have received help in every period of giving by the Joint, but today we stand before the dire necessity of building renovations in the small houses, and major repairs and new provisions. With hesitation I am writing the sum estimated as a minimum: Dm20,000—. Can the Joint help us, will you assist us personally, will you put in a good word with your friends? Since weeks I postpone writing this letter—as I have promised my colleagues—because it is so difficult to beg. Actually, the work should begin with the good season—it should have started already—, but only today did I give myself the necessary push, and I only hope that you don't take it amiss that I wrote you and not Mr. Bernhard Kahn in Vienna. If you want to have the exact figures of the details of the estimate, I am naturally willing to send them to you. But all in all, you can rely on me that I am careful and economical, and would not enlarge or change things if I could not really justify it.

I am expecting a speedy and positive answer from you and the Joint office.

Yours,
Bertha Pappenheim

Bertha often remarked that the younger generation had lost the ability to spend meaningful time alone, but in fact she herself rarely had time for introspection and reflection. Work in the Home proved particularly strenuous after the war. The focus of the Home before the war was the care for the unmarried mother and her child; after the war the Home expanded its mission to include the care of orphans from both the East and West. Since the economic situation of the Home had worsened and there were many "war babies" to look after, Bertha was thankful for an association of employees that she had founded for allowing her even some minimal free time.

Bertha wrote of a "delightful hour" she took for private celebration on the last day of Hanukkah, December 23, 1919. The holiday had always been important to her, though at times sorrowful. In 1881, during Hanukkah she had been kept from her dying father. In 1882, she began to mentally and emotionally relive the previous year. In 1919, she began her Hanukkah observance by lighting a cozy charcoal fire in the stove, which she pretended was a fireplace. At the "fireplace" she had an "economically criminal urge": she lit three candles in the brass ceiling lamp with its graceful branches. Since it was the last evening of Hanukkah, she actually should have lit eight candles to praise God, but she had only four, which softly lit her room. "The beautiful lamp on the table glowed, the yellow vase sparkled like an exquisite piece of amber. The yellow roses were no longer fresh, but I didn't mind; nor did the flirting clay shepherds—they sat on a pink ribbon and were lost to the world." When she looked to the right, she saw her collection of silhouettes. Always remembering Vienna, she placed a figure of Maria Theresa in laced-up camisole and court dress. Feeling unencumbered by historical knowledge and cultural history, Bertha believed she possessed more religious tolerance than the royal anti-Semite, so for Maria Theresa's salvation she hung two silhouettes of priests on either side of her, and with tenderness she then hung the image of the young Franz Joseph in the company of six smartly dressed Viennese girls.

She mused on the devastation of the war and on the economic depression in Vienna, writing that Vienna to which the world was indebted "for so much beauty and merriment is starving," and that people were sending contributions with such hypocrisy that her "cheeks get hot with shame." Vienna, she bemoaned, was "hungry and cold. Praise the Viennese children were lucky to be shadows before they ever heard of annexation and before they knew that the Vienna woods had been cut down."

Then Bertha became suddenly happy with the thought that she had translated Mary Wollstonecraft's *In Defense of Human Rights*—she had almost forgotten that she did. Bertha felt that there was a straight line from her "spiritual understanding in those days to my right to vote with full responsibility." She gazed in front of her at her beautiful commode given to her by her cousin Louise, and reflected: "beauty belongs to all. It may give joy for generations if it is shaped in precious material. . . . But common materials may also be precious; heavy, brittle iron, how exquisite it can be forced, charm and iron." She wished that more women could have both these qualities—usually felt to be in opposition. She mused again on Mary Wollstonecraft: "Dear woman, you were able to unite the opposites harmoniously." Bertha might well have been writing about the evolution of her own character.

As she contemplated the intricacy of women's handwork, her eyes followed her bell-pull with its many beaded parrots. She felt both envy and admiration for a woman who had time enough for this embroidery. She then looked at her black cabinet: "It was once to hold my father's collection of goblets." Since her childhood she found it had awed her. Now it served as her "comforter." It was empty. She felt ashamed that for three years she had not found the time, energy, or leisure to replace her thousand "dear, dear little things, or to pet them." She was particularly mournful that for five years, she "had not seen my laces, my greatest treasure, documents of feminine artistry, taste, culture." At the end of her hour she reveals herself more deeply: "What longing one can have for dead things. Maybe because my life has left me lonely. I extinguish the candles; my Hanukkah celebration is over!"

In August 1920, Hitler announced that "scientific" anti-Semitism had proved the dangers of the Jewish race to the German people. He felt it must be "our concern to arouse in our people instinctive feelings against the Jews." In 1923, he proclaimed, "The Jew may be a race, but not a human being. . . . The Jew is the image of the devil." Even in Bertha's tranquil town of Neu Isenburg, "nightly rampages of teenagers" made attacks on Jewish homes, and the local police had to be summoned to patrol Jewish homes and shops.

In the four houses of the Home, which Bertha called "invisible Isenburg," the joys of Jewish education and celebrations continued to be untouched by the outside world. The Home was a private haven, its milieu structured by Bertha's aesthetic and ethical principles. In an answer to a questionnaire, she asserted: "Without imagination it is completely impossible to organize anything at all. . . . The creative aspect of organizing seems to me to contain an artistic element. Success means so much to me in human terms that I have to react with a kind of hostility to the disruption of an organization that I have envisioned or desired, as a painter or a sculptor would who sees his work destroyed."

In the world outside Isenburg, Bertha continued her revolutionary activities as the president and emissary of JFB. She started a campaign to eradicate tuberculosis among Jewish children in 1922; the disease had been the cause of one of her sister's and her father's death. She organized an International Women's Conference in 1923 and a Jewish World Conference for the Creation of a World Guardianship of Abandoned Children in 1924.

Underneath this abundant philanthropic activity, Bertha became dismayed with the JFB leadership. In 1924, she resigned as its president, something she had threatened to do in both 1916 and 1922. Times had changed, new issues were at the forefront, and white slavery, Bertha's burning issue, was no longer a high priority for the organization. The 1920s were the Jazz Age; younger women bobbed their hair and wore short skirts, while Bertha retained her Victorian attire and her "old-fashioned" primness. This was the era of the emancipated "new woman" and the professional career woman. The JFB Berlin branch recorded the formation of eleven different professional sub-organizations for Jewish women, among them a medical group, an office and sales group, and a group for jurists and political economists. How far removed this younger generation was from Bertha's noblesse oblige philanthropy! Among the social issues that interested the younger generation were criminal law, constitutional law (citizenship), women in politics, women in public service, pacifism, standards of living, and a women's police.

In contrast to this new generation of women with professional ambitions, the girls in Bertha's Home were trained for menial factory jobs or domestic work. They settled into arranged marriages within their own class and background. Bertha had no higher aspirations for the poor Ostjuden than a smattering of education, pride and knowledge of Judaism, and a clean, hard-working life. Bertha also clung to her belief that the wealthy volunteer worker was superior to the trained professional social worker. At one discussion of this issue at a JFB meeting, an auditor made notes: "Talk was of social welfare work and of the work of official social workers. Then a delicate, fragile figure rose, whose lovely head radiated lightning of holy zeal. . . . She demanded that social work not be left solely to professional workers, that it be the moral obligation of everyone. . . . It was a prophetic function that she fulfilled."

On November 6, 1924, Bertha wrote a letter to her friend Mrs. Guggenheim, who was unable to have children. Bertha expressed her sense of fulfillment in her work:

> Dear Frau Guggenheim!
>
> I feel how sad you are that a woman's chief happiness may have been denied to you, but I would, however like to share with you a consolation that might not seem altogether like one at the moment, but which will become all the more vivid with time: Women who must do without the happiness of genuine, personal motherhood, may come to develop their capacity for spiritual motherhood if they follow the peaceful path of caring for children and young people, who have been partially or altogether denied their physical mothers. You can become a providence for these young people, whom you

> should learn to serve with entire warmth and spirit, doing both important work and learning to carry out "small holy deeds"—then you will learn to bear your fate with sorrow and perhaps you will be able to discover in it great, if also painful, laws and guidelines. And remember that as old as I am, I will also be there for you if you ever need me at a given point in your work.
>
> My best thanks for the beautiful little cloth—perhaps my home-life will again become such that I will make use of it with a cheerful spirit.

The phrase "small holy deeds" was Bertha's dictum for herself, an invocation of her spiritual duty.

Bettina Brenner was elected to succeed her as JFB president. Still a loyal member, Bertha visited Bettina often as an adviser. Bettina recalls the "wonderfully, beautiful hours" that Bertha spent in her Leipzig home. It was understood that a visit from Miss Pappenheim was only permitted if it had a "purpose"; it could not merely be for pleasure. Bettina wrote that "the much abused word 'culture' with all its potential attributes had no better embodiment than Bertha Pappenheim. . . . Whether it was at larger 'receptions' given in her honor where she shared the role of hostess, or within her closest circle—in a threesome—that she explained the most fundamental Jewish existential issues in her combative manner, with untiring energy until late in the night, whether she sat silently in a corner listening to the piano music that was often played at her request, she was always the same, charming, interesting—simply unique—woman."

Bertha also resigned from the BDF board. As Marion Kaplan has justly commented, Bertha's participation on the board reflected the symbiosis of her "feminist and Jewish loyalties." Bertha believed that Jewish women working as Jews within the

German movement could "fight anti-Semitism through personal interaction," and that friendship was possible through mutual interests and issues. Social work as a cause was intrinsic to Bertha's whole philosophy, for only a deeply felt and mutual commitment could provide a possible meeting ground for Jew and gentile.

The new generation of JFB social workers came from a variety of social classes; many had to earn their own living and could not work as volunteers. Their involvement in issues was practical, not passionate. In her letter of resignation, Bertha protested

> the chain of indifference, misunderstanding, not understanding, the putting off and always remaining half-hearted, concerning the issues that are important to me and which my conscience will not let me abandon. I name only sterilization, the kindergarten seminar, the waiving of school attendance, not to mention the evacuation and rescue of children. I know you will object that these things should not depend on JFB. Admittedly, but the posture in our circle was lame, only agreeing as long as I was part of it, otherwise indifferently rejecting and postponing. I cannot accept any responsibility for this pace or position, and this flirtation with the Central Welfare Agency disgusts me. It may be that there is no other way, but that too is no reason for me to remain, knowing I cannot succeed, grinning amicably, on the board.

Cora Berliner wrote that the sharp tone in Bertha's resignation was not rare in her correspondence. Cora explained that "in this woman lived a volcano which erupted when her fury was aroused. Did she take pleasure in conflict? In part." When someone Bertha attacked tried to defend his or her point of view or accused her of unfairness or self-righteousness, she was not offended or angry. "On the contrary," Cora wrote, "[Bertha] felt a certain satisfaction in having goaded her adversary and was unable to see the wounds she inflicted. It is true only of matters which immediately related to her goals. Here she could mercilessly castigate what seemed to her cowardice, weakness, and dishonesty, and she could never be convinced that her opponent might have other material reasons for his position. . . . The tragedy of those battles did cause her pain. Combativeness was never an end in itself. Only when her mission was at stake, did she employ the heavy artillery."

Bertha's passion revolved around two circles of thought. First, Bertha believed that social work should depend on the voluntary participation of women in the Jewish community, and that only woman "with her maternal instincts, her life-preserving will is capable of truly empathizing with the distress of a suffering creature and can actually use this empathy to help it." She distrusted men and all professional social workers, male and female. She always suspected that among professional social workers, social issues served as a foil for the exercise of ambition and power. Cora asserts that Bertha had "such a proud, intractable, independent nature" that she held in contempt those who took a bureaucratic position and sacrificed their freedom. At the same time, she herself demanded subordination and discipline within her organizations.

Bertha's second circle of passion was focused on the abuse of women as sexual objects, which "caused her an almost physically felt pain." She felt that people's indifference to this issue was a disgrace she would never overcome. She traveled around the world, calling upon all nations and religions to work with her in her battle against white slavery. When they failed "she threw her complete contempt at their heads . . . because here her deepest womanhood was utterly wounded. . . . Conflict was her life element and the expression of her strength. Combat was as holy to her as good deeds and love."

In 1928, Bertha gave a speech on the silver anniversary of the Girl's Club she had founded twenty-five years before. At the age of sixty-nine, she asked: "Is it a tragedy or a grace to be old and to get old? It is a tragedy when one realizes what things we still want, which in our head are still like frames yet to be filled. . . . But to be old in some moments is grace . . . grace, if one feels that one has created something, that one has not passed by great things without taking an interest. . . . In this moment I feel grace." The same year, Bertha purchased a small house near the Home, which she hoped would eventually serve as a center for Jewish cultural life. In contrast to her almost obsessive work and attention to the details of daily life, she organized Tuesday evenings at the house and Friday Sabbath at the Home as celebratory events.

Tuesday evenings were conducted in the manner of a traditional European artistic salon, but without the artifice, pretension, or men that had dominated the salons of Bertha's young adulthood in Vienna. These occasions were both sacred and joyous to the circle of women she entertained. Bertha bountifully recreated the Viennese *maîtresse de maison extraordinaire*. Though far removed from the social grandeur of her youth, she reproduced the aura of a gracious patrician home within the austere provincial environment of the larger Home in Neu-Isenburg. She called her friends jokingly "my little circle" and prepared the evenings with love. She consciously chose Tuesday, because it was the day that is twice called *ki-tov*, from the invocation of "God is good" in the story of creation. The social composition of the "circle" underwent changes in the course of almost ten years, but a core

Bertha's house in Neu Isenburg, 1920. [Photo © Leo Baeck Institute]

group of members remained part of it to the end. Bertha rarely deviated from the democratic principle of allowing her *ki-tov* people the right to make suggestions and objections.

Bertha spent every Tuesday afternoon in town, buying delicacies for her dinner. As Sara Eisenstaedt described it, "Her imagination was inexhaustible in the invention of new dishes, and the Lucullan delights she offered us were as varied as the patterns of her necklaces." The necklaces themselves were often given as gifts to her friends. Bertha gave them fanciful names, such as "First Ball," "Old Vienna," "Eros," "Hazelnut," and "Turtle," and in their design they were as elegant and intricately varied as the laces she collected and tatted. She believed that as social workers it was improper for her colleagues to wear real pearls, fine jewelry, or furs, so she gave them these handmade ornaments, lest they feel unadorned. With the rise of the Nazi party,

Jewish women, out of fear, chose to become increasingly inconspicuous and to abjure ostentation in dress and manner.

Sara was awed by the sensuous decor and repasts, recounting, "We were offered everything in an amplitude and with such beauty that is difficult to describe in words." Bertha created menus and table decorations in a variety of fanciful colors and shapes, reflecting both her overflowing imagination and the extravagances of her Viennese upbringing. Sara believed that the richness of her offerings did not contradict Bertha's austere approach to life in the Home, because of Bertha's belief in the high educative value of the aesthetic: "It was with a boundless joy that she decorated the table for us and spoiled us with delicacies, but she would not have done to that degree purely for her own pleasure. And how much did she teach us through this!"

According to another guest, Bertha was "the refined hostess of the old school, meticulous—even when dressed with the utmost simplicity—." In spite of the fashionable lure of short skirts and bobbed haircuts, Bertha continued to attire herself as a Victorian lady. When she entered Bertha's house, the guest was greeted by a hearty handshake from a "small, delicate, black-clad lady. I use this word purposely; there is no one whom it suits better. . . . 'How did you spend the day?' was the typical first question, typical of the woman who allows no hour of the day to pass without devoting herself to the good, useful, and not least, beautiful. No task that contradicts her feeling for the beautiful satisfies her. . . . The flowers, the furnishings, the room's wallpaper, the sofa pillows, etc.,—a symphony of color; the atmospheric room with the lights somewhat dimmed in consideration of the eyes." Bertha's house was appointed with fine carved cupboards, skillful engravings from Old Vienna, amusing French watercolors on the staircase, all manner of upper-class refinements

French watercolors on Bertha's stairway. [Photo © Leo Baeck]

that were in stark contrast to the rude, pedestrian architecture of her house on Zeppelinstrasse 41. Her guests could view her garden with green fruit on the peach trees, red berries on the bushes, and a sweep of green lawn that vanished into the curvaceous Taunus hills.

The outward glory of the evening suited the splendor of its spiritual content. The cycle of the Jewish year was observed on these evenings. They celebrated Hanukkah, Purim, and the Tuesday evening before Pesach. It was Bertha's invention that a symbolic place be laid for the possibility of a miraculous visit by the Prophet Elijah every Tuesday, not just on Pesach, which was traditional.

When the guests entered Bertha's house they were released from the fetters of mundane life and enveloped in a warmth that might only have been duplicated in the homes of their parents in bygone years. She had a maternal concern for the well-being of her guests. Their cheer often reached the level of Bertha's exuberance. Bertha also adored gossip and her wit and humor were always present, with such teasing as, "Now, children, I am going to tell you something under greatest discretion. By that of course, I mean, repeat it!"

The conversations she commanded and stimulated were remarkable for the acuity of her questions and the intensity of her concentration. She was never rude or nasty, and nothing obscene was ever ventured. One guest noted that her "total honesty hovers above everything like a conductor, directing all that comprises the core of her personality, dominating in the beauty of form and expression. Her self-discipline educates her surroundings."

No one dared confront her with the prevailing mood of the time, made ominous by the beginning of the persecution of the German Jews. If anyone alluded to it, she would reply, "We are not in the ghetto," and to the objection, "Miss Pappenheim, we Jews have no space!" she would answer, "We don't need space, we have spiritual space that knows no limits." Bertha allowed her guests to relax and forget their personal worries; year after year she kept these evenings unaltered by the increasingly threatening political events. Bertha shared everything with her guests: collections, travels, reports, resolutions, her books, her poems, fairy tales, and Reminders. Both *grande dame* and *sage,* she spoke about what had impressed her deeply during the week, and over the years as well. "Not one of us ever imagined to elevate herself, even for a moment, to Bertha Pappenheim's level," Sara wrote in awe. Bertha loved and affirmed the Jewish destiny and life in its many forms. She refused to tolerate despair in these soirees; letting oneself go was strictly forbidden, as was any form of banality.

Bertha's sitting room in Neu Isenburg. [Photo © Leo Baeck]

"This Viennese woman's sensibility that was born of art, revealed itself when she decided periodically to resume her almost forgotten piano playing, and her pleasure in the works of the local giants, in the melodies of Mozart and Haydn, charmingly felt and interpreted, inspired pleasure around her, too," reminisced another guest, Käthe Mende.

"The picture of Bertha Pappenheim sitting on the sofa in the lamplight, stringing her beads is unforgettable," Sara remembered vividly, "her beaming face, the movements of those lovely hands. Thus we, her '*ki-tov*' people, will remember her always."

Bertha arranged Friday evenings, the Sabbath, as the high point of the Home's Jewish education. For her the observation of the Sabbath was spiritually deeper than the strict observation of a kosher household, deeper too then the superficial honoring of the Holy Days or of the commandments, which were in any case a priori incontrovertible laws of the house. Bertha wrote in a 1924 work report that "naturally in Isenburg there is religious instruction, graduated according to experience, or rather ignorance; one endeavors to teach the girls to read Hebrew and understand the prayers. In recent years through the congregational solidarity of Isenburg's Jewish families . . . services have been held in a room of the Home placed at their disposal on the Holy Days, during which a child might have seen a Torah scroll and heard a shofar for the first time."

Bertha felt that the most important education in the Home was the Sabbath, which developed its own tradition. Gertrude Ehrenwerth, who worked in the Home, described Bertha's shaping of the Friday evenings and holidays as "The loveliest of all her gifts to us—these evenings were unforgettable to everyone. They were so simply yet overwhelming, that every child could carry some of the glitter and festiveness away in himself." The evening began with a prayer which Bertha wrote for the children:

> Blessed be the one who remembers the Sabbath and observes it. Blessed be the Jews who are happy, proud, and upright in their community, which brought the divine idea of the day of rest into the world. Six days of honest work, industry, and effort, but on the seventh day, rest for the lifting of the spirit in holy form. May every Sabbath, from its beginning, give us the strength to identify ourselves anew as true Jews, to the unchangeable laws of custom, and to the beautiful traditions of our Father.

After the prayer, the evening's activities consisted, in Bertha's description, of "a happy gathering over a good meal, under the light of the candles, singing, reading, presentations by the children, cheerful parliamentarian discussions, fruit, chocolate, and

Children at the Home on the Sabbath. [Photo © Leo Baeck]

sweets (whenever we receive these as presents). We are happy when guests spend the Shabbas with us and make their own spiritual contributions. All of our discharged children are homesick for these evenings. If only we could be successful in teaching all of them to make the content of Judaism—according to

Hillel—in the practice of the commandment of neighborly love and in the understanding of the Ten Commandments find the guiding principle of their lives, it would be a pleasurable result of our efforts."

After the dinner, everyone crowded around her. Each child wanted to sit next to her. Some evenings she gave her own interpretation of the Ten Commandments. Once she said that if the people of Israel had given humanity nothing more than the Ten Commandments and the Sabbath, "these alone would have been enough to justify their existence." She considered the Sixth Commandment, preserving the sanctity of life, to be a specifically Jewish obligation.

She always strove to impart new festivals and customs. She gave the children a Sabbath prayer to sing at noon. She was happy when the two-year-olds were already able to say a blessing over the bread. Bertha, beloved by her wards for her storytelling, told "big" stories and created her own religious themes. She was always overflowing with love and wittiness, whether telling her own tales or reading from Dr. Dolittle, or the "flying classroom." "With her exquisite humor she brought these fairy tales to life before us. At her suggestion and with her enthusiastic participation stories from the Dolittle book were transformed into a shadow-play," wrote Gertrude admiringly.

When she read aloud, she always interrupted herself and encouraged the children to express their own opinions and explain what had already been read. Her sensitivity to language revealed itself on the so-called "Question Nights." On these nights children could ask questions or request the explanation of words they did not understand. Bertha "introduced turns of phrase as comparisons, and enough ideas to think and read about for days." She was especially pleased if the children made up stories themselves,

Stork Fountain, donated by Bertha to the Home c. 1928.
[Photo © Leo Baeck Institute]

put on plays, or sang folk songs. Bertha radiated a "child-like" joy in these gatherings.

Hannah Karminski lovingly remembered a Friday evening during which Bertha recounted a journey she had made to Rome. She spoke of the beautiful Fontana di Trevi that one would always yearn for. "I only wish there could be such a Fontana di Trevi, such a fountain of yearning, in Isenberg too, so that everyone who lived here would think of it afterwards—yearning for what is beautiful." Bertha donated a fountain called "The Stork" to the Home, its motif of the mythical bringer of babies hearkening back to one of her first fairy tales, *In Storkland*. Later, the fountain was destroyed, but a description and picture of it remain:

> The fountain is an entertaining piece of sculpture. It lies embedded in the greens and varied colors of the orchard

> and lawns which surround the Home, and invites one to pause, quietly observe and enjoy it. The bonds between human beings and all the creatures of the earth, the deepest meaning of motherhood, and the wishful sadness that the enchanting fairy veil lends these creatures—all this through the language of art is made understandable to the imagination of a child. On the first part of the triptych is a She-bear protecting her cub from falling from a tree; in the middle portion a hen protects her chicks under her wing; and the third section shows the stork Adebar, threatened by an insolent monkey.

Apart from her Tuesday and Friday evenings, Bertha remained sharply attuned to issues in the outside world. While socialist and communist feminists called for both contraception and abortion after the war, most bourgeois feminists, especially the JFB, remained opposed. The Frauenbund leaders worried about the declining Jewish birthrate and encouraged Jewish women to raise larger families. Both contraception and abortion were condemned on religious grounds, but other means of birth control had become widespread among Jews.

By 1925, however, JFB was willing to join BDF in supporting the legalization of abortion for medical and social reasons, although they warned of the "physical dangers for women."

In 1927, Bertha wrote sharply about both the death penalty and abortion:

> I would like to see the words "Death Penalty" and their meaning encoded in the new penal laws in a manner that would make ethical spillers of blood come to be known as judges, not murderers.
>
> The deadly electrical current should come into practice as the sole method of execution. There should be no appointed executioner.

> Any judge believing it necessary to impose such a sentence would also be required to carry it out—by throwing a switch or pressing a button—as an act of the highest responsibility of conscience. His unwillingness to do so would call his judgment into question.
>
> Those who oppose the death penalty must also oppose abortion. The death penalty destroys a life that has been proven harmful to the community, but abortion robs the community of countless opportunities to bring up and witness the blossoming of life's precious values.

Bertha published *Sisyphus-Arbeit II* in 1929. This volume is a collection of letters Bertha sent to international leaders protesting the white slave trade and calling for world guardianship of abandoned children. Again, she felt frustrated in realizing her mission. In her introduction to the volume, she wrote that those "who promote the enjoyment of alcohol, the enjoyment of opium, and who want the unrestrained, irresponsible enjoyment of sex . . . regard prostitution as merely a cheerful 'affirmation of life.'" On the other hand, the representatives of the opposite approach believe that prostitution as a social ill cannot be eliminated any more than "theft, swindle, robbery and murder." However, Bertha would not tolerate silence, especially when the victims were Jews, who were particularly vulnerable in this underworld. She insisted that "Jewish women and girls constitute a kind of fair game, partly as a result of complications (statelessness, difficult marriage law), partly as a result of antagonistic attitudes in their countries of residence (anti-Semitism); their position becomes still more difficult for the homeless and uprooted creatures as a result of repatriation laws." Bertha was particularly distressed that the world regarded the slave trade as "a Jewish business," and noted that even before the war, the protection of girls and women turned out to be "a labor of Sisyphus."

At the age of seventy, Bertha once again turned her back on JFB by not attending their twenty-fifth anniversary celebration. By now JFB had 52,000 members, more than one fifth of the adult Jewish women in Germany. Hannah Karminski referred to the absent Bertha in her address to the celebration: "When the leader, the creator of a movement, reveals the plan for which she is 'called,' she alone bears responsibility for it. . . . Her will is to a certain extent—absolute. These creative people, who create movement, therefore also experience the tragedy of their message in that moment when the urge, which lives, motivates and fulfills them, can no longer have an absolute effect. They are, like every powerful artistic nature, inwardly attached to bringing the idea to fruition without distortion, without compromise."

Bertha did continue to work within the framework of JFB. On July 29, 1929, she penned a petition for JFB to the Rabbinical Conference in Vienna, begging for assistance for the *agunah* (abandoned wife). Once again she protested the Jewish law that made out of these Jewish women outcasts, unable to remarry, and vulnerable to male victimizers. She pleaded, "we ask the Conference of Rabbis to turn its attention, with the deepest Jewish pity that demands love of all creatures, to the destiny of those women . . . crushed under the wheels of an outmoded interpretation of the laws. The agunah, those women neglected by Jewish law and its exponents and judges, loyal to the tribe and its ethical demands, until—lonely and cast out—they come to understand that for them, the laws governing morality effect their opposite, because asceticism is demanded of them, self-denial, prostitution and abnormality, rather than joyous preservation of life. Do not bury a large number of women alive as widows—in the East they speak of 20,000—alongside the great multitude of male victims claimed by the world war from Jews of all countries, or force them into an un-Jewish life. . . . We women speak for those whose sad fate prevents them from knowing how to demonstrate collectively before your forum!"

Chapter Thirteen

LETTER TO FELIX WARBURG*

Isenburg, December 7, 1923

Dear Mr. [Felix] Warburg:

A few days ago, I told Louise in my sanatarium "Praunheim" [the Frankfurt street where L. Goldschmidt lived] about an inspection trip I had made to children in foster homes. She felt that I should write a record of my trip as a characteristic of the year 1923 and I should send it to you.

Crumstadt is located near Pfungstadt, beyond Darmstadt. A small Jewish island of 16 families, six children, three of school age—a dying community. There never was rail connection, but one needs only a few hours for the visit. I am well equipped for such trips; not only my competence but my Austrian passport makes it easier and less expensive. My visit had been announced. I was to be met at Pfungstadt and planned to return the same day. I left Isenburg at 7:30 A.M. and, to make the trip more worthwhile, took along three-year-old Emmy who was to be sent to Holland.

Isenburg used to have good connections and a decent station. Since the French have occupied the station, one buys tickets in a

*Text by Bertha Pappenheim. Bertha wrote many letters to Felix Warburg requesting funds for the Home, reporting on conditions there, and describing her charitable activities and travels. She wrote him this letter at the end of 1923.

shack in the woods. The weather was awful—snow mixed with rain. I had a choice to walk through underbrush, roots, holes, fallen leaves or to take a longer path, which I and a young helper did for Emmy had to be wheeled in a baby carriage, naturally without tires or a hood—otherwise we would never had received it as a gift. The child enjoyed her bumpy trip; Miss Faber pushed and I pulled through the worst spots. Rubber soles are no good if water is pouring in the top of your shoes. When I and others have to plod the path at dawn or dusk, I wish Poincaré had to take it too. It was unusually nasty that morning. We heaved a surprised Emmy into the car with the help of a hand. "Granny," he said, "a few bounds, and you'll be on, too!"

We traveled from Isenburg to Frankfurt, where Emmy debarked, then continued by a roundabout way. It was cold; heat did not reach our car. We changed trains at Eberstadt. To understand the conditions in Germany, one only has to look and listen in a fourth-class car; tired, worn, angry faces. And what rags, what talk! How one has to slave to earn nothing at all. All those millions buy nothing. Bread is 600 billions (today, 850 billions). A pale sickly woman sitting next to me seemed not have learned the price yet. She bobbed up, repeating desperately, "600 billions!" The others griped about the young folks who earn money but won't help, they only smoke cigarettes and wear sheer stockings. And about the peasants who hide potatoes, feed them to the livestock and sell them for dollars only.

I waited for remarks about Jews, which did not come—the women were too preoccupied with themselves and their own burning problems—they seemed to have no strength left to think about anti-Semitism. Change from Eberstadt to Pfungstadt. The "parlor" car, fourth class, was crowded; a laborer gave me his seat. I noticed a red-haired Galician Jew involved in a loud exchange in the middle of the car, with seats only around its walls. Two packages were on the floor next to him, his yardstick pushed into his high boot. He was being battered by violently hostile words as by a hailstorm; his answers in Yiddish evoked furious laughter.

"What did we pay for potatoes in peacetime?" asked the main haranguer.

"Three marks for a hundred pounds," yelled the chorus.

"What did we pay for apron fabric?"

"80 pfennige."

"And this dirty Jew here's asking today hundred pounds of potatoes for one meter of apron fabric!"

A roaring belched out. A woman cried, "*Junghans* ask just as much!"

"He's even worse than a Jew," screamed another woman, "You should be strung up."

"All of them should be hung. A stone round their neck, dumped into a river, all of the *mishpocheh!*" Laughter. A certain humor was at the bottom of this terrible scene—a kind of coarse joke, which could have become an ugly, bitter outbreak through something in the atmosphere—maybe a drop of alcohol. We got off at Pfungstadt, where Mr. Bergen, the teacher, was to meet me with a car.

No Bergen, no car; all quite deserted. I waited a little in a cutting breeze and then decided to make a call or walk to Crumstadt. I asked a man for directions. He looked me over and advised against a walk; two-and-a-half hours: he underestimated my strength.

The phone at the station did not work—it was 12:15—no chance to proceed. Finally, I asked a quite good-natured looking woman whether there were any Jews in Pfungstadt. "Plenty," she said, "Blum lives near by." So I went to the Blum General Store.

The front entrance was locked; I walked through the yard, found a mezuzah on the door frame, and felt a bit reassured. A young woman, wearing an impressive wig, met me. She took me to a heated room and I gave my name. She knew me from Cassel. The grandmother remembered that I had raised her late husband's sister-in-law's cousin at Theobaldstrasse (Girl's Orphanage). The little flower in the baby buggy did not yet know me, else it would not have sucked thumb so happily. Within five minutes, a plate of hot potato soup and carrots was brought in, and a phone call made to Max Bruchfeld III at Crumstadt. He knew that no one had met me and that a mail coach would leave at 4:00. The store people were not so sure, but the well-known firm of Bruchfeld Hardware was positive: Bergen would meet me at the French-occupied border. What else was left to do but to look over Blum's general store? I asked of course about pots and pans for Isenburg where so many now are "bottomless." Surprise! In Pfungstadt, there's an enamel pots shop with a Jewish partner, Katz. Phone call: "Are you Mr. Katz who has an aunt and a sister in Kattowitz?" "Of course!" "Councillor Wiener?" "But of course!" An introduction, a visit, hope to get cheap or seconds of pots and pans. He insisted that I take along a rug for the trip to Crumstadt. (Bless him, whose energy prevailed over my carelessness!)

Walk back to the inn. There I met the red-haired peddler again. He sat there quietly, then left. The local worthies, drinking beer, derided him less coarsely but otherwise in the same vein as the people on the train. They felt that people who had no "right" to exploit Germany's poverty should be treated the same way as in Munich. Did I remain silent out of cowardice, twice witnessing such vulgar drivel? [Perhaps], but there was no hope to convince any one in a few minutes. One has to look for better chances.

I stood at the window of the inn waiting for the mail coach. Finally I learned that the open cart with a nag was the mail coach, for the French do not permit any connections, and take away the horses. The result: the teacher could not meet me. Mail is hauled by a potato wagon. It was 4:30 P.M. I climbed into the coach box, sat down on a board, trying to wrap myself into Mr. Katz's rug. Suddenly the red peddler sat next to me, then the driver, and slowly the critter took off. It got dark, the landscape was unattractive. Icy wind and half-freezing rain—rather unpleasant. I wore an old military coat, heavy, stiff, but not warm. All three of us were freezing. Then a fourth passenger joined us and we went on, freezing, now all four of us.

The red-headed Jew wore unusual glasses. His eyes seemed too large and his face kind of vacant. I was anxious to question him about the price of the potatoes and the aprons, but did not dare because the "Aryans" might have mistreated him. I asked in a low voice whether he had felt terrible this morning in the train. No, he was used to it! I asked him his name: Kupfermann, Frankfurt. Do you live in Stadelhof? Yes. I knew who he was. He has a sick wife who a few days ago underwent surgery; three small children. There was great distress—another member of my select circle of acquaintances.

We continued quietly in the dark and cold. The eyes of the Semites watered but not those of the Aryans. I wonder whether that's a racial distinction. After almost two hours the cart stopped. Someone called my name. It was Bergen, the teacher. We had arrived in occupied Crumstadt.

The last passenger and the red-haired peddler disappeared. I climbed carefully from the cart into the arms of Bergen—the fare, fifteen billions. He asked if I would make a detour of a climb over a small wall. Of course I climbed, and a minute later I was in his living room. Oh, was it good, wonderfully warm, and cozy. The kindness of the people is so heartfelt and direct. Frau Bergen was quite beside herself, well, I might have looked somewhat pitiful. They placed me on a couch, set as an exhibit, considering conditions and the sickly grandmother and nice potatoes. I had been expected at noon. Arthur, the foster child, an Isenburg alum (i.e. illegitimate), well-cared for, treated with kindness, happily unpacked a writing tablet, a gift from Sister Emma. Finally I asked where I would spend the night. Bergens and Bruchfelds had thrown dice; I was glad to stay at the Bergens, on the couch on which I was sitting, opposite a chest with the most marvelous wedding presents—and they talked and talked; I could scarcely keep up.

The main reason for my trip, to take Irmchen Weingart, an Isenburg child, back from a bad foster home, had to wait until next morning. Herr Bergen said encouragingly, "Grünbaum will not dare to refuse." I quite agreed, yet I was unable to sleep. But I had an excellent idea, highly recommended to all friends of winter sports: I had made a vest out of newspapers, worn it underneath my normal dress, and really felt quite warm. But, since there are no newspapers in the occupied zone, people have no idea of what may have happened during the last months. My stuffing did not protect my lower limbs.

Imagine how people live in the occupied zone! I heard the same complaints at Ems, where I recently visited the orphanage. People are cut off if they do not have some business connections. I won't mention the harassment with letters, money orders, and packages. In the morning Frau Bergen reappeared, brought nice ersatz coffee, good bread, homemade jam. I definitely had to refuse a pat of butter and a small creamer with milk which she proudly brought for her guest. Turli (Arthur) asked what holiday it was, and I felt quite strange when the child was told that I was the holiday. I made thousands of good resolutions for my entire life to be worthy of this word.

Now, to Grünbaum, to get Irmchen. This rogue—he was said to have beaten up his wife two days before his confinement—did not let me wait too long. "I want to get the child," I purred sweetly when he appeared. "Got any dough?" "No." Silence. "You may have it right away. She's got nothing to wear, anyway." He told me what Herr Bergen also had said: that the office at Frankfurt pays so little for foster children and so late that one can keep them only if one loves them. They are right but don't know how hard it is to get money at all. Frau Freimann could tell. Yes, if I had a Jewish mint, I could print without fear of inflation, and would pay, and we, the Jewish social workers, would live in our institutions just as well as the French live in Germany.

Irmchen soon showed up with a big chunk of bread spread with farmer's cheese and some apples for the trip, and a cardboard box with her few belongings. She happily announced that she would never come back. I was pleased that this operation was much less painful than expected, but would not have suggested G. treat me otherwise.

Back to Bruchfeld III. Lina, also one of our charges, was working there for three weeks: after Isenburg, her cheeks filled up. "There's everything here one needs." Herr Bruchfeld has a hardware store, sells for French francs only, or barters grain, potatoes—you can't imagine what it means. I seriously advised Lina to stay on, since "there's everything one needed." It's a nice household. I was invited for dinner: we had preserved meat and beans. Lina and, in the old-fashioned way, the apprentice were there too. He had such an appetite that I expect him to be quite successful once he has a hardware store of his own. The little Bruchfeld IV, six months old, ran the whole show. Everything was nice, only the outhouse at quite a distance. We discussed for half an hour how to get back home: by "mail coach," with two friends of the family to the border of the occupied zone, or to walk and then take a street car to Frankfurt. We decided on the latter. My child and I were hurriedly packed into a small open carriage. Bruchfeld III was driving—we arrived just ten minutes after our train had left. Noon. It had been quite cold—forty-five minutes—but my newspaper vest had proved successful. Suddenly, a thought occurred to me: if the French had noticed a slight rustle, would they have asked me to undress? No one would have believed that I had innocently carried forbidden newspapers. Luckily nothing happened—but the next train left at 5:22 P.M. and I was to pay ninety centimes for a ticket. No German money was accepted. Loaded down with Irmchen's box, a bag of food, an umbrella, my briefcase, and Irmchen, I tried in vain to buy a franc. Finally in an inn a man sold me a franc. Germans were eating dinner there. There was a table for Frenchmen. Someone talked equally bad French and German, obviously a fellow from Alsatia who selected his patriotism by currency. I ordered a cup of coffee, and some kind of liquid arrived which I could not drink. You see, Germany's poverty has not subdued me yet. Also, I've an Austrian passport! I was born in Vienna. That excuses what Irmchen could not understand: that I could refuse something worth 100 million, or anything at all. It was cold, since there is no coal in the occupied zone. Irmchen was a dear, chattered all the time. She predicted that I would die soon "for my hair was so old." Then she asked whether all my many children at Isenburg had a bed of their own. "Yes." "And where is your husband?" "I have none." "Where were you married?" "Not at all." "Oh!" A cookie helped me out of this difficult situation and Irmchen's underwear kept us busy, but finally I felt I was overstaying my coffee. We returned to the station. There it was even colder. Bilingual notices interested me for a short time only. The little one who had entertained me by indiscretions about her origins became noticeably tired and quiet and gave me her cold hands to rub.

Everything ends at last, even the waiting at the station. The train arrived when I already was to have been in Frankfurt. It was barely heated. It was night, kosher evening with moon and stars. The French and a Moroccan with a fez did not object to my passport. But now I would have to walk through the woods with the tired child and my many parcels. I was undecided: it was an hour's walk. A good old Frankfurt cab driver noticed my problem and, as a talkative widower who had raised seven children, he offered to wait for half an hour (still more waiting) for passengers from the next train. It was late: no one got off. The kind driver took us on. Autos passed us, but our good horse trotted faithfully: at last, at last, we arrived in Frankfurt, where I left Irmchen with friends for the night. The fare was quite reasonable: only a billion and a half. I walked home.

I arrived about ten in my once pleasant home, now spoiled by uncouth tenants. My bedroom can't be heated. I could not go to sleep in my beautiful canopied bed from 1705. I.H.S. is beautifully carved on the canopy, with a cross and a sun, but *Lev.* 19:34 is on my mind. I felt as if modern times had really brought no progress in practice, nor in motivation. I heard the clock strike twelve, and one, then two. I could not get warm, nor fall asleep, until a good cry gave me some release from my tension. But why need I, an old, lonely woman, wake up in the morning? I'm still afraid of a day when I won't have the strength to go to Crumstadt, or, since I will soon have to go to Wittlich on the Moselle. With best regards.

Yours,
Bertha Pappenheim

Chapter Fourteen

FASCISM AND ILLNESS (1930-1936)

The inexorable, expansive and yet smallest, always appropriate and all-encompassing in logical and lawful form is God. To suffer what is lawful with humility—to feel oneself obligated as an active part of the law—that is religion. [February 7, 1930]

• • •

God is unimaginable, we can only recognize him by his attributes: justice, truth and the will to live. To seek this understanding, to be zealously active, is to love God. God is one and all, and all encompassing. [April 16, 1935]

• • •

Every experience, regardless of how lovely or difficult, uplifting or oppressive, is worth living. [August 20, 1935]

Bertha Pappenheim

"We are responsible for each other. We are tied to a community of fate. For us German Jews, the terrible blow of the Third Reich on April 1, 1933, Nazi Boycott day—how it has hit us! How will be survive? How will we bear the hatred and misery? By the suicide of individuals? By the suicide of the community? Shall we lament and deny? Shall we emigrate and change our economic status? Shall we act foolishly or philosophically? The Diaspora, even Palestine is exile—yet we may see in the distance the summit of Mt. Sinai."

Late in her life, when Bertha finally acknowledged the desperate situation of the German Jews, confusion and outrage broke out inside her after so much time spent denying the Nazis' intentions. She began to imagine the unimaginable.

In the early thirties, as the Nazis gained a majority in the Reichstag, the feminist ideal of the emancipated woman, and the feminists themselves, were among the first to be persecuted. The New Woman of the Weimar Republic was replaced by the Nazi image of the sturdy peasant mother, which returned women to the female sphere of *Kinder, Küche, und Kirche* (Children, Kitchen, and Church). This image was propagandized by Gertrude Scholtz-Klink, who was asked by Nazi leaders to form a "ladies' auxiliary." For her the word "lady" had foreign connotations suggesting a beautiful and useless socialite. Feminists, she said, threatened men by demanding entry into male-dominated fields. She considered both "ladies" and "feminists" selfish. In forming the Frauenwerk (Women's Bureau), she offered an alternative to these role models. According to Claudia Koonz, the Nazi revival of motherhood, like other aspects of Nazi social policy, was carried to grotesque extremes. She emphasizes that the "thoroughness of Nazi policy followed from the Nazi leaders' frankly misogynistic view of women." The creation of the image of the New Mother "was the perfect solution to the Woman's Question, by mobilizing women as mothers into active public service within areas that kept them far from men's political and economic concerns."

Koonz insightfully demystifies the myth of the exaltation of the peasant family. Although the family was idealized as the "germ cell" of the nation, eugenic laws interfered with private choices related to marriage and children. "The demand for total loyalty to the *Führer* undercut fathers' authority. As indoctrination supplanted education, youth leaders and teachers rivaled mothers for children's devotion." Hitler made the revolutionary implications of National Socialism clear, declaiming, "Anyone who interprets National Socialism as merely a political movement knows almost nothing about it. It is more than a religion. It is the determination to create the new man." Scholtz-Klink encouraged women to "Say to yourselves, I am the 'Volk'; the tiny individual self (*ich*) must submit to the great you (*Du*)." Because women exerted no force in politics and economics, Koonz notes that "women would provide a constant backdrop to men's history . . . within the context of Nazi social beliefs . . . all individualism in men and women was to be destroyed." Koonz laments that the history and records of women within the Jewish community have all but disappeared. Gestapo searches destroyed family records, individuals burned family papers to avoid suspicion, the press was censored, and few women wrote memoirs.

In her pious devotion to Judaism, Bertha entered more profoundly into the spiritual world of her heritage and intensified her activity in the area of conserving the Jewish women's literature. Bertha's gift with languages, particularly her knowledge of both Hebrew and Yiddish, made her well suited for this work. Having first translated her ancestor Glückel's life from the Yiddish in 1910, she again immersed herself in translation two decades later. By 1930, she had translated from the Yiddish and published in German *The Woman's Bible*, the *Tse'enah u'ree'nah*, and *All Manner of Tales*, the *Mayseh Bukh,* which intermixed the tales from the Talmud with oriental myths and medieval folktales. Bertha wrote with some bitterness in her introduction to the *Woman's Bible* that Jewish scholars thought "women's mental faculties were not meant to be developed beyond the intellectually limited circle to which they were confined by men."

Unlike other acculturated and assimilated German Jews, who disdained Yiddish as an inferior language and a sign of the crudity of the Ostjuden and who severely punished their children for using any Yiddish phrase, Bertha praised Yiddish as the Jewish woman's language. This was another profound way in which she embraced the "low-brow" Ostjuden culture as equal to the high-minded Germanic culture. She showed no shame at being identified as Jewish or alien to the gentile community. Bertha also began work on a history of the French Revolution, in which a Jewish woman took a prominent part. Bertha Badt-Strauss, an author, recalled an evening at a friend's house in which Bertha read *The Grateful Animals,* accompanied by soft music, while Frankfurt artists performed a shadow-play. "No one who experienced that evening," wrote Bertha Badt-Strauss, "can forget the magical effect of the folktale's childlike wisdom or the noble presence of its reader."

In 1932, at the age of seventy-five, in a state of seething anger against the reign of anti-Semitism, Bertha wrote a prayer:

> Thunderous rage fills me! I will preserve it, it shall burn in me—as long as what rightfully arouses it exists. I will not become lenient, I will not be blind to shameful, harmful activity, I will not excuse what is dishonest and unforgivable. I hope that I may retain the strength to cry out in passionate anger, again and again, to condemn every injustice!

Bertha also wrote in one of her two thousand *Denkzettel* (Reminders) that she wished for "mildness" in old age, a sharp contrast to her desire for "severity," which she had revered in her middle years.

In 1932, although still a staunch anti-Zionist, Bertha now supported the candidacy of Munich physician Dr. Rahel Straus for president of JFB. In 1910, Straus had been refused ordinary JFB membership on account of her Zionist position. When

Dr. Straus reminded Bertha of her previous opposition, she said, "Yes, but living Judaism is with you, tradition, and Jewish knowledge, hence [your] Zionism is the lesser evil, when compared to the utter un-Jewishness of other candidates under consideration."

When, in March 1933, Adolf Hitler was appointed Chancellor of Germany and the Parliament passed the first set of racial laws restricting Jewish civil rights, Bertha offered to take up the leadership of JFB, feeling that the Bund needed a strong personality to deal with the crisis. Bertha withdrew her offer after a "deficiency in direction, following, loyalty and courage" in the leadership and the movement once again alienated her. Bertha wrote a letter describing her fears to the board on March 19, 1933:

> When I saw the connection between recent events in Germany and the fate of German Jewry and became convinced that only a strong, not cowardly, silence on the part of Jewish women will give us the strength and ability to remain what we are, I saw in the wavering of BDF a certain moment of danger. . . . It is above all essential at this moment to transfer the outwardly visible leadership to . . . a woman who is neither Orthodox nor Zionist, neither stamped and bound liberal nor C.V. . . . As the threatening clouds hover ever darker upon the Jewish horizon, I offered on the fifteenth of March to assume the temporary leadership of JFB myself . . . whatever the future may bring to us Jews—you know that already once the Jewish women saved the community. . . . Let us try not to be weaker.

Adding to Bertha's lifelong outrage at conversions and intermarriages was the fact that terrifyingly such actions were having political consequences. She wrote a short parable entitled "The Legacy," which describes the "ironic" justice of "passing":

The Legacy

The year was 1933. Professor Goldenherz, baptized twenty-five years earlier, which enabled him to obtain a teaching post, attempted to obliterate any trace of Jewish origin from his life, and that of his wife and children. As he had made valuable contributions in his field, he believed he would never again have to confront his heritage.

When the racial laws were instituted and he lost his professorship, laboratory, and thus the possibility of engaging in further scientific activity, he was completely at a loss. His children, who had only the vaguest idea of their parents' background, were understandably bewildered.

Since his name had appeared in the press on the list of internationally famous experts, it came to pass that approximately six or eight weeks after his dismissal he received a letter from an American attorney, asking him to identify his ancestry. . . . If he could ascertain and incontrovertibly prove his origin, the undersigned lawyer and notary would confer on Professor Goldenherz a legacy from one of his grandfather's brothers. . . .

Professor Goldenherz was somewhat astonished by this news and did not quite know how he should react to it. . . . A few days later, Professor Goldenherz went to a lawyer who also had been dismissed from his post, and brought him the letter from America. Goldenherz was very convincing and asked his friend to send an affidavit to the lawyer in Chicago. . . .

Agitated, the Goldenherz family spent six weeks under stress until a registered letter did in fact arrive. The inheritance was a yellowed sheet of paper with religious commandments and prayers written on it. . . . A great inheritance, indeed. Were it only that all the discharged and baptized academics received one.

Mrs. Clem Cramer wanted to produce one of Bertha's plays. Bertha wrote to her on January 9, 1933 with her typical irony:

> I understand that a small circle of women want to make me happy with the performance of one of my immortal plays. I have to reject the plan for technical and personal reasons.
>
> The technical reasons are as follows: "Easter" does not conform with today's taste; "Scoundrels" with the distance of time will be important as a picture of Jewish culture. "Tragic Moments" would raise objections in Zionist circles today. . . . Of course, it is a good target, but I don't advise throwing explosives among the little women at a congregation of delegates. Personally, I don't want my author's fame established belatedly at the expense of so much money and trouble such production would demand. I don't have any inferiority complexes from which I need to be relieved.
>
> With sincere regards,
> *Bertha Pappenheim*

When in 1933, Gertrude Ehrenwerth, a social worker, was dismissed from her position as a government employee, she went to work at Isenburg. She remembers that she was "still reeling from the shock that had hit each and every one of us German Jews in particular. I knew little of Miss Pappenheim and 'her' home. I only knew that work was being done there that was also dear to my heart: education of young girls. Of the Jewish spirit and essence of our religion, I knew nothing." Coming from institutional social work, Gertrude found it difficult to fit in at first.

> Only gradually did I enter into a closer relationship with Miss Pappenheim. . . . She understood, in her particular, purposeful and ever so charming way, to impart the

> meaning, the seriousness, and also the beauty of the work to me again and again. She demanded involvement of the whole self, but she also gave of herself completely. And so she was, in her being, continually my inspiration. . . . She shared the joys and sorrows of each of her charges, knew each one and helped them all. . . . She always expected a telephone report early each morning about the children's well-being and about unusual events in the home.

Bertha, who had suffered from rheumatism for years, would have preferred to live in sunnier climes if it hadn't been for her work. Her rheumatism, combined with severe gallbladder attacks, left her in increasingly severe pain. In 1933, she was also suffering from the early stages of cancer. Her only concession to her illness was staying late in bed. She would rise late and spend the rest of the day in the Home. First, she would make the rounds of the youngest children. Her face became transfigured as she spoke to them. She noticed everything, whether a child was lying in an uncomfortable position, the sun was too bright, or a child was ill. She would watch over a child with severe fever until the doctor arrived, or take the child to the hospital herself. The toddlers greeted her with shouts of joy, tugged at her skirts, and played with the "pearls" she wore on a cord around her neck. She helped to feed and dress the children and aided the kindergarten teachers with their work, providing them with her endlessly innovative ideas. Gertrude wrote, "She was always inventive, and in her eternally young heart superior to us all."

Meals that Bertha shared with the staff and children were always festive. When she was absent the sparkle disappeared. A stickler for good manners, she would walk away from the long table if one of the children misbehaved, leaving the rest truly upset.

After lunch Bertha worked in her office. She always welcomed complaints and lent her ear to the needs of her charges. The older children found her to be both mentor and friend. In the afternoons she sat in the sewing room writing, making her necklaces or other handiwork, which was no longer fashionable among emancipated women.

Gertrude noted that Bertha especially enjoyed unpacking gift packages that arrived from all over Germany. These were particularly happy hours. She had a use for everything and was always brimming with ideas. She wrote thank-you notes herself. By the same token, if the gift was useless, she would become outraged and make her displeasure known to the donor.

In spite of the adoration all around her, a part of Bertha retained a sense of isolation. Rahel Straus wrote that when a gift table was set up in honor on her birthday, she was so moved that she could hardly speak. Weeping, Bertha said, "Excuse me, I am so unaccustomed to being loved that it easily overwhelms me."

In the 1930s, Bertha became reconciled to professional social workers, although she believed that they should have low salaries to ensure the integrity of their commitment. She instituted the "tea hour" at which she entertained professional workers, engaging in serious conversations focused on educational issues or the conduct of Jewish women. She often voiced sharp criticism, especially of the young, but she kept faith in the future.

Bertha harbored qualms about the work of the professionals. She sent a caustic letter addressed to three social workers who had been trained in the Home, and were among her closest associates:

> Dear Ladies,
>
> For some time an observation has haunted me, a sad thought, that a poorly carried out social work can have the same effect on the whole complex of a woman's life

> as the abusive use of nicotine and alcohol to which one becomes increasingly addicted. Three women from my closest working group make me uneasy . . . Mrs. Nassauer, Forchheimer, and Freimann. . . . As different as their backgrounds and upbringing are, they have one thing in common . . . that threatens to make themselves . . . into caricatures. . . . You do too much for the good, body and soul suffer under double and triple burden which you want to take from the needy women to save her for her family. . . . What a pity that ambition grows hand in hand with the good and the pure willingness to sacrifice . . . you are restless and wavering because the godlike is living in you and you feel it too much that you do not take care of your body, your spirit, your house as you should.

In Berlin on September 17, 1933, prominent Jewish leaders formed the Reich Representation of the German Jews. They chose as their leader Leo Baeck, a Berlin rabbi, and Otto Hirsch, a writer on Jewish philosophy, to represent them and unify the warring factions. Otto Hirsch wrote of Bertha Pappenheim:

> We were only together a few times, but the meetings were always meaningful and always had a lasting effect. She had a contentious nature, was aggressive. . . . She hated compromises. I knew her to be unjust, and became so especially easily if she believed that women had been undermined by men, or felt that her rights had been violated. Was this the result of the fact that she herself possessed a thoroughly masculine sensibility? She reminded me of Ibsen's words about the strength of those who stand alone . . . the essential trait of her character, unconditional honesty. . . . She was a tactician, in that sense she was an apolitical person. It did such good, it was pleasing to know such a person was alive in our time and it made me proud, that this person was Jewish.

Bertha never stopped writing fairy tales. Compared to her initial stories, which explored universal themes of spiritual life, her later tales reflected the horrors of being Jewish in Nazi Germany. "Human Fable," written on December 18, 1933, reveals the pitiable irony of the increasing valuelessness of human life and Bertha's deepened longing to connect to the Hebrew God. In this fable, an old woman is waiting to be admitted to heaven. Asked where she wants to go by an angel, whose traits were reminiscent of a Nazi youth, she answered, "To God." Another angel lectures her on the difficulty of procuring a "certificate" to see God, and further that "Someone, for example, who has given an awful lot of money to a university or written fat books, sent children to safety, held lotteries, and was always busy, always gentle and polite," could gain access to Him. The old woman replies that she has but her "life" to offer to Him. The two youthful angels laugh in the old woman's face, "Dear woman, life isn't worth a thing! Now, get lost!" The woman throws herself and her longing for God into space and disappears.

In 1933, the German League of Women Voters, an affiliate of BDF, invited Nazis along with other speakers to comment on the role women could be expected to play under Nazi rule. BDF sent a letter of apology to JFB. However, even the strongest supporters of JFB affiliation with BDF felt the rising anti-Semitic currents in the movement. The JFB resigned from the BDF in 1933; the BDF accepted the resignation "with deepest regrets." A few days later the BDF itself disbanded to avoid being taken over by Nazi activists and programs.

Bertha's friend Paula Ollendorf, who founded the local chapter of JFB in Breslau in 1908 and had served on the board since 1910, became disheartened by the behavior of her former BDF friends. They avoided her with "stupid excuses" so they "would not be caught with Jews."

In 1934, Ottilie Schönewald became the last elected president of JFB. She wrote, "It was clear to me from the very start that a Jewish organization under Nazi rule, even if relatively tolerated in the beginning of 1934, would have to employ new methods to do justice to its mission. This naturally led to differences of opinion with prior leadership, which had been attuned to normal conditions. Still it should be ascribed to the influence of Bertha Pappenheim that our essential task remained keeping families together; therefore, as long as there still remained a prospect for a further existence of our community in Germany, we opposed sending children, especially those not yet of school age, to Palestine, an action that had already begun in 1934. . . . I would like to merely record that our efforts were aimed at inspiring the Jewish women who joined with the spirit of resistance against the ruling powers. . . . In Hitler's Germany, we had to run our . . . institutions, which would be of only a brief duration, as if they were there forever."

In October 1934, Bertha wrote her specifically Jewish fairy tale:

The Hill of the Martyrs

An old city. An old Jewish cemetery—a good place.

Heavy autumn fog is hanging between the shadowy outlines of the stones. Gone are the paths between the stones which lie partly toppled, partly sunken into the ground; lost in this wilderness wanders a female figure—a trailing gown, a billowing veil, flying strands of hair, ageless in the field of graves, meandering among the stones.

Outside the wall a crowd of people has gathered,

muttering and fidgeting restlessly, rooted to the spot. The fluttering figure approaches a bluff overgrown by high grasses that seem to weep in the dampness. In this place, hundreds of years ago, men who died for their God were buried. The woman casts herself to the ground, the wind tugs at the folds of her robe, howling and whistling over the stones.

Drowning out the storm the woman cries: "Ye, holy ones, whose blood once soaked the earth for our God, whose bodies have crumbled to dust and whose souls ascend and descend from the depths of this hill's graves to the heavenly heights, pause a moment to answer the question which I have been asked to put to you by the people outside of this good place!

"Ye, holy ones—how should we poor creatures go on living, how to survive the burden of these times, under the pain and hatred that oppress us?"

The woman veiled her head, pressed her ear hard to the cold wet ground, and as she closed her eyes, breathlessly listening, she heard the voices of the saints, singing in wonderful unison, speaking to her:

"Shma Israel, Adonai Eloheinu, Adonai Echad!" (Hear, O Israel: the Lord is our God, the Lord is One!)

The sound was intoxicatingly beautiful and majestic to the woman's ears, as if she could not tear herself away from the surging, flowing song of the saints who had given their lives for Him.

But the mass of people outside the wall began to grumble.

The woman then tore herself away from the song of the saints; her gown billowing, she ran up the hill, to see the crowd and call out, over the wall.

The impatient multitude shouted, "Speak out, woman! We sent you to find out what the saints of days long past and those of this day have to say!"

> Then the woman shouted over the wall from the hill, *"Shma Israel, Adonai Eloheinu, Adonai Echad!"*
>
> "Is that all you have learned, is that all you have heard, you dimwit?" the mob bellowed, laughing and bawling contemptuously, way back to where some of the people still stood grumbling. An echo caught up the laughter, rolled back over the wall, and struck the woman like a mortal blow, and she collapsed on the hill of the martyrs.

Bertha's belief in justice was absolute. Since the essence of Nazi ideology was the overthrow of the transcendent God, Bertha became a warrior on behalf of the transcendence of spirit and faith over the eminence of the Nazi concept of the "Volk." Her spiritual resistance to the Nazis crystallized the heart of Judaism within her. She held the primacy of faith and prayer as an incantation over political evil. Unlike other German Jews who remained naive or in denial, Bertha was acutely aware of the circumstances, but kept her faith in a God of justice who would protect the Jewish people.

Like most people dying of cancer her circles of interest because increasingly smaller and more personal. She began to prepare an annual report of the Home, as if she were still living in ordinary times. She invited a social worker from Berlin, Käthe Mende, to aid her in selecting, compiling, and summarizing the files of the Home's work.

Käthe Mende describes the four months she spent as Bertha's guest and co-worker in Isenburg, from January to April 1934. At first Käthe had asked if she could come in May, but Bertha replied, "Come soon, who knows whether I will still be able to discuss the work with you in May." Käthe departed forthwith, with a "shadowy feeling" that there was not much time left. This "dark feeling" vanished completely under the "spell of Bertha's vibrant, restlessly creative presence." With inexhaustible zeal Bertha discussed every individual case with Käthe, some dated as far as thirty years back. Käthe was amazed that Bertha not only knew her present charges but remained spiritually close to those who had left the Home. By this time approximately fifteen hundred youths had passed through the Home. It was not unusual for Bertha to recall a particular characteristic that would not have been recorded in the files, but would always be confirmed by another source. Bertha never spoke impersonally, but always "with a warm lively feeling for each child, or young woman." Bertha had written innumerable long detailed letters to parents or to the girls themselves. She had "the heartbeat of a truly maternal caretaker who never sees file numbers before her, but God-given human beings." The letters to the girls were never written from a "lofty perch" and regardless of sad experiences and disappointments, she always remained their maternal adviser, "who saw not sin, but a sad fate or pathology and in her unerring womanly instinct she was on the course which has now been scientifically proved and systemically developed in the treatment of psychopaths."

Bertha and Käthe spent hours of delightful collaboration in the Frankfurter Community Building, studying names from the birth registry that might aid their project. Bertha loved the old Jewish names of poor maidservants who emigrated to Frankfurt, the *Vögelchen* (birdie), *Täubchen* (little dove) and, of course, the *Glückeles* (joyful ones), preferring them to the Agathas, Amalias, and Leonoras who began appearing from 1820 on and which she felt were the result of their parents' literary or musical education.

Käthe, like all the women who worked closely with Bertha, was inspired by her almost paradoxical persona: "a social worker of deepest passion, who spared herself no drudgery, she was also an aristocrat of life and taste in the finest sense."

Bertha refused to take the painkillers her doctors prescribed, and her pain-free hours became rarer. Nevertheless, Käthe found Bertha to be in "high spirits" as if she were a "young girl taking pleasure in a lovely piece of clothing, she moved around the room, posing playfully like a model." Bertha's living habits had become increasingly simple, which Käthe admired, writing, "with what natural grace she bore the sacrifice which may have been harder for her than for many others as her aesthetic sensibility . . . was always active."

Bertha continued to organize public performances, create ornamental requests for contributions, design medals, and display her handicrafts, all to raise money for her social work.

Bertha's collections still provided her with her purest pleasure, but also caused her the greatest pain; for she no longer had access to her beloved lace collection, which she had placed outside her home for safekeeping.

Käthe recalled a day when for the pleasure of a few friends Bertha's more accessible collections of Berlin iron jewelry, plackets, and candelabra were displayed at the Jewish Museum in Frankfurt.

In February 1934, Bertha spoke at the Community Hall, begging assistance for children's welfare. In the anteroom, displayed on rich cloth, were fifty of her necklaces. Lisbet Cassirer was astonished, writing in the *Blätter*, "Can this be the same Bertha Pappenheim, who speaks so sharply to the women of the Reich?" Bertha claimed that the necklaces compensated for the worries of day-to-day life. The more difficult times became, the more Bertha felt the need to busy herself with lovely things. To Lisbet, Bertha's creations "are an expression of her cultivation. As unerringly as she gives direction to the work, these necklaces are meant to resolutely illustrate to women the lasting value of culture. They serve as a reminder that a woman must create a balance within herself that will allow her to make her way through difficult times with greater ease." Margaret Susman wrote of these exhibitions that "the powerful hands, with angelic strength, which have held high the torch of religion and ethics in the storms of a benighted world, are the same fine and delicate hands from which spring the almost playful works of art which so entrance us. Is this not in its way a miracle?"

Everyone who spent an evening in Bertha's company was enchanted with her talents as a born storyteller who told riveting stories about the lives of her parents and herself. A jewel in Bertha's collection of humorous sketches was a hilarious story about her trip to a remote village to visit a Galician rabbi. A clever villager rounded up numerous "guests" and improvised an omnibus, for which she had to bear the entire cost. She also liked to speak of the "spiritual greed" in some Frankfurt circles of which she was not fond.

Visitors noted that surrounding the "surging intellectual wealth" of the lady of the house were few books and no bookcases. Bertha was always weighing the value of books against the value of experience. Alarmed over Nazi censorship and the public burning of Jewish books and those books of the intelligentsia that were unfavorable to National Socialism, she wrote to Hannah Karminski, who was renown for her book collection, on July 29, 1934:

> That books have been burned in our time is the symptom of a pervasive barbarity that stems from an over- as much as from an undervaluation of books. To grasp the flowing, the developing—that which is struggling in any

> way for definition—one needs human beings far more than books, and the dreaded spirit cannot be burned.
>
> You must not think, dear Hannah, that I have no respect for your bookshelves. On the contrary, I have an immense respect for all the knowledge I know that I do not know, and I believe that it is exactly my ignorance, my lack of education, that has caused me to be so intimidated by books.
>
> On the other hand, after some consideration, I also believe what I have become, as much as that which I have not become, can be traced back to this inadequate spiritual nourishment—I might almost say undernourishment. . . .
>
> I do not think that people who own and read many books are smarter than others, nor do I believe that they are better.
>
> Not all bibliophiles are mental giants, just as not all kleptomaniacs are thieves; they must only pretend to be. When I think of an unborn child, and see an infant in its crib, then everything that I want to learn, read, shape and form gathers and focuses on that developing being like a wish to God which I offer up to the spirit which lives scattered throughout books—a diaspora of the spirit.

One of Bertha's visitors, Helene Hannah Thon, a former member of JFB who had earlier emigrated to Palestine, paid a call on Bertha in the company of an eleven-year-old Jewish-Palestinian boy. The child, deeply affected by Bertha, who seemed to him like a holy biblical figure, told Helene: "She looks like Deborah."

Although Helene knew that her fantasy of Bertha's prophetic powers was illusory, because of Bertha's failure to support Zionism in time to save more German Jews; nonetheless, Helene still kept a photograph of Bertha on her desk. In Jerusalem, her new home, Helene derived inspiration by just looking at Bertha's eyes in the photograph. "The eyes of the woman in the picture before me spent their lifetime always looking at human suffering . . . especially at all Jewish suffering. . . . But they saw through this pain . . . the recognition of the immortal life of the Jewish people and the undying power of Judaism. Thus, anyone who saw those eyes in his lifetime was unable to forget them. They could look . . . severe . . . ironic . . . when unobserved, overflowing with love . . . these eyes could flash in holy rage. . . . This battle for truth—for what seemed to her, not always to us, to be the truth—gave her appearance something reminiscent of the prophets."

Although Bertha continued to plan trips to shore up sister Jewish institutions and aid children, she increasingly devoted herself to her writing and her profound spiritual relationship with God.

There are a score of remaining letters from Bertha's continuing correspondence with Martin Buber between 1916 and 1936. During this time Buber was a professor of Judaism and comparative literature at the University of Frankfurt. In 1933, when Jewish professors and students were expelled by the Nazis, Buber and other intellectuals organized adult education at the Freies Jüdisches Lehrhaus (Free Institute of Jewish Learning). The JFB associated with Lehrhaus in 1934, where Bertha attended workshops and led study groups on Judaism. Buber was sympathetic to women's education. Aubrey Hodes writes about his grandmother at sixteen reading German books in secret in her room, because Jewish girls in Galicia weren't permitted to read Goethe and Schiller. Buber inherited his grandmother's books, which he kept with him for the rest of his life. His work, grounded in mysticism and existentialism, inspired Bertha into a lively debate in writing. She chastised him for his pompous style, for not making his ideas more readily accessible to the masses, for his Zionism, and for much else.

Since Buber's retirement from his professorship in 1933, he and Bertha had shared in the intense activity of founding separate Jewish schools and encouraging Jewish education for both children and adults. Both Bertha and Buber considered education as a form of "spiritual resistance." Their implacable faith in the Jewish concept of God remained their deepest bond. Bertha's Home remained a haven of pragmatic social work for needy girls and a salon for bourgeois Jewish feminist discussion, which Bertha dominated and controlled; Buber's home became a refuge for both Jewish and Christian political strategists, intellectuals, and writers of all persuasions who engaged in free-flowing interchanges as they organized themselves in active resistance to the Nazis. In 1933, Buber announced that he would take primary responsibility for the establishment of a Jewish system of schools and culture. Before 1933, Buber was well-known among intellectuals as an esoteric philosopher; under the Nazis, by contrast, he became increasingly famous and profoundly influential among almost all Jewish communities. As a powerful leader, pathfinder, and comforter, he, along with Rabbi Leo Baeck, became one of the two prominent spokesmen for the German Jews. Dr. Bertha Badt-Strauss, who also greatly admired Bertha, wrote that Buber's lectures were like "an island of peace in the daily renewing and flaring-up of Nazi persecution." Buber more than any other single person re-awakened the Jewish consciousness of the assimilated German Jews, helping them to transmute their despair and suffering into a meaningful Jewish identity and to spiritually prepare them for emigration to Palestine. Bertha's identity as an acculturated German, with her crusty denial of the need for mass emigration and her hatred of the Zionists, still shrilly disputed with Buber, although she did plan to visit Palestine.

On June 7, 1935, Buber and his wife Paula, who had lived in Heppenheim for twenty years, finally accepted Bertha's long-standing invitation to visit the Home.

June 7, 1935

Dear Professor Buber,

I enjoyed your visit yesterday so much that I have to let you know this and thank you. Not only because I was able to show you the Home I had founded and defended in my [old] age in the fight against irrationality, shortsightedness, smoke-screens (wishful thinking) and the love of gossip (even today, I still have to shield "Isenburg" from all of it), but also because I always have had rather peculiar feelings toward you: in person, I feel your warmth and inclination to do good; when you are beyond personal reach however, I know cognitively and exactly where things are amiss and, forgive me, where you are wrong, for you are not demanding (do not urge, press). The prophets of old did not tell people what they wanted to hear, they spoke clearly and were demanding. With what success though? . . .

I think your wife knows very well what is going on in Europe and in Asia, at least in the basic concept of community—those who have not been spoiled through indolence, dishonesty.

How the Jewish press is ruining us, how mendacious it is, regardless of which party line it follows—and how the youth prevaricates. Perhaps one could achieve something with workers, if one explained to their children what's important.

That you wish to advise me on my trip to Palestine is

very kind of you. September is however still quite far away, and physically I am truly run down. . . .

Bertha Pappenheim

A week later Bertha again rebuked Buber for the intellectual complexity and unintelligibility of his writings for the uneducated but morally committed woman. She also expressed her sense of isolation and worthlessness, much as she did during her earlier travels of 1911–12, contemplating that her single-minded ideas resulted from living alone with no one to question her or complicate her thoughts:

June 13, 1935

Dear Professor Buber!

I am terribly sorry to have to tell you that I have not understood the book you sent me. It is likely I have not understood your preface either—and therefore replied to something you had never said—an incident, which, ordinarily, one would call stupid.

But I cannot understand either why ideas, which should belong to all people, to the many dullards as well, the mighty ones and to one's neighbors have to be so entangled that they become cold as ice, move farther and farther away, and devalue life. I think I love the mighty and the neighbor as I hate their opponents and attackers, daily, hourly. I'd like to make this love and hate accessible (open) to all, to implant [them with it]—that is neighborly love, never educational target; educational methods are many.

You probably won't understand this stuttering and ridicule it, but I do not want to let complicate for myself that which is so simple, so close, so salubrious.

Perhaps I believe so much on my way to be simply obvious, because I am and have always been alone, and no one, no fellow man has been around to complicate my existence.

At times, I feel as if I have fallen off a tree, as a fruit kernel in a burst skin, left on the road; nothing has become of it, probably as a consequence of the law and justice of the Almighty, and therefore I cannot understand those who are a thousand times more intelligent. (Miss Karminski will discuss with you the trip via Rome. Tuesday, the 18th, I am leaving for Vienna, if I don't trip over myself.)

With friendly regards,
Bertha Pappenheim

In Bertha's next letter two days later she resumed her cheerfulness and tried to make amends for her caustic letter. She reminded him that they shared the concept that the way to God is through loving "Thy Neighbor," but also insisted upon the necessity of Hate.

June 15, 1935

Dear Professor Buber,

Suddenly, I am pleased with our old-fashioned correspondence on the beeline between Isenburg and Heppenheim. Today, one doesn't engage oneself in something similar without objectivity and purpose! Still, I thank you for your kind letter that could not have been any different. I don't want to see myself as a human being who just accidentally crossed your path. That's not the way I want it. Obviously, I want to help everybody who is in need and do not want to refuse anyone, though that does not mean I love him. To love is something individual, as I am an individual—and as I always have hoped that one would help me.

I do not want to give my warm hate: I hate the rabbis, who consider women to be God's inferior creatures; I hate the Zionists, who want to build a land only on "political" grounds, without honor and justice (righteousness); I hate the officialdom—the organizations, officials wrapped in ethical cloaks, become fat. I hate the 1933's Jews with their fresh-coat-of-paint tradition—and possibly many others, all of whom I would fail if they needed me. Or should I love those who are forcing me to go to Vienna and smilingly part from my darlings[?] That is called turning the other cheek.

Love without [unintelligible sign] means to embrace, lead, hold fast, to radiate, teach to believe, give of all one has for the sake of another, who is exacting is, for he is righteous.

I read the commandment of loving thy neighbor to my children in a similar way you have explained it to me. But there is *more* to it[:] the hate of that which is not worthy of love.

Period, dash, and for the time being, the end of this so unfashionable correspondence!

With regards and thanks,
Bertha Pappenheim

In 1936, Bertha wrote of the difference between Christians and Jews; of the extent to which Christians always seemed so devoted to the Holy Scriptures; and of Buber's habit of referring to God as HIM and not as the Eternal One. In this letter her exquisite insight and knowledge of European culture and philosophy belied, somewhat coyly, her constant protestations of her ignorance and inferior intellect. However, the main purpose of her letter was to thank him for the beauty and inspiration of the Psalms he had translated and published, the fourteenth volume of his translation of the Bible, which was then being published by Schocken Verlag.

March 18, 1936

Dear Professor Buber,

I have been preoccupied, and not only since yesterday, with the thought of why the Bible has a totally different purport for the Christian than for us. In all circles and classes there were, and surely still are, Christians whose faith in reading the Bible is original, naive (or primitive), and who find devotion, support, and solace in deep grief,—the road to God,—to God, not to HIM. [The Buber-Rosenzweig translation of the Bible uses the personal pronoun instead of the name of God.]

I do not recall ever having met a Jewish person whom I would believe capable of such connectedness to the Bible, such as Rembrandt as beautifully and movingly depicted in the portrait of his mother reading the prayer book. . . .

In our times one should love the Bible, reach for it, though I believe that when in true inner need, many Jewish people reach in fact for "their Goethe," not for "their Bible." (I may say so, for I am neither well-versed in the Scriptures not in Goethe.) Now what do they do in the Central Office? They intellectualize the Bible to the extreme. [As if] one had to earn [access] to it. How dreadful. Using their method, one can perhaps draw closer to Shakespeare or Dante, Spinoza or Kant, and many others who illumine me like stars from the farthest distance; but the Bible would have to be brought so close to the Jews—to the simple-minded too—that they learn to love and hate (which is the same) nothing else[,] and know and feel that there exists an omnipresent justice[;] that time is timeless.

Bertha Pappenheim

In this fifth letter Bertha again thanked Buber for his astonishing translation of the Psalms. She showed her gratitude by alluding to a similar relationship she had had with an art collector in the past, who had opened a window to a world of Dutch art that she had not known existed.

March 21, 1936

Dear Professor Buber,

Your patience with me is truly touching, yet I believe that you are displeased with me for I don't understand you.

But: many years ago a collector showed me a portfolio of old etchings and through it the beauty of this Dutch art juxtaposed against the painters I believed were the only ones who had achieved greatness. He opened for me a window to a world about which I had no idea, or perhaps only the slightest idea. Today I am still grateful to that man for having enriched my life.

The same will happen with the Psalms to your listener; you have opened something of your accomplishment (work) of which she wasn't aware, and she is grateful to you.

Yours,
Bertha Pappenheim

In her letter dated March 10, 1936, Bertha wrote that she has almost used the familiar "Dear" in her address to him, but although she does not like him from afar, she enjoys being with him, writing "you are a mixture of attraction and repulsion." Both Bertha and Buber were "mystical activists." They both transmuted their absolute faith in the justice of their Jewish God into daring political action. In 1934, Buber lectured on "The Power of the Spirit," attacking the evil of the Nazis' paganism, racism, and false nationalism. He was courageous enough to speak to an audience in Berlin with 200 SS men in the audience. As Bertha was dying in 1936 she fearlessly confronted the Gestapo, who had made accusations against her.

Although Bertha was always chiding Buber about their intellectual and political disagreements, she was obviously proud to be associated with him, especially when he finally came to visit her in Isenburg. Beneath the formality and impersonality of their letters, Bertha insinuated herself into his life in the hope of gaining greater recognition and intimacy. They shared their "spiritual resistance" to the Nazis and their commitment to bring God and the World together. Both Bertha and Buber embodied Bergson's concept of "mystical activism" in their daily lives. Buber wrote about the Christian mystics, Bergson and Simone Weil, in his essay "The Silent Question," accusing both of them of stereotyping Judaism. In the essay on Bergson, "The Two Sources," he wrote that the true mystic does not isolate himself from the world, that "mystics and saints . . . have broken down natural resistance and raised humanity to a new destiny. . . . All mystics declare they have the impression of a current passion from their soul to God, and flowing back again to mankind. Let no one speak of material obstacles to a soul thus freed! Love for one's family, love for one's country, love of mankind . . . one single feeling growing ever larger . . . superabundant activity is the culminating point of the inner evolution of the great mystics."

In 1938, Buber was silenced and unwillingly emigrated to Palestine. "If other beings have forsaken us after we have spoken the true Thou to them, we will be accepted by God; but not if we have forsaken other beings," he wrote in *I and Thou,* which could have served as a comforting phrase to Bertha in her relation with God.

According to Margaret Susman, both Bertha's intimate and extended circles were privy to her pedagogical and social activity. There was no person who came in contact with Bertha who did not feel something of her "mental anguish, but few knew that this mind was not exhausted by its practical undertakings but . . . had a life of its own and many paths." Bertha's personality and life were "a burning protest" against the religious and ethical dissolution of the time in which she lived. "Amidst all the uprooted, unstable, and collapsing lives of our world . . . she had been given the ultimate gift a human being can receive . . . living in the chaos of monstrous upheavals: a path."

Bertha was devoted to her literary works, which still, according to Margaret, did not bear witness to what most deeply motivated her, "the primary relationship of the absolute to her life. . . . Bearer of the law in a lawless world . . . the fundamental orientation of the true Jew."

Late in life Bertha decided to take a private class in philosophy with Margaret Susman, where she discovered the world view of the pre-Socratic Greeks, particularly the concept of unity through infinite flux. In her studies, "she sought everywhere and found everywhere: the Great Law." The guiding principle of her life was the Law as God's commandment. From the cosmic, primary law of Greek antiquity, she found the just order of eternal change of becoming and dissolution; of birth and death. Bertha wrote, "It is infinitely difficult to be just, only the Great Law is irrevocably just." Margaret praised Bertha, who, in a time when people had become "spiritually and mentally lame . . . was still able to draw actively upon super-personal resources. As a true Jew . . . [she] was a collaborator in the realization of the kingdom of God. In a time of the deepest devastation of faith, she still lived . . . according to divine law and will."

Bertha's spiritual faith, which increasingly verged on the mystical, is most perfectly revealed through her third Jewish fairy tale entitled "The True Ring," inspired by the ring-fable in Lessing's play *Nathan the Wise* (1779). Ottilie Schönewald had remembered Bertha first discussing the play, upon which the tale is based, in 1912.

On December 16, 1934, Bertha wrote a letter referring to her leitmotif in "The True Ring":

> . . . no poet has ever experienced a Nathan (*Nathan the Wise* is a confessional book—but behind it is Lessing's friendship for Mendelssohn . . .) or a Shylock, or a Franz Moor, or an Iphigenia. . . . If a human being avows himself to the Jewish God, whose voice he claims to hear on quiet nights, then he must know that the Jewish God is a demanding God, a God who will not be content to have his followers hear His 'voice,' His 'word,' His 'way,' His 'wisdom' and to love and praise it. In one corner of his life, at least, the Jew must live his belief.

The climax of Lessing's play is a dispute between Nathan the Wise and the Sultan, Saladin, about whose faith is the greatest. Nathan tells the "Ring Fable," in which a king wanted to give each of his three beloved sons his magic opal ring, so he had two additional copies made. The three sons quarreled as to who had the "true ring," but the rings were indistinguishable. Faith, according to Nathan, is what gives the ring its power, nothing "magical" or intrinsic within the stone. By implication, Christians, Jews, and Muslims are equal to the degree that each has absolute faith in God, and lives a noble and righteous life.

During the Nazi era Lessing's play was banned because of its Jewish hero. His friend Moses Mendelssohn (1729–1786) was called the "archetypal German Jew." He was the first Jew to identify himself with German cultural concerns and use the German language in his literary works; he is generally regarded as having initiated *Haskalah,* or the Jewish "Enlightenment" movement. Martin Buber describes the symbolic significance of the friendship between Lessing and Mendelssohn, as "the earliest stage of the symbiosis between the German and the Jewish spirit." Mendelssohn wrote a dialogue entitled *Phädon,* modeled after Plato's *Phaedo,* to prove the immortality of the human soul. He was called the "German Socrates." Bertha and Mendelssohn both believed that Judaism was distinct from all other religions, not as much in matters of doctrine but "of law, commandment, and ways of serving God." Mendelssohn influenced Bertha's tale with his concept of the messianic goal of history; the triumph of pure monotheism over degenerate beliefs.

Bertha was inspired by Lessing's belief in the creative nature of God; in the continuous and progressive evolution of the universe; and in God's eternal revelation, ever more complete in history.

Bertha, a female Mendelssohn, embodied the highest form of the acculturated German Jew. Bertha's version of "The True Ring" was conceived several days after one of her Friday evenings. Bertha and her friends had spent the night discussing Lessing and *Nathan,* which Bertha read to a small circle of friends on a following night, February 27, 1934. One of Judaism's basic tenets is the belief in the messianic age, in the coming of the messiah. Bertha's tale is a parable of how salvation symbolized through an orbiting "magic" stone, is historically attained through those "messianic" people who, born of superpersonal love, are chosen to guide humans out of the darkness into the radiant light of God's consciousness toward the day when everyone will live out the unity of the One God, and the "stone will rest."

Plagued by constant pain, Bertha had written a confessional work. She was blessed by an illuminating faith. She continued to work through the storms of Nazi persecution. For example, with faith and courage she took a group of children, some from Isenburg, to the safety of a Jewish orphanage in Glasgow.

Chapter Fifteen

"THE TRUE RING"*

A man in the East owned a ring. The power of the ring made its owner agreeable in the eyes of God and men. The man had three sons he loved equally and could not decide on the one to whom he should leave the ring.

So he had an artist come to him, gave him the ring—a golden band set with an unusually beautiful opal—and commissioned the artist to make two more identical rings. Before he died, the man from the East gave his three sons the three rings. Many years later it came to pass that the artist felt his final hours approaching and was tormented by his conscience because he knew that he had committed a terrible ruse. Trying to copy the ring entrusted to him, he had found he was unable to make a

*Text by Bertha Pappenheim

[Bertha's tale "The True Ring" is a variation on Lessing's parable found in *Nathan the Wise,* which Bertha had treasured and contemplated upon since she was fifty-three. This tale is Kabbalistic, and mysterious—far removed from her early tales like "The Pond Sprite," which is infused with German Romanticism. Although the moral of Lessing's tale finds that the True God is found in all three major religions: Judaism, Christianity, and Islam, by contrast, Bertha's parable written under Nazi terrorism and the godless Volk, holds faith that the True concept of God is only expressed by messianic Orthodox Judaism. Although Christians have faith in Jesus as the Messiah, and Islamics have faith in Mohammed as the Messenger of God, Orthodox Jews believe that the True Messiah has yet to appear. Bertha uses the metaphor of the "glowing eye" revolving in space for the mysterious ways God has illuminated the lives of many Jewish mystics through Love and Harmony (I would include Bertha). When the True Messiah is revealed, the "glowing eye" will come to rest because there will be a radical transformation of the universe, particularly in the inner spirit of humanity.]

similar work of art. In his rage he had even broken the stone out of the band to make a wax imprint of its delicate design. Now he had the beautiful glowing stone and the band in his hand, yet every attempt by his practiced hand failed to reproduce the small great work of art.

Partially in acknowledgment of his artistic inadequacy, partially in rage, he melted the golden band with his little blowtorch until the precious work was nothing but a small lump of gold. He cast it into the heavens where it shone like gold, as the newest star in the Milky Way. Then he took the stone, too, and cast it into space.

Afterward he crafted three identical rings, which the man from the East then gave to his sons.

Then the stone, which in addition to its great beauty possessed a great power, began to fly around the world like a glowing eye. Everywhere a natural disaster occurred, it lit up. It might have been a storm raging over the earth with zig-zag lightning, a rainbow connecting heaven and earth in a magical display of color, the eruption of a fire-spewing mountain laying waste to vast expanses of earth, tidal waves whipping up the sea, or snow-capped mountain peaks ignited in glowing color, there always would be people with the fortunate ability to observe the momentary flashing of the stone. But those people would never say anything about it.

But the stone's movement through space seemed not to be exhausted by manifesting itself in such exaggerated, widely visible natural phenomena. There are other ways. Sometimes, on quiet nights in small rooms, when from the harmony of two people a unity, a child aspired to life, it could happen—but only did so rarely and at great intervals—that the stone would light up over this creature without anyone noticing, except that perhaps the mother in a renewed desire to live regarded the child auspiciously as a chosen one and blessed it.

Throughout the history there were but a few people who had been completely enveloped by the radiance of the magic stone. Outwardly, their fate may have been rough and painful, but the inner glow of the magic stone's illumination has flooded them throughout their lives and given them the capacity to recognize the good, the true, and the beautiful, and through light, warmth, and a special strength have an illuminating, warming, strengthening effect on others.

Only a few people know of the stone's orbit in space. They call its strength the *shechinah*, the Divine Presence. And they wait for it to encounter their Messiah. When it does, the stone revolving in space will finally come to rest.

Chapter Sixteen

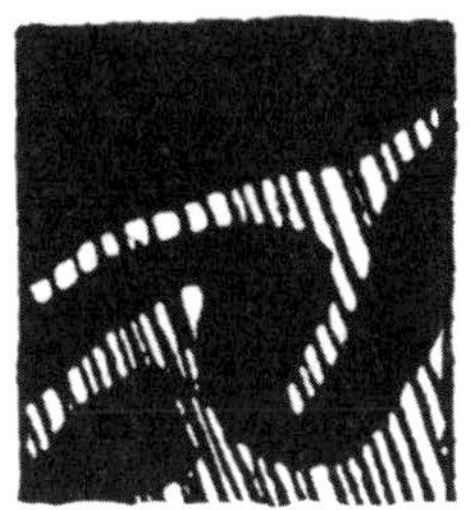

DEATH (1935-1936)

Afraid of death? No!—afraid for what? For the life of the living that (God forbid) it should be terminated before having gazed—if only once—upon the Eternal. B.P., November 30, 1934

Satirical Self-Obituaries, May 1, 1934

The Family Page: She was a woman who for decades stubbornly defended her timely ideas, but did so in a fashion and ways that sought to anticipate development in a manner that was not to every man's liking and taste. What a shame!

The Israelite: By background and upbringing an Orthodox woman who, in the course of the decades and under the evident influence of the revolutionary ideas of the Women's Movement, thought to tear herself away from her roots—often conducting herself with hostility—yet did not denounce them. According to her good family—we remind you that her father was one of the founders of the "*Schiffeschul*" in Vienna—she ought to have rendered Orthodoxy better service. What a shame!

C.V. Zeitung: A woman of good abilities, dedicated equally to the combative Jewish essence and German culture, but who in her sharpness and rejection of any ideology she did not agree with, consciously placed herself outside our ranks. What a shame!

Die Judische Kundsdiau (Jewish Review): A zealous old opponent of our movement, whose Jewish consciousness and strength cannot be denied. Where she believed herself to be a German, she was only an assimilationist after all. What a shame!

> *Blaetter des Jüdischen Frauenbundes:* In 1904 she founded the Jüdischer Frauenbund, whose importance has still not been fully grasped. World Jewry—men and women—could be thankful to her for this social (altruistic?) act. They are not. What a shame!

In 1935, at the age of seventy-nine, Bertha was dying of a fatal tumor. In the last summer of her life, although often in great pain, she traveled home to Vienna and left her collection of antique laces and glass to the Museum for Arts and Crafts, where it remains. While in Vienna, it is possible that she destroyed any documents referring to her early breakdown and requested that family members not give out any information after her death.

On her way back from Vienna, she stopped in Bad Ischl, both the happy resort of her youth and the place where her emotional disorders began when she was twenty-one. In Bad Ischl she became so ill that she was rushed to a hospital in Munich. She returned to Isenburg, where her beloved physician, Dr. Minkel, cared for her.

Still filled with extraordinary energy and multiple plans and projects, Bertha made arrangements to travel to Holland and Poland. In September 1935, she went to Amsterdam to meet Henrietta Szold, the American Zionist leader who was organizing the emigration of young German Jews between the ages of fifteen and seventeen to Palestine. Bertha, still believing that somehow under Nazi rule there was a place for Jews in Germany, fought this plan with all the strength she could muster. It was not until the passage of the anti-Jewish Nuremberg Laws in 1935 that she recognized her error.

In November of that year she learned of the death of two leaders of the Jewish education of girls, both attendees of the Beth Jakob Seminary, a teacher training institute in Cracow. In response to their deaths, she undertook a strenuous journey to Cracow to plead for the addition of a department of social workers and nurses to serve this population of student teachers. She promised to return in the spring of 1936. Tragically, after Bertha's death, ninety-three girls at the Beth Jakob Seminary committed suicide after the Nazis announced plans to turn their home into a brothel. The girls took ritual cleansing baths, then poisoned themselves. A letter smuggled out by one of them contained the following poem:

> Death does not terrify us; we go out to meet him.
> We answered our God while we were alive;
> Pity, oh merciful Father?
> Oh, pity the people that knew Thee,
> For there is no more pity in men.

In the spring of 1936, Bertha's tumor had metastasized to her liver and she became bedridden. Because of her vanity, she only allowed a few of her close friends to visit her. Throughout this period of great suffering, all the complexities of her personality remained intact. When Ottilie Schönewald brought her a gift of yellow roses, she retorted with her typical dry humor, "How lovely, they match my complexion."

Her closest friend, Hannah Karminski, visited her on April 6 during Pesach. They had planned to take a trip to Spain to celebrate Bertha's eightieth birthday. Despite her weakness and pain, Bertha wanted to celebrate Pesach with the children in the main house. Dr. Minkel advised further bed rest, but Bertha knew her condition and wanted to spend a last evening among the children; and she was happy with all the festivities around her.

A young man from *Bachad* led the Seder. She interrupted him to translate from the Hebrew or to explain passages to the children. Her spirituality was at its peak. She continued to transcend others' attempts to understand her through materialist theories or reason. She was, in the end, a woman who took a Kierkegaardian leap of faith and found God in the core of her being. She spoke of the slavery of the Jews in Egypt: "Laboring in Egypt was unbearable because at the time there was no Sabbath. With the prospect of Shabbat, anyone can bear such heavy work. Without Sabbath, everything is bondage and slavery."

She wrote many beautiful prayers in 1935, including one confirming her faith:

> My God, you are no God of soft words and incense—no God of the past. You are an everpresent God. To me you are a demanding God. You hallowed me with your "you shall"; you await my decision between good and evil, you demand that I prove to be the strength of your strength, that I strive toward you, sweeping others along with me, helping with all that I am able. Demand! Demand, so that with each breath of my life, I will feel in my conscience: there is a God.

The day after the Seder she took to bed, her skin jaundiced from the cancer, but still planning to return to Poland. On April 9, the Gestapo summoned Bertha to a hearing on April 14. A feeble-minded boy who had been raised for a short time at the Home had made anti-Hitler remarks. Bertha Pappenheim was being held responsible for the boy's behavior.

Although Dr. Minkel advised her not to undertake the trip, or at least to try to arrange for the hearing to be held at her house, Bertha insisted, saying, "I will travel."

With Hannah Karminski she went to the police station for the hearing. Bundled up, Bertha actually enjoyed the trip. The sunshine shone on the blooming fruit trees, the young saplings,

Bertha and Hannah Karminski, 1935. [Photo © Leo Baeck Institute]

the fresh green of the trees. She sucked in this beauty with all her senses, the scent of the blossoms and meadows, and retorted to Hannah, "This is what you would not allow me to enjoy!"

The interrogation lasted an hour and a half. During the course of it, Bertha learned that a personal denunciation had been made against her. According to Hannah, Bertha displayed a kind of superhuman strength, in her honest indignation and her unshakable calm and even in this hour showed a bit of humor, which unmistakably proved her superiority. Standing up to the Gestapo was her last great act.

On the way home, as she traveled through the blooming countryside, Bertha spoke of the anxiety and disappointment this denunciation had caused her. "And you will see that Mrs. X will be sorry that she did that. Perhaps she is already suffering for it—and regrets it."

After this ordeal, Bertha never left her bed again. Hannah encouraged her to try to stand up a few more times, but it didn't work. "I wouldn't get up for all the tea in China!" Bertha replied.

The problem of the emigration of Jewish children to Palestine continued to worry Bertha, since she loathed the idea of the separation of families. "Just think," she told Hannah, "of the children over there alone, and of the parents. What they have to put up with!" Everyone tried to reassure her about the fate of the children. Bertha responded, "But even if nothing happens to them, the effect on their nerves is horrifying enough."

Until her last days, Bertha wanted to know what was going on in Palestine and in the rest of the world. And her narrower world, the world of the Home, also concerned her.

Hannah wrote of Bertha's beauty in every phase of her illness. Bertha herself described each new stage of her illness and apologized for taking so long to die.

Hannah wrote that Bertha's poor body, which had to "live" for fourteen days on ice—iced drinks and a few foods—made her increasingly worn and haggard. Her features, however, became increasingly knowing, wise, and soft. "If I were to see myself in a mirror now," she said ten days before her death, "I would surely look like Dürer's mother in that picture he drew before her death. She must have had something similar to what I have."

Bertha's friends and doctor joined her in laughing at this remark. She emphatically refused to look in a mirror. Her pain became so intense that Dr. Minkel started to treat her with morphine. It is a great irony that the medicine to which she became addicted as a young woman was given to her again in extremis. After the first morphine injection, her face took on a hard, almost masculine quality, as if she was standing before the Final Judgment fearless and undeterred.

Until the end, Bertha continued her "talking cure." She narrated a tale to Hannah called "The Twisted Rose," based on a Grimm fairy tale. She interwove all the themes that she loved: youth, home, sorrow, and yearning after personal happiness. With the beautiful hands of which she had always been vain, she made stiff, dramatic gestures to reinforce the story.

On Thursday, May 20, she continued to refuse all visitors, saying repeatedly, "Don't let anyone in." On several occasions she also spoke warmly about Martin Buber. Her room had to be kept dark because light and brightness caused her pain, and she protected her head and eyes from them. She vomited repeatedly

Hannah Karminsky at Bertha's house, 1935.
[Photo © Leo Baeck Institute]

and that evening she vomited blood for the first time. She asked Dr. Minkel if he treated all the sick so well, "the poor as well," and stressed that she had "undeservedly good care." "Just think," she remarked, "of the sick in Palestine. They have no water, and certainly not such care."

On Friday, May 21, seven days before her death, Bertha dictated a final poem to Hannah:

Quietly, quietly, without direction,
Goes the time,
Quietly, quietly without direction,
Am I ready to go with You.

Quietly, quietly, without direction,
One must be ready
For time and eternity.
Who is that, You?
Give me peace.

She tried to dictate a second story to Hannah, which amounted to two or three sentences. The story was to have been called "Coup de Grace."

On May 22, Bertha called for Hannah very early in the morning. When Hannah arrived at her bedside, she was agitated and sobbing. Bertha told her, "Tonight the old man was near me—he came quite quietly. He stood there at the end of the bed. At first, I thought he was the doctor. But then I realized that he was very old and had a furrowed face and long beard. He looked at me very kindly, and gestured thus [she moved her hand in the air in an act of blessing], and then he was gone. I must tell the doctor as well. But he must not laugh. If he laughs, he will never be allowed to come in here again!" Dr. Minkel did not laugh; he was deeply moved by this vision.

At the end, in her last not-quite-lucid hours, she spoke often of Vienna. She also referred to the Book of Job, wondering if Job had not had a similar disease. Hannah reminded her that he had leprosy and that his friends had avoided him, while Bertha was surrounded by loved ones. Bertha then recalled that Job had had a "happy ending," since God spoke to him out of the whirlwind.

Bertha repeated the watchword of her faith, the Sh'ma Yisroel, every day before her death. Hannah remarked that Bertha's hands were, until the end, noble, beautiful, and unwilted. According to her, Bertha frequently used these hands to elucidate her thoughts—often her mouth was silent and only her hands spoke. During her last few days, Bertha kept Hannah at her bedside. When the doctor came, he was allowed to hold her hand.

Late in the afternoon of May 28, Dr. Minkel lifted Bertha's feather-light figure and took her to the sofa. She laid both hands firmly on Hannah's. She didn't move again. Along with Hannah Karminski, the members of her inner circle were present in her room during her last hours: Stephanie Forchheimer, Paula Niedermeyer, Gertrude Ehrenwerth, Helene Krämer, and Jenny Wolf.

Bertha was facing the wall because of pain on her left side. Hannah and Dr. Minkel rearranged her bedding so that she could face the room and gaze on the loving faces and her beautiful artifacts in her final moments.

Bertha was buried next to her mother on the liberal side of the Old Jewish Cemetery in Frankfurt. According to her wishes, no eulogies were given. The rabbi read Psalm 121, her favorite psalm:

> I will lift up mine eyes unto the
> hills, from whence cometh my help.
> My help cometh from the Lord,
> which made heaven and earth.
> He will not suffer thy foot to be
> moved: He that keepeth thee will not
> slumber.
> Behold, he that keepeth Israel shall
> neither slumber nor sleep.
> The Lord is thy keeper: the Lord
> is thy shade upon thy right hand.
> The sun shall not smite thee by day,
> nor the moon by night.
> The Lord shall preserve thee from
> all evil: he shall preserve thy soul.

> The Lord shall preserve thy going
> out and thy coming in from this time
> forth, and even for evermore.

Bertha's friend, the philosopher Martin Buber, wrote the following words of commemoration in her honor:

> There are people of mind, and there are people of passion; neither is as common as one thinks. More rare are people of mind and passion, and rarer still is the passion of the mind. Bertha Pappenheim was a being of passionate mind.
>
> Did she not have to become strict—oh, not hard—but simply severe, lovingly severe, mightily demanding and mightily raging since everything was the way it was and remained that way? She stood in an era that was no match for that white fire—a time which could not have been because it cannot even recognize its inability to believe that such a thing exists.
>
> But it does exist. That while flame burned in our day. Now it has gone out and only her image lingers eternally reflected in the hearts of those who knew her. Pass on this picture, hand down the memory, testify that it still exists!

In her Last Will and Testament, Bertha stated how she wished to be remembered:

> Not with words, which fade away, not with flowers, which do not last, shall anyone approach my final resting place; if you remember me, bring a little stone, as the silent promise and symbol of the establishment of the idea and mission of women's duty and woman's joy in serving unceasingly and courageously in life.

Chapter Seventeen

AFTERMATH (1936–1954)

The entrance to the Old Jewish Cemetery in Frankfurt, where Bertha was laid to rest, is framed by a large neo-Grecian portico with Doric pillars and protected by an art nouveau iron gate. Cicily Neuhaus' reflections on Bertha's burial epitomize the devotion of her followers. Cicily wrote:

> As the coffin with her mortal shell was drawn into the cemetery hall it was difficult not to kneel, not to bow in mute respect before the woman whose entire life was a singular path of purity and greatness, the strictest fulfillment of duty, of quality, and of truth.
>
> In this hour of parting, Bertha Pappenheim stood before us as alive as ever. So insistent and obligating was this impression, that the silence she demanded seemed natural—yet it was exactly from that silence that the majesty of her being spoke to the small, awe-inspired community of women.
>
> Our Jewish law does not recognize "saints" among our people, even if in the purity and the integrity of their lives they are worthy of this description. We bow and kneel before God only, not before people. Only in the majesty of death, in the majesty of God's presence, can the Jewish person become a "saint." As it is said, "In death the righteous are larger than in life."
>
> We thank you, God, for what you gave us in Bertha

Pappenheim, we recognize in your taking her from us, our task and our obligation.

Two weeks after the funeral, JFB held a memorial service to celebrate Bertha's achievements and honor her. One speaker felt that Bertha "stood too far from the things of the time"; another spoke of the power of her "spellbinding" personality; a third said that Bertha realized "the holy commandments through her actions, the unity of religion and life."

Irene Barmstädter gave a eulogy for Bertha at the Girl's Club on June 14, 1936. She evoked the tears of a gathering of mourners who had lost their "mother" and became "orphans." She spoke of Bertha's "always going her own way." She also mentioned that "even in her reading, everything took on a personal note. She was the kind of woman who left her mark on everything."

After Bertha's death, Helene Krämer because the director of the Home. One of Bertha's beloved "daughters," she first met her "mother" and mentor in 1889 as an eight-year-old orphan. In 1907, she had gone to Tarnopol in Galicia to direct an orphanage founded by Weibliche Fürsorge. Bertha visited her there several times. After the outbreak of World War I, Helene directed an orphanage in Posen and in 1922 she returned to Frankfurt.

Under Helene's direction the daily routine of the Home did not change until the fall of 1937, when the Nazis enacted laws that forbade Jews to attend public school. The principal of the Isenburg public school requested that the children be transferred to a Jewish school. Twenty-four children then commuted to a Jewish public school in Frankfurt, accompanied by an officer. However, the Home itself, housing fifty children, remained undisturbed until November 10, 1938, the date of the infamous

Kristallnacht, when many synagogues and Jewish-owned businesses, schools, and other buildings were destroyed by mobs.

As the Nazi cruelty towards the Jews had been intensifying in the weeks before *Kristallnacht,* Helene "was terribly worried and prepared for horrible events." She had decided to leave the teens and other schoolchildren in the main building and the infants and small children in what was called the Children's House.

At 7:00 P.M. on November 10, "the barbarians" came with pitch torches and called to the inhabitants of the Home, "Open up, we bring you meat." The rioters forced their way into the overcrowded building, screaming, "Jews out!" Their cruel deed took five minutes at most. The leader of the pack, a man named Schmidt who had laid the electrical wiring in the Home, demanded the cash box from Helene. She was barely able to grab the children's coats before the main building was burned down and the side building was seriously damaged.

The infants were carried out in baskets. All the employees and children stood in the cold autumn night for an hour watching the horrible sight of the building burning.

The JFB President, Paula Nassauer, spent the whole night at Isenberg, moving more than 100 children and adults into one of the two remaining buildings. The electrical wiring failed and the "screaming and wailing of the children was so horrifying and heartbreaking" that the "barbarians" took pity on them and allowed them to go to a neighboring house to ask for money to buy candles. Since several girls had suffered heart attacks, a Christian doctor was called and found his way to the ruins by candlelight. The fire engine arrived much too late. The house smoldered until the next day, when Helene was forced to dismiss the Christian employees who had worked in the home for years; the schoolchildren were taken to the orphanage in Frankfurt.

After *Kristallnacht* JFB was ordered dissolved. Its treasury and institutions were absorbed by the *Reichvereinigung der Juden in Deutschland,* and the remaining leaders—Cora Berliner and Hannah Karminski, among others—actively worked in this organization on emigration aid.

Helene Krämer remained at the Home until October 31, 1941, when she fled to Cuba, before moving to New York in November. In 1955, she wrote a vivid account of the destruction of the Home's buildings on *Kristallnacht.* After her emigration the Home was run by Sophie Sondheim. On March 31, 1942, the Home was closed. Sophie Sondheim and Hanna Königsfeld, the housekeeper, were taken to Darmstadt on April 5, 1942. On October 9, 1943, they were deported to Auschwitz to be gassed. They stayed together until their deaths. The Home nurse, Selma Strauss, was also sent to Darmstadt. On September 19, 1942, after she learned of the transports to "the East," she hanged herself.

The last "complete and supplementary list" of missing Jews cites fifty-eight people. Nineteen children taken to Frankfurt were deported to "the East" in May 1942. The remaining occupants of the Home were "handed over to their homelands." There they were seized by the Gestapo, who were engaged in making these areas *Judenfrei* (free of Jews), and put onto transports for the death camps.

The path of the suffering was difficult to follow. Ten inhabitants of the Home were carried off to various ghettos and death camps in "the East." Three employees and fourteen students, among them eight children under six, were deported to Auschwitz between July 11, 1942 and October 23, 1944. In spite of thirty years of systematic searching on the part of the International Tracing Service, no further information has come to light. "Only in a single case is there a vague hope that a five-year-old boy survived."

Bertha, transcending her anti-Zionist stance, helped many friends and acquaintances emigrate to Palestine. Willi Goldman, who had lived at the Home and worked in Frankfurt, was summoned to her home in early 1933. He had lost his job in Frankfurt as a result of Nazi activities and wanted to leave for Palestine, although that too was becoming increasingly fraught with peril. He later reminisced that whenever Bertha wanted "something from us children, we went in with a thumping heart. Her majestic appearance made us shy." Bertha described her impressions of Palestine and gave him practical advice on the conditions there and what trade to follow. He observed that Bertha was still anti-Zionist, and believed herself to be a "real German citizen of Jewish faith. But she did see the shadows on the horizon." Since the yearly quota for German emigrants was limited to one thousand Jews, Willi felt fortunate to receive his visa, a one-way ticket out of Germany. The day before his departure, in August 1933, Willi saw Bertha Pappenheim for the last time.

> [Bertha] asked me to come and see her in the Home and said to me: "I have here a little note book for you in which I have written down addresses of people in Jerusalem, Haifa, and Tel-Aviv, to whom you can turn if you need help." Also, all of the welfare organizations for immigrants were listed there. On the first page there was also a personal dedication to me. Then she stood up—I was sitting on a chair in front of her—laid both hands on my head and said nothing. Because I kept my head bowed, I couldn't see her face. Then she turned around and went into the corner of the room and said to me without turning around, "God protect you, now please go."

After 1933, the emigration quota became totally inadequate. Hanni Glenn, a twenty-year-old wife of a Jewish shopkeeper in

Neu-Isenburg, with no connection to the Home, testified to Bertha's boundless compassion and pragmatism:

> I will never forget how some time before our departure from Neu-Isenburg the doorbell rang and Miss Pappenheim was standing there: we were all thunderstruck. She had never done this before. . . . Miss Pappenheim never made private calls. . . . Through the efforts of Miss Pappenheim I got a private audience with the British Consul General in Frankfurt. . . . Miss Pappenheim's assistance even went as far as writing me a letter of recommendation to a renowned lawyer from Frankfurt who was already established there (Palestine) and who employed me as a secretary two weeks after my arrival. . . . Most immigrant girls had to earn their living by doing hard physical work. . . . For Neu-Isenburg there were no days of glory. After 1933, former students, with whom I had spent years together in school, from one day to the next behaved as though I had overnight become leprous. In shops, people made dirty remarks within earshot, directed at me, and on the street I was harassed. . . . Our housekeeper, Christian Hafele, stayed true to us to the last moment. . . . When I took the five o'clock train to the Consulate, Christian Hafele was already up on a ladder, painting over the nightly graffiti in the color of our shutters.

Most of the JFB leaders, including Cora Berliner and Hannah Karminski, were deported in 1942. The few who survived emigrated and formed, in Bertha Pappenheim's honor, an organization called Care By Women, based in both New York and Palestine. Hannah Karminski wrote about her visit with Cora Berliner on the day of Cora's deportation:

> Cora and our other friends took books along. They agreed on the selection. To my knowledge, C. took

West German postage stamp from "Helpers of Humanity" series, 1954. [Photo © Leo Baeck Institute]

> Faust and I an anthology. When I went to visit them on the last day, shortly before their departure, they were sitting in the garden reading Goethe.

In 1953, Ernest Jones revealed that Anna O.'s real name was Bertha Pappenheim. Bertha's cousin, Dr. Paul P. Homburger, the executor of her estate, protested Ernest Jones's revelation of her identity as "Anna O." in an open letter.

In 1954, in a series entitled "Helpers of Humanity," the West German government issued a stamp in Bertha Pappenheim's honor, with her face engraved upon it.

Chapter Eighteen

GEBETE (PRAYERS)*

I. Memorial Prayer

Mother, on these days I light a yorzeit candle for you and place a small stone on your grave—in remembrance. But such tokens are not necessary. As time passes, I find myself, while engaged in the most seemingly trivial actions and words, remembering you—I remember you infinitely often, as well as Father—your treatment of each other, your shared convictions, devotion, and mutual respect as husband and wife, to whom I owe my life.

I remember you, Mother, your goodness, your intelligence that was never harsh, your industry, your dexterity, your delicacy, and your modesty.

You lived as a link in a chain of noble generations.

The little flickering light conjures and animates the shadows of the past.

Blessed be your memory, Mother.

II.

The wind blows over the graves, and the sunlight falls across the stones. Memories trickle through my thoughts in little drops.

*Text by Bertha Pappenheim. These prayers were selected and edited by Jüdischer Frauenbund and published by Philo Verlag in 1936.

As I place a little stone upon the beloved spot, I wish for myself, the childless one, for small stones of remembrance to be placed on the rim of the red sandstone that bears the inscription: “She was quite severe!”

III. Prayer of Thanks

A little one grasps my finger, tugs at my hair, and laughs at his successful attack, teeth glinting.

I am so happy to have provided a shelter for this little human seedling, which might otherwise have been trampled in the dust and left us one hope poorer.

How good it is, that this little human seedling and I encountered each other in the universe. Let us thank our Creator for the good fortune of love and life.

IV.

Resentment rages in me! I will harbor it and it shall burn within me as long as that which justifies it exists. I will not become negligent, I will not be blind to shameful, harmful acts; I will not excuse what is dishonest and inexcusable.

May I but retain the strength to cry out, again and again, in indignant rage to condemn all injustice!

V.

Thanks that I am able to preserve for myself alone the power that grows, unasked and unforced, in my consciousness, as if in a cool mill dam.

But thanks, too, for the hour when I found the words to express what moves me and, with them, moves others.

To feel power is to live—to live is the desire to serve. . . .

VI.

Often deeply pained and injured by others—what of it? Let me summon the strength to tread the one and only path—the Royal Road.

And not heard, misunderstood—what of it? Let me continue to speak and to tell the truth.

And when it is cold, and when it is dark, and the air becomes rank and hard to breathe,—when I discern the truth and wish to proclaim it, and people are stupid, what of it? I can proclaim the truth through action—soundlessly, without words.

That I may have the strength to do so, now and always!

Amen.

VII.

Fill me, you force of goodness, of which to be merely one atom should fill us with proud humility. Strengthen and sharpen my sense so that without becoming lost and confused, I may tread the only path that you prescribe. To depart from a life of stinging disappointments is not painful, it would be painful to have lived without ever having known your sublimity.

Force of goodness and truth, protect me.

VIII.

Shall I give thanks that I still exist?

Shall I lament that I still exist?

It was a year of insight,
Thus a year of self-denial,
So do I lament that I still live:
That I wasted time,
That I squandered love—
Not only this year,
But in many others.
But to waste and squander
Is to be rich, and live.
Thus I give thanks for having been able to live
And long for death.

IX. A Prayer for Women

Spirit of the universe, who has bound the world
Together with just laws, give us the insight to
recognize them, a creative work ethic, and a willingness
for acts of love:

We shudder—there is a death that stalks the land; women can no longer give birth and have lost their desire for it. The organs of respiration and procreation are poisoned—a vapor of egotism, hypocrisy, and dishonesty hangs over Jewish homes, which can no longer be distinguished from the others to which they are to bring the great word from Mount Sinai.

That the sound of the Shofar could shake the community, that trivial letters would no longer obstruct the paths of women, that the specter of the great death might disappear and that a generation might arise out of strength and love and respect for the Holy Spirit, who blesses those who live and govern with a pure heart.

Amen.

X.

Time, ancient and revered, source of help and healing, you have built and bestowed upon me so much. You have animated the ancestral heritage that so enriched my life and revealed to me the pulsing filaments that hold existence together. All merciful Time, bring me mildness with the ripeness of age.

XI.

Only not to become blind—not with the soul, to no longer distinguish the small from the great, the narrow from the wide, the exalted from the burdened, or that which shines in eternal light.

Only not to become blind—not with the soul!

ACKNOWLEDGMENTS

To the Divine in each of us which leads us to create our lives with Love. For my friends and their families in the Chicago milieu in which I was raised: for their high culture; beautiful manners; formal households glittering with art, books, and music; passionate philanthropy; and loving loyalty. My Chicago milieu so paralleled that of Bertha Pappenheim's—my imaginative entrance into Bertha's world was in many ways seamless. In memory of my mother, who taught me unconditional love and love of Beauty; in memory of my father, who taught me historical perspective and the limits of genius, even his own; in memory of my maternal grandparents, who were the incarnation of generosity and pure joie de vivre; in memory of my paternal grandparents, whose aristocratic Viennese ancestors passed on from generation to generation a passion for justice, and the wisdom that with privilege comes responsibility. In memory of my second mother, Colleen Young, whose soulfulness and playfulness ensured me a happy childhood, and who taught me the concept of "soul."

Bless all my teachers! For this book, I am in debt for my healthy sense of ignorance and the joy of process to Distinguished Professor Daniel Gerould, and his distinguished wife, independent scholar Yadvega; to the luminous mind of Distinguished

Professor Linda Nochlin; to the breathtaking work of Lydia Gasman; and to philosophy professor Joan Stambaugh, who counseled me to stay close to the spiritual world.

Among my colleagues at CUNY, I was blessed by my racquetball partner of ten years, art historian Marlene Park, whose loving-kindness and insights are saintly. I owe my deepest gratitude for the intellectual sources of this work to the compassionate and profound Professor Marion Kaplan; to my role model, Distinguished Professor Blanche Cook, for both her politics and genius at biography; to Professor Holly Hill, who continued to love reading about Bertha for a decade; to my chairman for almost a decade, Patrick Collins, who supported me with endless devotion and patience. In memory of professor and author Flora Rheta Shreiber, whom I miss terribly; to Professor Georgiana Peacher, my spiritual mother and Jungian scholar and author of streams of unconsciousness. I wish to thank the visionary president of John Jay College of Criminal Justice, Gerald Lynch, for giving me such an extraordinary life; Professor David Willinger for his creativity and faith; Professor Daniel Gasman for his love of truth; and all my feminist colleagues in the founding years of the Women's Committee for the inspiration; Professor Lilia Milani, whose successful class action on behalf of CUNY women protected my academic career; and my best friend, Professor Irving Portner, for the precious diamonds of his heart.

For knowledge and wisdom about Bertha Pappenheim and psychoanalysis, I am in great debt to Freud scholars and renaissance geniuses and pranksters Peter and Julia Swales: for their ingenious detective work; for their valiant spirits in savoir vivre; for making my parties internationally famous; for all their acts of love and kindness; and of course, for all the archival material of which one could dream. To my guardian angel, renowned psychiatrist and psychoanalyst Dr. Susan Lazar, for her lifelong friendship and heroic acts on my behalf. Her work will bring new consciousness on the planet. To professor and author Phyllis Chessler, whose ur-work on women and madness and forensic psychology is legendary; I am awed that she has taken time to read my manuscript, aid in its publication, and offer me friendship; may her life and work be blessed. I wish to thank psychoanalyst Brett Kahr of London—brilliant colloquy and many peak experiences; and Jeffrey Masson for his friendship, infectious enthusiasm for serious research in unraveling the truth in psychoanalytic history and the Holocaust, and for making our visits enormous fun with surprise introductions to extraordinary people. To John Kerr for his belief in revelation through chronological order; to Professor Albrecht Hirschmuller, whose depth and detailed research in the life of Josef Breuer and our small meetings are much treasured; to Professor Sander Gilman, who holds so many chairs he could hold a dinner party, for reading my manuscript and giving me wondrous suggestions; to my beloved dance therapist, Jane Wilson Downes, for her insights into creativity and healing and for giving me the courage to create my own dance and the courage to perform; to pioneer self-psychologist Robert Stolorow for serving as a theoretical consultant on my work, to all the members of Women in German On-line, sponsored by Berkeley, University of California, for the high level of their work and support for many years now; to Armando Verdiglioni, who gave me adventurous trips and meetings with the most innovative psychoanalysts of our time; to philosophy professor and author, Françoise Collin, who published my first book, and who has written letters and published my work for two decades in Paris and Belgium; to Lloyd DeMause and the Institute of Psychohistory for treating my work with respect; and their courageous enterprises; and to my "monster mind," Dr. Zvi Lothane, psychiatrist, psychoanalyst, author, and friend whom I love dearly, and whose unquestioned support and aid in the writing of this book is without precedence, as well as teaching me the word "spa" during the dark times. May he receive the recognition he deserves for his innovative work on Schreber and Love therapy, and his famous salons in his penthouse garden. I owe my deep respect to Dagmar Hermann, whose trilingual reading of my early manuscript and exquisite translations of letters to Martin Buber inspired me to reach to a higher level of work; and to independent scholar Roberta Schwartz, who so generously shared her videos, the letters to Martin Buber, and the correspondence with Felix Warburg with me; who with selfless devotion produced an education film about Bertha Pappenheim.

For the production of this book I would like to thank my divine agent, Loretta Barrett, who first sold it to my greatly beloved mentor, the legendary Arthur Rosenthal, founder of Basic Books and director of the Harvard University Press, who in turn, along with Vassar soulmate Jane Gregory Rubin, helped it find a home at Moyer Bell; my deepest gratitude to founders Jennifer Moyer and Britt Bell; my editorial director, Sam McGregor; and brilliant line editor, Arabella Meyer.

This work would not have been possible without the generous support of three City University of New York grants and a grant from the Lucius Littauer Foundation.

I would like to thank everyone at the following institutions who aided me in my archival and photographic research:

The Leo Baeck Institute of New York, especially to Dr.

Diane Spielmann for her gracious support of my efforts for many years.

The Jewish Museum of Frankfurt, Germany

The Stadt Museum of Neu-Isenberg, Germany

The City Archives of Vienna, Austria

The secretary of Sanatorium Bellevue, Kreuzlingen, Switzerland

The Jewish Community of Frankfurt, Germany

The Library of the Hebrew University of Jerusalem, Israel

Union Theological Seminary, the American Jewish Archives, Cincinnati, Ohio

I also wish to thank Ian Caramitru, the minister of culture of Romania, and Princess Sophie of Romania for my research on orphans, and the opportunity to experience "spiritual motherhood." In my various trips to Eastern Europe, I was treated as a celebrity, due to the efforts of the remarkable U.S. Director of the International Theatre Organization, Martha Coigney.

The great joy I had over the years was supported by my research assistants from Barnard College, New York: Robin Aronson, Amy Sanders, Bronwyn Miller, and Mona Sanders. They taught me what Bertha Pappenheim meant by "spiritual daughters" who gave more than they received. May their lives be ever filled with gaiety, love, and recognition; may all their dreams come true!

My literary translators, who are listed in the book, gave eloquent voice to previously untranslated material by Bertha Pappenheim, especially the exquisite work of Donald Flannell Friedman.

Last, I would like to thank everyone who supported my performance piece, "Anna O.'s Private Theatre": my co-creator and director, George Ferencz; and the awesome Marshall Coid, violinist, composer, counter tenor who traveled the world with me; and who has accompanied me not only in the performance piece but in my multimedia lectures for almost two decades, with such astounding creativity and radiant spirit that I love him with my whole being. I wish to thank the American Psychoanalytic Association; Anne Louise Silver, the president of the American Academy of Psychoanalysis, for her undeserved praise; the Oxford Psychoanalytical Forum, Frederic Flammand of the International Theatre Festival of Le Plan K., Brussels; the great love of Fernand for my "writing room" in 5 Square du Val de la Cambre; my beloved lawyer, Kenneth Burrows; the Department of Women's Studies, Yale University; the graduate program in history, Sarah Lawrence College; and the Graduate Center of the City University of New York, among my favorite venues and audiences.

Bless everyone I have met on this joyous and transforming adventure.

NOTES

Introduction

p. 1. Just as a person . . . : The quotes at the top of chapters, unless otherwise designated, are among the 2,000 "Reminders" or *Denkzettel,* dated from 1922–35, translated by Amy Sanders. Frankfurt: Archives of the Jewish Museum, unnumbered; typewritten.

p. 3. Breuer published the case history: Josef Breuer and Sigmund Freud, *Studies on Hysteria,* trans. James Strachey and Anna Freud (New York: Basic, 1955), 21–47.

p. 4. "a girl suffering from hysteria": Sigmund Freud, *Five Lectures on Psycho-Analysis,* trans. and ed. James Strachey (New York: Norton, 1977), 9.

p. 4. "psycho-analysis is my creation": Sigmund Freud, *On the History of the Psycho-Analytic Movement,* trans. Joan Riviere (New York: Norton, 1966), 7.

p. 4. broke the code of confidentiality: Ernest Jones, *The Life and Work of Sigmund Freud* (New York: Basic, 1957), 1:223.

p. 5. "private theatre": Ibid., 22.

p. 5. "talking cure": Ibid., 30.

p. 5. anthology: Dora Edinger, *Bertha Pappenheim: Freud's Anna O.* (Highland Park, Ill.: Congregation Solel, 1968).

p. 6. classic social history: Marion Kaplan, *The Jewish Feminist Movement in Germany: The Campaigns of the Jüdischer Frauenbund, 1904–1938* (Westport, Conn.: Greenwood, 1979).

p. 6. studious explorations: Ellen M. Jensen, *Streifzüge durch das Leben von Anna O./Bertha Pappenheim: Ein Fall für die Psychiatrie—Ein Leben für die Philanthropie* (Frankfurt: ZTV, 1984).

p. 6. most recent monograph: Mikkel Borch-Jacobsen, *Remembering Anna O.* (New York: Routledge, 1996).

p. 6. "creative illness": Henri F. Ellenberger, *The Discovery of the Unconscious: The History and Evolution of Dynamic Psychiatry* (New York: Basic, 1970), 447.

p. 7. Bertha wrote of the super-earthliness: *Denkzettel (1922–35)* (Frankfurt: Archiv Bertha Pappenheim).

p. 7. original biblical quotation: Michael Fishbane, *The Kiss of God: Sprirtual and Mystical Death in Judaism* (Seattle: University of Washington Press, 1994).

p. 9. the value of the impermanent self: Joan Stambaugh, *The Formless Self,* (Albany: State University of New York Press, 1999), 28.

p. 10. French radical feminists: Hélène Cixous, "La Rire de la Meduse," in Elaine Marks and Isabelle de Courtivron, eds. *New French Feminisms* (New York: Schocken, 1981), 253.

p. 10. "great poetic and imaginative gifts": Breuer and Freud, *Studies on Hysteria*, 21.

p. 10. "part of all libations": Ibid., 252.

p. 10. celebrates the superiority of women's bodies: Luce Irigaray, *Ethique de la Différence Sexualle* (Paris: Les Editions de Minuit, 1984).

p. 10. crisis in masculinity: Elaine Showalter, *Sexual Anarchy: Gender and Culture at the Fin de Siècle* (New York: Viking, 1990), 10. The entire book was inspiring. See also Showalter, *Hystories: Hysterical Epidemics and Modern Media* (New York: Columbia University Press, 1997).

p. 11. no boundary of unified consciousness: Ken Wilber, *The Collected Works of Ken Wilber* (Boston: Shambala, 1999).

p. 11. awareness of false boundaries: Ibid., 86.

p. 11. "identities" are forged: Erik Erikson, *Life History and the Historical Moment* (New York: Norton, 1975).

p. 11. flowing from the imaginal: James Hillman, *A Blue Fire,* ed. Thomas Moore (New York: HarperCollins, 1989).

p. 12. "the infinite I AM": I. A. Richards, ed., *The Portable Coleridge* (New York: Viking, 1961), 516.

p. 12. continually threatened: See especially Diana Tietjens Meyers, ed., *Feminists Rethink the Self* (Boulder: Westview, 1997); Ruth-Ellen Boetcher Joeres, *Respectability and Deviance: Nineteenth-Century German Women Writers and the Ambiguity of Representation* (Chicago: University of Chicago Press, 1998).

p. 12. "If I were not an enemy": Bertha Pappenheim, *Sisyphus-Arbeit* (Leipzig: Verlag Paul E. Linder, 1924).

p. 13. German scholar: Albrecht Hirschmuller, *The Life and Work of Josef Breuer* (New York: New York University Press, 1978).

1. Public Theatre/Private Theatre (1880–1881)

p. 21. "she embellished her life": Josef Breuer and Sigmund Freud, *Studies on Hysteria* (New York: Basic, 1955), 22.

p. 21. "almost a physically felt pain": *Blätter des Jüdischen Frauenbunds: Für Frauenarbeit und Frauenbewegung,* Vol. XII, July/August 1936, 30.

p. 22. a nervous cough: Breuer and Freud, *Studies on Hysteria,* 40.

p. 22. Austrian resort: Peter Swales, "Freud, Breuer, and the Blessed Virgin" (privately printed, 1986), 1. Peter Swales is a playful, magical genius of a Freud historian. Peter and his wife, Julia, gave me a copy of the first fairy tales Bertha wrote, which they had discovered in the Frankfurt City Archives, as well as a constant flow of secret or freshly unearthed archival material during the course of this project.

p. 23. influential circle: Helga Heubach, *Das Heim des Jüdischen Frauenbundes in Neu-Isenburg* (The Home of the League of Jewish Women) (Magistrates der Stadt Neu-Isenburg: 1986), 8.

p. 24. a magnificent view: I visited the house in July 1990, thanks to the research of Freud historian Peter Swales. The house, garden, and vistas remain as they were a century ago.

p. 24. at a critical stage: Breuer and Freud, *Studies on Hysteria,* 38–39.

p. 24. how distorted and enormous its face had become: Ibid., 39.

p. 24. *massa confusa:* French term for secondary or altered consciousness.

p. 25. children's verses: Breuer and Freud, *Studies on Hysteria,* 38.

p. 25. her arm would contract: Ibid., 39.

p. 25. addressed her in English: Albrecht Hirschmuller, *The Life and Work of Josef Breuer* (New York: New York University Press, 1978), Appendix C, 279.

p. 26. rich and fashionable: Carl Shorshke, *Fin-de-Siècle Vienna,* (New York: Vintage, 1961), p. 49. The second and third floor apartments of the Ringstrasse District were called "Nobelstock."

p. 26. "theatromania": Stefan Zweig, *The World of Yesterday* (London: Cassell, 1953), 18.

p. 26. majestic spectacle: Ibid.

p. 27. "its intellectual character": Marsha L. Rozenblit, *The Jews of Vienna, 1867–1914: Assimilation and Identity* (Albany: State University of New York Press, 1983), 2.

p. 28. A formative influence: Heubach, *Das Heim des Jüdischen Frauenbundes,* 7.

p. 29. Orthodox Schiffschul: The Schiffschul was destroyed on Kristallnacht, 1938. A plaque marks its remains.

p. 29. "Torah True" *Yiddishkeit:* George E. Berkley, *Vienna and Its Jews* (Cambridge: Abt, 1988), 46.

p. 29. arranged marriage: Ellen M. Jensen, *Streifzüge durch das Leben von Anna O./Bertha Pappenheim: Ein Fall für die Psychiatrie—Ein Leben für die Philanthropie* (Frankfurt: ZTV, 1984), 9.

p. 29. social and business capital: W. E. Mosse, *The German-Jewish Economic Elite: 1820–1935, A Socio-Cultural Profile* (Oxford: Clarendon, 1989), 164.

p. 29. families of the first order: Ibid.

p. 29. "crowned glory": Ibid., 167.

p. 31. Imperial Parades: Heubach, *Das Heim des Jüdischen Frauenbundes*, 7.

p. 31. "more Jews in Vienna": Berkley, *Vienna and Its Jews*, 29.

p. 31. "sages of Vienna": Ibid.

p. 31. deported to Hungary: Paul Hofmann, *The Viennese: Splendor, Twilight, and Exile* (New York: Doubleday, 1988), 36–42.

p. 31. executed or exiled: Ibid., 29.

p. 31. expelled once again: Ibid., 30.

p. 32. number of visiting merchants swelled: Ibid., 31.

p. 32. intellectually powerful salons: Ibid., 32.

p. 32. prevented from trading . . . : Ibid.

p. 33. largest conversion rate: Rozenblit, *The Jews of Vienna*, 7.

p. 33. precursor . . . of anorexia: Dijkstra, *Idols of Perversity: Fantasies of Feminine Evil in Fin-De-Siècle Culture* (New York: Oxford, 1987), 29.

p. 33. not unlike . . . Rossetti: Showalter, *The Female Malady* (New York: Pantheon, 1985), 134.

p. 34. the family physician: Breuer and Freud, *Studies on Hysteria,* 23.

p. 34. quintessential female malady: Showalter, *The Female Malady,* 129.

p. 34. Egyptian papyri: Ilza Veith, *Hysteria: The History of a Disease* (Chicago: University of Chicago Press, 1965), 2.

p. 35. "to drive it away": Ibid., 3.

p. 35. standard prescriptions: Ibid., 13.

p. 35. "lability and capriciousness": Showalter, *The Female Malady,* 129.

p. 36. "Resistant to medical treatment": Barbara Ehrenreich

and Deirdre English, *For Her Own Good: 150 Years of the Experts' Advice to Women* (New York: Doubleday, 1978), 137.

p. 36. "reorganized around the patient": Elaine Showalter, *The Female Malady,* 133.

p. 36. new freedom and power: Carroll Smith-Rosenberg, "The Hysterical Woman: Sex Roles and Conflict in 19th-Century America," *Social Research* (Winter 1972): 663.

p. 36. usually short and routine: Hirschmuller, *The Life and Work of Josef Breuer,* 309–310.

p. 37. "sharp and critical common sense": Breuer and Freud, *Studies on Hysteria,* 21.

p. 37. "extremely monotonous existence": Ibid., 22.

p. 38. "silent struggles and silent opposition": Hirschmuller, *The Life and Work of Josef Breuer,* 277.

p. 39. powerful intellect: Breuer and Freud, *Studies on Hysteria,* 21.

p. 39. "just once more!": Jensen, *Streifzüge durch das Leben von Anna O./Bertha Pappenheim,* 20.

p. 40. "completely sterilized atmosphere": Zweig, *The World of Yesterday,* 77.

p. 40. "an ironic sense": Bertha Pappenheim, *Ethische Kultur* (weekly journal), February 1898.

p. 40. "crossing oneself": Jensen, *Streifzüge durch das Leben von Anna O./Bertha Pappenheim,* 14–15.

p. 42. "from December 11, 1880": This narrative is constructed from two sources: the first is the classic case history written by Breuer and published in *Studies on Hysteria* (1895); the second is a handwritten manuscript of Breuer's earlier notes discovered in Sanatorium Bellevue in 1970 by Henri Ellenberger and published by Hirschmuller in 1980.

p. 42. In the 1880's: Rosemary Agonito, ed., *History of Ideas on Women* (New York: Paragon, 1977), 200.

p. 43. "they have no genius": Will Durant, ed., *The Works of Schopenhauer* (New York: Frederick Unger, 1928), 456.

p. 44. characterized women as superficial: Walter Kaufmann,

ed., *The Portable Nietzsche, Thus Spoke Zarathustra* (New York: Viking, 1967), 389.

p. 44. A deep soul: Agonito, *History of Ideas on Women,* 269.

p. 44. traditional characteristics: Ibid., 250.

p. 44. triply demeaned Jewish women: Otto Weininger, *Sex and Character* (London: Heinemann, 1906), 304.

p. 44. "the absolute Jew is devoid of a soul": Ibid., 313.

p. 45. Romantic hero: Janik and Toulmin, *Wittgenstein's Vienna* (New York: Simon & Schuster, 1973), 71.

p. 45. blame others: Hirschmuller, *The Life and Work of Josef Breuer,* 281.

p. 46. she resumed speaking: Breuer and Freud, *Studies on Hysteria,* 25.

p. 47. child feels merged with the mother: Melinda Guttman, "Performing A Case History", *Women and Performance* 2 (78). See also Diane Hunter, "Hysteria, Psychoanalysis, and Feminism: The Case of Anna O." in Shirley Nelson Garner, Claire Kahane, and Madelon Sprengnether, eds., *The (M)other Tongue* (Ithaca: Cornell University Press, 1985), 89–93, for a brilliant Lacanian interpretation.

p. 47. speaking it . . . became unbearable: Sander Gilman, *Jewish Self-Hatred* (Baltimore: Johns Hopkins University Press, 1986), 260.

p. 47. a fantastic referent: Daniel Boyarin, *Unheroic Conduct* (Berkeley: University of California Press, 1997), 335.

p. 49. profound, complex morality: James Hillman, *A Blue Fire,* ed. Thomas Moore (New York: HarperCollins, 1989).

p. 49. "rising into a new life": Henri Ellenberger, *La Notion de Maladie Creatrice* (my translation), Dialogues, Vol. III, Canada, 27.

p. 50. new "Thousand and One Nights": Hans Christian Andersen, *Picture-book Without Pictures,* trans. Hanby Crump (Celle: E.H.C. Schulze, 1856), 5.

p. 50. "observer brain": Hirschmuller, *The Life and Work of Josef Breuer,* 283.

p. 50. "the greater part remained in perpetual darkness": Andersen, *Picture-book*, 97.

p. 51. speaking perfectly: Hirschmuller: *The Life and Work of Josef Breuer,* 282.

p. 51. "would have made any sacrifice": Ibid., 283.

p. 51. Bertha had seen her father rarely: Breuer and Freud, *Studies on Hysteria*, 26.

p. 52. begged to be told the truth: Hirschmuller, *The Life and Work of Josef Breuer,* 284.

p. 52. profound agitation: Ibid.

p. 53. "I know my father is dead": Ibid.

2. The Talking Cure (1881–1882)

p. 53. violent outburst: Breuer and Freud, *Studies on Hysteria,* (New York: Basic, 1955), 26.

p. 53. Her vision: Ibid.

p. 57. Bertha suffered: Ibid., 28.

p. 57. Breuer lied: Ibid.

p. 57. Inzersdorf sanitorium: Albrecht Hirschmuller, *The Life and Work of Josef Breuer* (New York: New York University Press, 1978), 286.

p. 57. avoided the use of narcotics: Breuer and Freud, *Studies on Hysteria*, 30.

p. 58. "A subservient female nurse and a godlike male doctor": Elaine Showalter, *The Female Malady* (New York: Pantheon, 1985), 139. Showalter here cites several contemporary feminist interpreters. She cites the controversy some feminists believe: that enforced dependency and childlike obedience to a "charismatic physician may have actually been restorative."

p. 58. All of these techniques proved ineffectual: Hirschmuller, *The Life and Work of Josef Breuer,* 104.

p. 58. to accomplish the elimination of hysteria: Wilhelm Orb, *Handbook of Electro-therapeutics* (New York: William Wood, 1881), 293.

p. 59. tearful worship in front of his picture: Hirschmuller, *The Life and Work of Josef Breuer,* 291–292.

p. 59. look after poor, sick people: Breuer and Freud, *Studies on Hysteria,* 31.

p. 59. "sultan with Scheherezade": Showalter, *The Female Malady,* 156.

p. 60. the permissive company of her Jewish doctor: John Murray Cuddihy, *The Ordeal of Civility: Freud, Marx, Levi-Strauss, and the Jewish Struggle with Modernity* (Boston: Beacon, 1974), 42.

p. 60. "thereupon the disturbance vanished": Breuer and Freud, *Studies on Hysteria,* 34.

p. 61. transcending the "ego" and becoming her "inner witness": Ken Wilber, *No Boundary* (Boston: Shambala, 1979), 55.

p. 63. "she knocked up against the stove": Breuer and Freud, *Studies on Hysteria,* 33.

p. 65. "it was not herself that she saw": Ibid., 37–40.

p. 65. denied herself the pleasure of reading: Hirschmuller, *The Life and Work of Josef Breuer,* 279.

p. 66. the exhaustive manner . . . alleviated her hearing problems: Breuer and Freud, *Studies on Hysteria,* 36.

p. 68. practicing witchcraft: Ilza Veith, *Hysteria: The History of a Disease* (Chicago: University of Chicago Press, 1965), 59.

p. 68. a variety of sexual delusions: Ibid., 67.

p. 68. "magnetic" illness: Henri F. Ellenberger, *The Discovery of the Unconscious: The History and Evolution of Dynamic Psychiatry* (New York: Basic, 1970), 484.

p. 68. unusual coexistence: Ibid. Also, the importance of this aspect has been brilliantly speculated on by Peter Swales in his unpublished manuscript, "Freud, Breuer, and the Blessed Virgin," 1986.

p. 68. "prodigious mnemonic feats": Ellenberger, *Discovery of the Unconscious,* 484.

p. 69. verified as accurate: Swales, "Freud, Breuer, and the Blessed Virgin," 20.

p. 69. "could be compared to Emmerich's nightly visions": Ellenberger, *Discovery of the Unconscious*, 484.

p. 69. cured her as she predicted: Swales, "Freud, Breuer, and the Blessed Virgin," 21.

p. 69. "one of those cases so frequent": Ellenberger, *Discovery of the Unconscious,* 484.

p. 70. a contradiction: Swales, "Freud, Breuer, and the Blessed Virgin," 30.

p. 71. a supreme means of expression: Louis Aragon and André Breton, "Le Cinquantenaire de l'hystérie," *La Révolution Surréaliste* 11 (1928).

p. 71. similar to an actor's physicalization: See also Diane Hunter, "Hysteria, Psychoanalysis, and Feminism: The Case of Anna O.," in Shirley Nelson Garner, Claire Kahane, and Madelon Sprengnether, eds., *The (M)other Tongue* (Ithaca: Cornell University Press, 1985).

p. 72. "she has enjoyed complete health": Breuer and Freud, *Studies on Hysteria,* 40–41.

p. 72. fled from her phantom pregnancy: Ernest Jones, *The Life and Work of Sigmund Freud* (New York: Basic, 1957), 1:224.

p. 72. fathered a child named Dora: "The Journal of My Analysis," 1925–1926 (unpublished), courtesy of Dr. Frank R. Hartman, New York City, 225.

p. 72. Breuer did not abruptly abandon his patient: Breuer referred several cases, Bertha's among them, to Sanatorium Bellevue that document this.

p. 72. before the legendary event: Henri Ellenberger, "The Story of 'Anna O.': A Critical Review with New Data," *Journal Hist. Behavioral Science* 8, (1972): 267–279.

p. 72. she became despondent: Hartman, "Journal."

p. 73. "fairer and more immortal": *Plato, Symposium and Phaedrus,* eds. Stanley Appelbaum and Candace Ward (Mineola, N.Y.: Dover, 1993), 31–32.

p. 73. "safely in your care": Hirschmuller, *The Life and Work of Josef Breuer,* 294.

3. Asylum and First Stories (1882–1887)

p. 75. traveling to a second sanatorium: Frederic Morton, *Thunder at Twilight* (New York: Scribners, 1989), 1. Morton's books on Vienna are splendid. In this book he describes Austria as an apocalyptic ballroom.

p. 76. a theatrical spectacle: Georges Didi-Huberman, *Invention de l'Hystérie* (Paris: Editions Macula, 1982), 5.

p. 76. "bound to reason": Michel Foucault, *Madness and Civiliaztion,* trans. Richard Howard (New York: Random House, 1965), 64.

p. 76. Musée Carnavalet: Didi-Huberman, *Invention de l'Hystérie,* 1982), 15.

p. 77. unchaining the madwomen: George Drinka, *The Birth of Neurosis* (New York: Simon & Schuster, 1984), 41.

p. 77. romanticization of madness: Robert Castel, *The Regulation of Madness* (Cambridge: Polity, 1988), 42.

p. 77. "physical" maltreatment: Ibid., 100.

p. 77. "image of rationality": Ibid., 76.

p. 77. unless she capitulated: Ibid.

p. 78. "moderately severe neuropathic heredity": Josef Breuer and Sigmund Freud, *Studies on Hysteria* (New York: Basic, 1955), 21.

p. 78. family tree: Dora Edinger, *Bertha Pappenheim: Freud's Anna O.* (Highland Park, Ill.: Congregation Solel, 1968), 15. (Bertha had shown Edinger this chart.)

p. 78. status as a "virgin": Nuns, virgins, and old maids were considered prime targets for hysteria because of its alleged sexual etiology.

p. 78. "astonishingly undeveloped": Breuer and Freud, *Studies on Hysteria,* 21.

p. 78. "cure": Clitoridectomies are still widely performed in Africa and other parts of the world in the 1990s as part of a girl's initiation into the religious culture of her tribe.

p. 79. "by reason of their sexual organs": Mary Daly, *Gyn/ecology: The Metaethics of Radical Feminism* (Boston: Beacon, 1978), 227.

p. 79. "female castration": Ibid.

p. 79. the "moral" cure: Yannick Ripa, *Women and Madness: The Incarceration of Women in Nineteenth-Century France*, trans. Catherine du Peloux Menage (Minneapolis: Polity, 1990), 121.

p. 79. normal people: "Normalcy" is no longer a psychiatric construct as has been extensively written about and studied in the last several decades.

p. 80. "'mad' in another cultural setting": Hendrik Ruitenbeek, ed., *Going Crazy* (New York: Bantam, 1972), 52. Thomas Szasz, R. D. Laing, and Phyllis Chessler (*Women and Madness*) were leading counterculture theorists who have been succeeded by the primacy of hereditary and chemical theories of mental illness led by contemporary psychopharmacologists.

p. 82. condominiums: I visited Bellevue in 1986, prior to its conversion. Dr. Binswanger was out of town; his assistant, Ruth, gave me a thorough tour, articles, and archival photographs.

p. 82. autobiographical account: Albrecht Hirschmuller, *The Life and Work of Josef Breuer* (New York: New York University Press, 1978), Appendix C: Archives of Sanatorium Bellevue (handwritten manuscript, conclusion missing, transcribed by Hirschmuller), 298.

p. 86. letter to Robert Binswanger: Ibid., 298–299.

p. 88. quinine and electrotherapy: This pain in the nerve of the jaw is still prevalent today. It is still considered to be the result of a combination of physical and psychological causes, and is almost impossible to treat.

p. 88. Recha Pappenheim: Hirschmuller, *The Life and Work of Josef Breuer,* 300.

p. 90. observe a woman's period: Ripa, *Women and Madness,* 129.

p. 90. "direct explosion of insanity": Henry Maudsley, "Suppression of the Menses," 87, cited in Vieda Skultans, ed., *Madness and Morals: An Anthology of Primary Source Documents* (London: Routledge & Kegan Paul, 1975).

p. 91. "without the noise of a large city": Hirschmuller, *The Life and Work of Josef Breuer,* 303.

p. 91. "Bertha will not learn of the contents of this": Ibid., 304.

p. 92. a letter of thanks: Ibid., 305–306.

p. 93. cheerful despite her continuing pain: Ibid., 307.

p. 94. "education will help": Anna Ettlinger, "Lebenserinnerungen für ihre Familie verfasst" (n.p.: Leo Baeck Institute, 1920).

p. 94. concentrate on her literary work: Ibid.

p. 94. Karlsruhe Women's Association: Ellen Jensen, *Streifzüge durch das Leben von Anna O./Bertha Pappenheim: Ein Fall für die Psychiatrie–Ein Leben für die Philanthropie* (Frankfurt: ZTV, 1984), 45.

p. 94. Fritz Homburger wrote . . . : Hirschmuller, *The Life and Work of Josef Breuer,* 306.

p. 95. Pappenheims were known to Freud: Peter Swales, "Freud, Breuer, and the Blessed Virgin" (unpublished manuscript, 1986), 25.

p. 95. He wished she would die: Ernest Jones, *The Life and Work of Sigmund Freud,* eds. Lionel Trilling and Steven Marcus (New York: Basic, 1957), 225. Also, Swales, "Freud, Breuer, and the Blessed Virgin," 25.

p. 96. "Can you be silent": Ibid., 27.

p. 96. "she is totally healthy": Ibid., 29.

p. 96. one of their first visitors: Ibid., 31.

p. 96. she still suffered: Jones, *The Life and Work of Sigmund Freud,* 225.

4. "The Pond Sprite" by Bertha Pappenheim

Kleine Geschichten für Kinder (Short stories for children) (Karlsruhe: Druck der G. Braun'schen Hofbuckdruckerei, 1888), 35–

107. This text was given to me by Freud's historian, Peter Swales, who discovered it in the Vienna Public Library. Julia Swales provided me with the first English translation. This translation is by Donald Flannell Friedman.

5. Frankfurt (1888–1899)

p. 105. restricted to certain occupations: Whiteside, Rogger, and Weber, 9.

p. 105. reflection of the vagaries of economic prosperity: Peter Gay, *Freud, Jews, and Other Germans: Masters and Victims in Modernist Culture* (New York: Oxford University Press, 1978), 12.

p. 106. she published her second book: Anna Ettlinger, "Lebenserinnerungen für ihre Familie verfasst" (n.p.: Leo Baeck Institute, 1920).

p. 106. she and Bertha . . . traveled to Vienna: *Blätter des Jüdischen Frauenbundes: Für Frauenarbeit und Frauenbewegung,* Vol. XII, July/August, 1936, 28.

p. 108. special privileges: Eugen Mayer, *The Jews of Frankfurt: Glimpses of the Past,* ed. and trans. Israel Meir (Frankfurt am Main: Verlag Waldemar Kramer, 1990), 10.

p. 108. "Shimon Hadarshan" (the preacher): Ibid., 10.

p. 108. general massacre and devastation: Ibid.

p. 108. earliest tombstones . . . are those of women: Ibid., 15.

p. 109. Karl IV's efforts to intervene: Ibid.

p. 109. "child whom the Church eventually canonized": Heinrich Heine, *The Rabbi of Bacherach* (New York: Dutton, 1906), 23–24.

p. 109. under military escort: Mayer, *The Jews of Frankfurt,* 22.

p. 110. "this really is something": Johann Jakob Hasslin, *Frankfurt: Stadt und Landschaft* (Munich: Wolf and Sohn, 1955).

p. 111. princes, diplomats, and avant-garde intelligentsia: Joeres and Maynes, *Respectability and Deviance* (Chicago: University of Chicago Press, 1998), 275.

p. 111. "pioneers in social assimilation": Ibid., 271.

p. 111. politics, philanthropy, the arts, and feminism: Dora Edinger, *Bertha Pappenheim: Freud's Anna O.* (Highland Park, Ill.: Congregation Solel, 1968), 15.

p. 112. charities had been created: Marion Kaplan.

p. 113. as far west as Warsaw: Stephen Berk, *Year of Crisis, Year of Hope: Russian Jewry and the Pogroms of 1881–1882* (Westport: Greenwood, 1985), 35.

p. 113. "scrolls were torn to shreds": Ibid., 35–36.

p. 113. "rape mothers and daughters in sight of each other": Ibid., 36.

p. 115. "paradigm of literature": Gordon Birrell, introduction, *German Literary Fairy Tales,* eds. Frank G. Ryder and Robert M. Browning (New York: Continuum, 1983), xix.

p. 116. "inherited, bartered or collected": Jennifer Waelti-Walters, *Fairy Tales and the Female Imagination* (Montreal: Eden, 1982), 2.

p. 117. *In the Junk Shop:* Bertha Pappenheim (P. Berthold), *In der Trödelbude* (Lahr: Druck und Verlag von Moritz Schauenburg, 1890).

p. 120. "how it is used": *BJF,* February 1929, "Gedanken über Erziehung, aus Notizender letzten 10 Jahre." In Dora Edinger, ed., *Bertha Pappenheim: Leben und Schriften* (Frankfurt am Main: Ner Tamid Verlag, 1963), 12–13.

p. 120. "psychoanalysis will never penetrate my establishments": Ibid.

p. 121. "all kinds of housework": *BJF,* Vol. XII, July/August 1936, 5.

p. 122. committed . . . as an hysteric: Albrecht Hirschmuller, *The Life and Work of Josef Breuer* (New York: New York University Press, 1978), 120.

p. 123. "to find and keep a position in life": *BJF,* Vol. XII, July/August 1936, 6. See also Ellen M. Jensen, *Streifzüge durch das Leben von Anna O./Bertha Pappenheim: Ein Fall für die Psychiatrie—Ein Leben für die Philanthropie* (Frankfurt: ZTV, 1984).

p. 123. "remained their deeply caring adviser": *BJF,* Vol. XII, July/August 1936, 3–5.

6. "The Coffee Mill's Story" by Bertha Pappenheim

p. 125. P. Berthold, "Was die Kaffeemülle erzählt," *In der Trödelbude* (Druck und Verlag von Moritz Schauenburg, 1890), translated by Donald Flannell Friedman.

7. Feminism and White Slavery (1899–1905)

p. 129. *Frauenrecht*: P. Berthold [=Bertha Pappenheim] *Frauenrecht: Schauspiel in drei Aufzügen* (Women's Right) (Dresden: Verlag Pierson, 1899).

p. 129. "irrelevant to . . . female pupils": Anna Taylor Allen, *Feminism and Motherhood in Germany: 1800–1914* (New Brunswick: Rutgers University Press, 1991), 125.

p. 129. gender difference, or spiritual motherhood: Ibid.

p. 130. "an article about Wollstonecraft": Bertha Pappenheim, "On the Women's Question A Hundred Years Ago."

p. 130. "share in rights to the benefit of mankind": Ibid.

p. 130. the author of *Frankenstein:* Ibid.

p. 131. hung a picture . . . on her living room wall: Marion Kaplan, *The Jewish Feminist Movement in Germany: The Campaign of the Jüdischer Frauenbund, 1904–1938* (Westport: Greenwood, 1979), 42. Kaplan's classic book on this subject should be read by anyone who wants a brilliant, full account of the Jewish feminist movement. Most of my discussion on this movement was inspired by this book. Kaplan's recent works mark her as the leading historian of Jewish women in Germany.

p. 131. "love is not to be bought": Mary Wollstonecraft, "The Effects of Discrimination Against Women," in Rosemary Agonito, ed., *History of Ideas on Women* (New York: Paragon, 1977), 148.

p. 131. "How much more respectable": Mary Wollstonecraft, *A Vindication of the Rights of Woman,* 2nd ed. (London: J. Johnson, 1979), chapter 9.

p. 134. "That is my right as a woman": Berthold, *Frauenrecht.*

p. 134. "they're nothing without us": Ibid.

p. 135. "fathers forget and disown them": Ibid.

p. 135. well-known author (*bekannte Schriftstellerin*)

p. 136. "she is worse than the others": *Allgemeine Zeitung des Judentums* (1901).

p. 136. "learn something from their non-Jewish sisters": Ibid.

p. 137. "A greater and deeper morality has long ruled": Ibid.

p. 137. "Their private interests": Kaplan, *The Jewish Feminist Movement in Germany,* 43.

p. 137. "rootedness": *Blätter des Jüdischen Frauenbundes: Für Frauenarbeit und Frauenbewegung,* ed. Hannah Karminski (Berlin, 1936), 6.

p. 137. "in order not to miss anything": Ibid.

p. 137. "sparkle of her personality permeated everything": Ibid.

p. 138. "keep a corner of your heart free": Ibid.

p. 138. German National Conference on the Struggle Against the White Slave Trade: Ellen Jensen, *Streifzüge durch das Leben von Anna O./Bertha Pappenheim: Ein Fall für die Psychiatrie—Ein Leben für die Philanthropie* (Frankfurt: ZTV, 1984), 74–75.

p. 139. "dealers, goods for sale, consumers": Jewish Association for the Protection of Girls and Women, *Official Report of the Jewish International Conference on the Suppression of the Traffic in Girls and Women* (London: Wertheimer, Lea & Co., 1910), 146.

p. 139. many committed suicide: Edward J. Bristow, *Prostitution and Prejudice* (New York: Schocken, 1983), 13.

p. 140. displacement and poverty: Edward J. Bristow, *Vice and Vigilance: Purity Movements in Britain Since 1700* (Totowa, N.J.: Rowman and Littlefield, 1977), 178.

p. 140. "no idea of what he was getting into": Bertha Pappenheim, *Sisyphus-Arbeit II* (Berlin: Druck und Verlag Berthold Levy, 1929), 4.

p. 140. "I cannot say what he did with me": Bristow, *Prostitution and Prejudice,* 98.

p. 141. they refused to help: Ibid., 99.

p. 141. prostitution at home or abroad: Ibid., 103.

p. 141. argue against the emancipation of women: Ibid., 43.

p. 141. Moro . . . wrote in 1903: Ibid., 1.

p. 142. the whole Jewish people: Ibid., 99.

p. 143. "great economic knowledge": Jensen, *Streifzüge durch das Leben von Anna O./Bertha Pappenheim,* 55.

p. 143. *On the Position of the Jewish Population in Galicia*

p. 143. large Jewish and Ukrainian populations: Ezra Mendelsohn, *The Jews of East Central Europe Between the World Wars* (Bloomington: Indiana University Press, 1983), 12.

p. 143. "component of the Polish landscape": Aleksander Hertz, *The Jews in Polish Culture* (Evanston, Ill.: Northwestern University Press, 1988), 6.

p. 143. "Jewish question in Poland": Ibid., 11.

p. 144. a national community: Ibid., 26.

p. 144. congratulated the authors: Jensen, *Streifzüge durch das Leben von Anna O./Bertha Pappenheim,* 75.

p. 145. "refusing to admit them as equal partners": Kaplan, *The Jewish Feminist Movement in Germany,* 44.

p. 145. "cowardly and dishonorable to defect": Ibid., 42.

p. 145. "Christian girls know much more": Ibid., 43.

p. 148. "one of the highlights of their life": 43

p. 148. "consciousness . . . spiritualization": *BJF,* 1936, 8.

p. 148. "the psychological victory of JFB": Ibid.

p. 149. a legacy from its Jewish sisters: Kaplan, *The Jewish Feminist Movement in Germany,* 67.

p. 150. "able to nod their approval": Ibid., 68. This discussion is based primarily on Kaplan's research.

p. 150. the driving spirit and the dominant personality: Ibid., 44.

p. 150. "chain that fastens a life's work to eternity": *BJF*, 1936, 10.

p. 151. "the great man theory": See also Kaplan, *The Jewish Feminist Movement in Germany,* 33.

p. 151. battles in their later life: Erik Erikson, *Identity and the Life Cycle* (New York: Norton, 1980); also noted by Marion Kaplan in *The Jewish Feminist Movement in Germany.*

p. 151. "responsibility for a segment of mankind": Frank Manual, *The Use and Abuse of Psychology in History*, 201.

8. Excerpts from *On the Condition of the Jewish Population in Galicia: Impressions of a Voyage* by Bertha Pappenheim

Bertha Pappenheim and Sara Rabinowitsch, *Zur Lage der jüdischen Bevölkerung in Galizien, Reise-Eindrücke und Vorschläge zur Besserung der Verhältnisse* (Frankfurt: Neuer Frankfurter Verlag GmbH, 1904).

9. From Spiritual Motherhood to Matriarch (1905–1910)

p. 169. withdraw from all contact: Ernest Jones, *The Life and Work of Sigmund Freud* (New York: Basic, 1957).

p. 169. "dragon lady": Ibid.

p. 170. prayer for her mother: *Blätter des Jüdischen Frauenbundes: Für Frauenarbeit und Frauenbewegung*, ed. Hannah Karminski (Berlin, 1935–1936), 40.

p. 172. "eyes were put out": Simon Dubnow, *History of the Jews in Russia and Poland: From the Earliest Times to the Present Day* (Philadelphia), 73–74.

p. 173. "the terrible 'work' was going on": Ibid., 74.

p. 173. Jewish mothers: Pappenheim Collection (handwritten, unnumbered), Leo Baeck Archives.

p. 175. "oppressed by the burden which they had to carry": *Allgemeine Zeitung das Jüdentums*, Vol. 27 (1906), 227–228.

p. 175. emigration hall of the Hamburg-American Line: Photo not cited or published in Jensen.

p. 175. until they were safely settled: Ellen Jensen, *Streifzüge durch das Leben von Anna O./Bertha Pappenheim: Ein Fall für die Psychiatrie—Ein Leben für die Philanthropie* (Frankfurt: ZTV, 1984).

p. 175. "Help by Women for Women": Marion Kaplan, *The Jewish Feminist Movement in Germany: The Campaigns of the Jüdischer Frauenbund, 1904–1938* (Westport: Greenwood, 1979), 133.

p. 175. Nazis forbade JFB from continuing: Ibid., 134.

p. 176. "prevent her from becoming saleable market goods": Bertha Pappenheim, "Zur Geschichte des Heimes 1907 bis 1936 Unter Leitung: Der Plan" (On the welfare for female youth at risk). In *Das Heim des Jüdischen Frauenbundes in Neu-Isenburg, 1907 bis 1942*, ed. Helga Heubach (Neu-Isenburg, 1986), 23–25.

p. 176. she would miss her little girls: Lucy Freeman, *The Story of Anna O.* (New York: Walker, 1972), 44.

p. 177. "On Welfare for Female Youth at Risk": Heubach, ed., *Das Heim des Jüdischen Frauenbundes*, 23–25.

p. 179. All were members: Ibid., 17.

p. 179. cram themselves in the center of cities: Bertha Pappenheim, "On the Morality Question," *Frankfurter Israelitsches Familienblatt* Vol. 11 (1907), 9.

p. 179. "a kind of divine justice": Ibid., 13.

p. 180. "a woman is not an individual": Ibid., 129–138.

p. 181. protest in the *Frankfurter Israelitischer Familienblatt*: Dr. Isaak Unna, *Frankfurt Israelite Family Journal,* October 1907, 2.

p. 181. pride in her Jewish heritage: Heubach, ed., *Das heim des Jüdischen Frauenbundes,* 28.

p. 182. a visual metaphor: See photos from my visit.

p. 184. "the great Jewish perspective": *BJF*, March 1934, 9.

p. 184. "larger perspective into which each task fits": Ibid.

p. 184. "uplift others along with her": Ibid.

p. 185. unwed Jewish mothers: Pappenheim, "On the Morality Question," 11.

p. 185. London, May 1909: *BJF,* 1934.

p. 186. race hatred outweighed woman-to-woman sympathy: Edward Bristow, *Prostitution and Prejudice* (New York: Schocken, 1983), 266–267.

p. 187. almost completely restricted: Kaplan, *The Jewish Feminist Movement in Germany,* 119.

p. 187. victims, not sinners: *Frankfurter Israelitisches Familienblatt* (August 5, 1906), 11. Also Kaplan, *The Jewish Feminist Movement in Germany,* 119.

p. 187. Henry Street Settlement: No material on or discussion of this trip remains.

p. 187. sense of aesthetic superiority: *BJF,* 1935–1936, 26.

p. 188. "opinion in Jewish circles was strongly divergent": Bristow, *Prostitution and Prejudice,* 265.

p. 188. "gathering ought not to have been held": Ibid.

p. 188. "saddest chapter": Bertha Pappenheim, speech at Jewish International Conference on the Suppression of the Traffic in Girls and Women, London 1910 (official report), 44–46, 133–134.

p. 190. "antiquated ideal": Ibid.

p. 190. "a battle cry": Ibid.

p. 191. "image of a woman who . . . stood out": *BJF,* 1935–1936, 31.

p. 192. instructions to her children: *The Memoirs of Glückel of Hameln,* trans. Marvin Lowenthal (New York: Schocken, 1977), 2.

p. 192. danced around her as he painted: Dora Edinger, *Bertha Pappenheim: Freud's Anna O.* (Highland Park, Ill.: Congregation Solel, 1968), 101. The portrait was lost but was reproduced in the first calendar of the JFB, April 4, 1932.

10. *Sisyphus-Arbeit* by Bertha Pappenheim

Bertha Pappenheim, *Sisyphus-Arbeit: Reisebriefe aus den Jahren 1911 und 1912* (Leipzig: Verlag Paul E. Linder, 1924).

p. 193. 1924 reissue: The following letters were translated by

Donald Flannell Friedman and Dora Edinger. I have indicated Dr. Friedman's translations; the rest are by Edinger in *Freud's Anna O.*

p. 193. September 1924: Translated by Donald Flannell Friedman.

p. 195. March 12, 1911: Translated by Donald Flannell Friedman.

p. 196. "Blessed is he": Goethe, *Iphigenia.*

p. 198. April 23, 1911: Translated by Donald Flannell Friedman.

p. 199. April 26, 1911: Translated by Donald Flannell Friedman.

p. 204. May 6, 1911: Translated by Donald Flannell Friedman.

p. 205. May 7, 1911: Translated by Donald Flannell Friedman.

p. 206. May 23, 1911: Translated by Donald Flannell Friedman.

p. 208. May 10, 1912: Translated by Donald Flannell Friedman.

p. 210. May 26, 1912: Translated by Donald Flannell Friedman.

11. Struggles (1911–1918)

p. 216. "it can also take place in joy": Albert Camus, *The Myth of Sisyphus and Other Essays* (New York: Vintage, 1955), 88.

p. 218. "So I try to look upon death,/A friendly face": Handwritten manuscript, unnumbered, Leo Baeck Archives.

p. 218. Bertha was bitterly opposed: Edward Bristow, *Prostitution and Prejudice* (New York: Schocken, 1983), 279.

p. 219. their mothers threw stones: *Blätter des Jüdischen Frauenbunds: Für Frauenarbeit und Frauenbewegung*, ed. Hannah Karminski (Berlin, 1935–1936), 20.

p. 219. *Tragic Moments*: Bertha Pappenheim, *Tragische Momente: Drei Lebensbilder* (Frankfurt: J. Kauffmann, 1913).

p. 221. military coats . . . helmet protectors: Ellen Jensen, *Streifzüge durch das Leben von Anna O./Bertha Pappenheim: Ein Fall für die Psychiatrie—Ein Leben für die Philanthropie* (Frankfurt: ZTV, 1984), 74.

p. 222. without means of support: Bristow, *Prostitution and Prejudice*, 284.

p. 222. profiteers and probably agents: Ibid., 287.

p. 223. "all individual stories are of no importance": Dora Edinger, *Bertha Pappenheim: Freud's Anna O.* (Highland Park, Ill.: Congregation Solel, 1968), 31.

p. 223. "hatefulness towards Jewish women": Marion Kaplan, *The Jewish Feminist Movement in Germany: The Campaign of the Jüdischer Frauenbund, 1904–1938* (Westport: Greenwood, 1979), 84.

p. 225. "inscribed their own anxieties": Regina G. Kunzel, *Fallen Women, Problem Girls* (New Haven: Yale University Press, 1993).

p. 225. "little more than their 'origin'": *Allgemeine Zetung des Jüdentums,* vol. 18, no. 51 (1916), 602.

p. 226. early structure dates from 1919: Martin Buber, *I and Thou,* 2nd ed. (New York: Charles Scribners Sons, 1958), 49.

p. 227. Frankfurt A.M.: Bertha Pappenheim, letter to Martin Buber, May 28, 1916, (handwritten, two pages), Buber Archive, the Jewish National and University Library, Jerusalem, 568, 1:1.

p. 229. May 30, 1916: Bertha Pappenheim, letter to Martin Buber, May 30, 1916, (handwritten, two pages), Buber Archive, The Jewish National and University Library, Jerusalem, 568, 1:2.

p. 230. "a pity that you have gone astray": quoted in Maurice Friedman, *Encounter on the Narrow Ridge: A Life of Martin Buber* (New York: Paragon, 1991), 88.

p. 230. the root impulse of drama: Eric Bentley, *Tragedy and Melodrama: Versions of Experience*, 85.

p. 230. "Finding the terms to express it": Peter Brook, *The Melodramatic Imagination* (New Haven: Yale University Press, 1976).

p. 230. Neither comic nor tragic: Ibid., 12.

p. 231. "undoes the moral order": Ibid., 33.

p. 234. "I'll send you the 3 speeches": Bertha Pappenheim, letter to Martin Buber, Letter No. 394, Buber Archives, Hebrew University. Translated by Dagmar Herrmann.

p. 234. "Judaism has not yet done its work": Martin Buber, *On Judaism* (New York: Schocken, 1967), 20.

p. 235. "Judaism's primary reality": Ibid., 9.

12. Tuesday and Friday Evenings (1919–1929)

p. 238. they did not organize: Claudia Koonz, *Mothers in Fatherland: Women, the Family, and Nazi Politics* (New York: St. Martin's, 1987), 34.

p. 238. the word "feminist" became . . . anathema: Ibid., 35.

p. 238. "women's rights have been won": Ibid.

p. 238. revived Romantic ideas: Ibid., 32.

p. 238. forced male leaders: Marion Kaplan, "Sisterhood Under Siege," in Renate Bridenthal, Atina Grossman, and Marion Kaplan, eds., *When Biology Became Destiny: Women in Weimar and Nazi Germany* (New York: Monthly Review, 1984), 180.

p. 239. "determined my fate": Ottilie Schönewald, *Jewish Life in Germany,* translation of manuscript from Leo Baeck Archives, 340.

p. 239. exemplar of Bertha's maxim: Ibid.

p. 239. *Mein Kampf:* Ruth Gay, *The Jews of Germany: A Historical Portrait* (New Haven: Yale University Press, 1992), 249.

p. 240. "Rembrandt Room": Ron Chernow, *The Warburgs* (New York: Random House, 1993), 246.

p. 241. "even when the circumstances are uncomfortable": Bertha Pappenheim, letter to Felix Warburg, September 6, 1920, the American Jewish Archives, Cincinnati, Ohio, box no. 163.

p. 242. "expecting a speedy and positive answer": Bertha Pappenheim, March 28, 1924, the American Jewish Archives, Cincinnati, Ohio, box no. 163.

p. 242. last day of Hanukkah: Bertha Pappenheim, "The Hanukkah Celebration," December 23, 1919 (typewritten manuscript, unnumbered), Frankfurt Archives.

p. 244. "the Jew is the image of the devil": Dieter Rebentisch and Angelika Raab, *Neu-Isenburg zwischen Anpassung und Widerstand* (Neu-Isenburg, The Ministry of the Stadt of Neu-Isenburg, 1978), 263.

p. 244. patrol Jewish homes and shops: Ibid.

p. 245. "have to react with a kind of hostility": *Blätter des Jüdischen Frauenbunds: Für Frauenarbeit und Frauenbewegung*, ed. Hannah Karminski (Berlin, 1936), 12.

p. 245. social issues: Bundesarchiv, former East Berlin, listed under JFB, League of Professional Women.

p. 246. "a prophetic function": Ellen Jensen, *Streifzüge durch das Leben von Anna O./Bertha Pappenheim: Ein Fall für die Psychiatrie—Ein Leben für die Philanthropie* (Frankfurt: ZTV, 1984), 120.

p. 247. "with a cheerful spirit": Archives of the Jewish Museum, Frankfurt, unnumbered.

p. 247. "simply unique": *BJF,* 1936, 25.

p. 248. mutual interests and issues: *BJF,* August 1936, 29.

p. 248. "I cannot succeed": Ibid.

p. 248. "Did she take pleasure in conflict?": Ibid.

p. 249. "the heavy artillery": Ibid.

p. 249. "an almost physically felt pain": Ibid.

p. 249. "Conflict was her life element": Ibid.

p. 250. center for Jewish cultural life: Jensen, *Streifzüge durch das Leben von Anna O./Bertha Pappenheim,* 92.

p. 250. consciously chose Tuesday: Sara Eisenstadt in *BJF,* August 1936, 23–24.

p. 252. "difficult to describe": *BJF,* August 1936, 24.

p. 252. "the refined hostess": Ibid.

p. 252. "atmospheric room": Ibid.

p. 254. "I mean, repeat it!": Ibid.

p. 254. "Her self-discipline educates her surroundings": Ibid.

p. 254. “we have spiritual space”: Ibid.

p. 255. Käthe Mende: Ibid., 23.

p. 255. “will remember her always”: Ibid.

p. 256. “there is religious instruction”: Ibid., 13.

p. 256. “so simple yet overwhelming”: Ibid., 14.

p. 256. “the beautiful traditions of our Father”: Gertrude Ehrenwerth, “Memories of Bertha Pappenheim” (1961) (typed manuscript, unnumbered), Frankfurt Archives.

p. 258. “a pleasurable result of our efforts”: *BJF,* August 1936, 13.

p. 258. “these alone would have been enough”: Ibid., 14.

p. 258. “enough ideas”: Ibid.

p. 259. “yearning for what is beautiful”: Hannah Karminski, “Commemoration Speech,” in Jensen, *Streifzüge durch das Leben von Anna O./Bertha Pappenheim,* 101.

p. 259. description and picture: unnumbered, Frankfurt Photo Archive.

p. 260. other means of birth control had become widespread: Marion Kaplan, *The Jewish Feminist Movement in Germany: The Campaigns of the Jüdischer Frauenbund, 1904–1938* (Westport: Greenwood, 1979), 70.

p. 260. “physical dangers for women”: Bridenthal, Grossman, and Kaplan, eds., *When Biology Became Destiny,* (New York: Monthly Review, 1984), 184.

p. 260. Bertha wrote sharply: *BJF,* May 1927, 3.

p. 261. “merely a cheerful ‘affirmation of life’ ”: Bertha Pappenheim, *Sisyphus-Arbeit II* (Berlin: Druck und Verlag Berthold Levy, 1929), 2.

p. 261. “their position becomes still more difficult”: Ibid., 4.

p. 261. “a labor of Sisyphus”: ibid., 5.

p. 262. Bertha once again turned her back: *BJF,* August 1936, 30.

p. 263. “We women speak for those whose sad fate prevents them”: Ibid., 31.

13. Letter to Felix Warburg by Bertha Pappenheim

Dora Edinger, *Bertha Pappenheim: Freud's Anna O.* (Highland Park, Ill.: Congregation Solel, 1968), 55. Felix Warburg was Bertha's second cousin. The letter was translated from a copy owned by Jenny Wolf, Chicago, Illinois.

14. Fascism and Illness (1930–1936)

p. 275. "the summit of Mt. Sinai": Bertha Pappenheim, 1934.

p. 276. she offered an alternative: Claudia Koonz, *Mothers in Fatherland: Women, the Family, and Nazi Politics* (New York: St. Martin's, 1987), 177.

p. 276. "frankly misogynistic view of women": Ibid.

p. 276. "far from men's political and economic concerns": Ibid.

p. 276. "youth leaders and teachers rivaled mothers": Ibid., 176.

p. 277. "create the new man": Ibid., 180.

p. 277. "submit to the great you": Ibid., 178.

p. 277. "all individualism . . . was to be destroyed": Ibid.

p. 278. high-minded: Bertha Pappenheim, "The Jewish Woman" (1934).

p. 278. "magical effect": Koonz, *Mothers in Fatherland,* 32.

p. 279. "Zionism is the lesser evil": Ellen Jensen, *Streifzüge durch das Leben von Anna O./Bertha Pappenheim: Ein Fall für die Psychiatrie—Ein Leben für die Philanthropie* (Frankfurt: ZTV, 1984), 121.

p. 279. "let us try not to be weaker": *BJF,* 1936, 10.

p. 279. "ironic" justice: *Frankfurter Israelitsches Gemeindeblatt,* July 1936, 277–278.

p. 281. wrote . . . with her typical irony: Bertha Pappenheim Archive, Leo Baeck Institute.

p. 282. "telephone report early each morning": *Blätter des Jüdischen Frauenbundes: Für Frauenarbeit und Frauenbewegung*, 1936, 13.

p. 282. "in her eternally young heart superior to us all": Ibid.

p. 283. "unaccustomed to being loved": Rahel Strauss, "Memoirs," 68, Archives of the Leo Baeck Institute.

p. 284. unify the warring factions: Ruth Gay, *The Jews of Germany: A Historical Portrait* (New Haven: Yale University Press, 1992), 257.

p. 284. "it made me proud": *BJF,* 1936, 29.

p. 285. throws herself . . . into space: Ibid., 38.

p. 285. "with deepest regrets": Marion Kaplan, "Sisterhood Under Siege," in Renate Bridenthal, Atina Grossman, and Marion Kaplan, eds., *When Biology Became Destiny: Women in Weimar and Nazi Germany* (New York: Monthly Review, 1984), 189.

p. 285. the BDF itself disbanded: Ibid.

p. 286. "would not be caught with Jews": Ibid.

p. 286. "as if they were there forever": Ottilie Schönewald, *Jewish Life in Germany,* 341; fragment (unnumbered), Frankfurt Archives.

p. 286. "The Hill of the Martyrs": *BJF,* 1936, 37. This text has never been reprinted, translated, or cited.

p. 288. "collapsed on the hill": Ibid.

p. 289. "systematically developed": Ibid., 23.

p. 290. "was always active": Ibid.

p. 290. at the Jewish Museum in Frankfurt: Ibid.

p. 291. "a woman must create a balance within herself": Ibid.

p. 291. "a miracle": Margaret Susman in *BJF,* 1936, 34.

p. 291. she had to bear the entire cost: *BJF,* 1936, 23.

p. 292. "a diaspora of the spirit": Letter to Hannah Karminski (typewritten, unnumbered, two pages), Frankfurt Archives.

p. 293. "something reminiscent of the prophets": *BJF,* 1936, 38.

p. 293. attended workshops and led study groups: Marion Kaplan, *The Jewish Feminist Movement in Germany: The Campaigns of the Jüdischer Frauenbund, 1904–1938* (Westport: Greenwood, 1979), 202.

p. 293. weren't permitted to read Goethe and Schiller: Aubrey Hodes, *Martin Buber: An Intimate Portrait* (New York: Viking, 1971).

p. 294. "an island of peace"

p. 294. spiritually prepare them: Maurice Friedman, *Encounter on the Narrow Ridge: A Life of Martin Buber* (New York: Paragon, 1991), 221.

p. 296. "September is . . . far away": Bertha Pappenheim, June 6, 1935 (handwritten, two pages), The Jewish National and University Library, Arc. Ms. Sas. 350/568. I am in great debt to Roberta Schwartz, who gave these letters to me and referred me to a most exquisite translater and linguist, Dagmar Hermann, for whose brilliant work and insights I am profoundly grateful. It was a particularly difficult task because the letters were handwritten.

p. 297. "no fellow man has been around": Bertha Pappenheim, 1935.

p. 298. "this so unfashionable correspondence": Bertha Pappenheim, June 15, 1935, (handwritten, two pages), Buber Archives.

p. 299. "time is timeless": Bertha Pappenheim, March 18, 1936 (handwritten, two pages), Buber Archives.

p. 300. "attraction and repulsion": Bertha Pappenheim, March 10, 1936, Buber Archives.

p. 300. SS men in the audience: Hodes, *Martin Buber,* 107.

p. 301. accusing both of them of stereotyping Judaism: Martin Buber, "The Silent Question," *On Judaism* (New York: Schocken, 1967), 208.

p. 301. "the culminating point": Henri Bergson, "The Two Sources," *Selections from Bergson* (New York: Doubleday, 1962), 147–150.

p. 301. "not if we have forsaken other beings": Buber, *On Judaism,* 153.

p. 302. "a path": Margaret Susman in *BJF,* 1936, 34.

p. 302. "the Great Law": Ibid., 35.

p. 302. "according to divine law and will": Ibid., 36.

p. 303. "the Jew must live his belief": Bertha Pappenheim in *BJF,* 1936, 34.

p. 304. "symbiosis": Alexander Altmann, "Moses Mendelssohn as the Archetypal German Jew" in Juhuda Reinharz and Walter Schatzberg, eds., *The Jewish Response to German Culture: From the Enlightenment to the Second World War* (Hanover: University Press of New England, 1985), 20.

p. 304. "law, commandment, and ways of serving God": Ibid., 25.

p. 304. Bertha read to a small circle of friends: Ibid., 23.

15. "The True Ring" by Bertha Pappenheim

Blätter des Jüdischen Frauenbundes: Für Frauenarbeit und Frauenbewegung, ed. Hannah Karminski, 1936, 37. This important text has never been reprinted, translated, or cited.

16. Death (1935–1936)

p. 311. *Satirical Self-Obituaries: Gedenkuummerder Blätter des Jüdischen Frauenbunds: Für Frauenarbeit und Frauenbewegung,* ed. Hannah Karminski (Berlin, July/August 1926), 28.

p. 312. not give out any information: Dora Edinger, *Bertha Pappenheim: Freud's Anna O.* (Highland Park, Ill.: Congregation Solel, 1968), 20.

p. 313. plans to turn their home into a brothel: *The reconstructionist* (New York, 1943) cited to Edinger. This story may be apocryphal. This issue is presently being debated.

p. 313. visited her on April 6th: Hannah Karminski, "Letter to Distant Friends of Bertha Pappenheim," June 7, 1936 (unnumbered), Jewish Museum, Frankfurt. The rest of this narrative is reconstructed for the most part from this letter.

p. 314. "there is a God": *Blätter des Jüdischen Frauenbundes: Für Frauenarbeit und Frauenbewegung,* August 1936, 1.

p. 317. gestures to reinforce the story: The story was lost.

p. 321. words of commemoration in her honor: *BJF,* August 1936, 1.

p. 321. "bring a little stone": Ibid., 39.

17. Aftermath (1936–1954)

p. 324. "our task and our obligation": *Blätter des Jüdischen Frauenbunds: Für Frauenarbeit und Frauenbewegung,* ed. Hannah Karminski (Berlin, 1936), 39.

p. 324. "left her mark on everything": Irene Barmstäder, Frankfurt Archives, June 1936 (unnumbered, typewritten).

p. 326. she wrote a vivid account: This narrative is derived from two sources. One is an account by Helene Krämer written in New York on November 15, 1955; the other is Krämer's notarized account as a witness, requested by the town of Neu-Isenburg, on December 19, 1951, published in *Neu-Isenburg zwischen Anpassung und Widerstand,* ed. Dieter Rebentisch und Angelika Raab (Neu-Isenburg: The Ministry of the Stadt of Neu-Isenburg, 1978), 265–266.

p. 326. "Only in a single case": Ibid., 236–237.

p. 327. Willi saw Bertha Pappenheim for the last time: Ibid., 266–267.

p. 328. "painting over the nightly graffiti": Ibid., 267–268.

p. 328. her visit with Cora Berliner: Hannah Karminski, "Letters to Berlin," Frankfurt Archives, 312. Also cited in Marion Kaplan, *The Jewish Feminist Movement in Germany: The Campaigns of the Jüdischer Frauenbund, 1904–1938* (Westport: Greenwood, 1979), 205.

p. 329. protested Ernest Jones's revelation: Richard Karpe, letter to Paul Homburger, September 30, 1958 (one typed page), Frankfurt Archives.

18. *Gebete* (Prayers) by Bertha Pappenheim

These prayers were selected and edited by Jüdischer Frauenbund and published in 1936 by Philo Verlag as a manuscript, in Bertha Pappenheim's handwriting. The book is in the Pappenheim Archives of the Leo Baeck Institute (unnumbered). This translation is by Mona Sanders.

SELECTED BIBLIOGRAPHY

This bibliography is highly selective since the intended audience is the general reader. The majority of books, periodical articles, and archival materials that are cited in the book or that influenced me are cited here; the remainder of the citations in the book are found in the notes.

Books

Allen, Anna Taylor. *Feminism and Motherhood in Germany: 1800–1914.* New Brunswick: Rutgers University Press, 1991.

Andersen, Hans Christian. *A Picture-book Without Pictures.* trans. Hanby Crump. Celle: E.H.C. Schulze, 1856.

Berk, Stephen. *Year of Crisis, Year of Hope: Russian Jewry and the Pogroms of 1881–1882.* Westport: Greenwood, 1985.

Berkley, George E. *Vienna and Its Jews.* Cambridge: Abt, 1988.

Borch-Jacobsen, Mikkel. *Remembering Anna O.* New York: Routledge, 1996.

Boyarin, Daniel. *Unheroic Conduct.* Berkeley: University of California Press, 1997.

Breuer, Josef and Sigmund Freud. *Studies on Hysteria.* trans. James Strachey and Anna Freud. New York: Basic, 1955.

Bristow, Edward J. *Prostitution and Prejudice.* New York: Schocken, 1983.

———. *Vice and Vigilance: Purity Movements in Britain Since 1700.* Totowa, N.J.: Rowman and Littlefield, 1977.

Brook, Peter. *The Melodramatic Imagination.* New Haven: Yale University Press, 1976.

Buber, Martin. *I and Thou.* 2nd ed. New York: Scribners, 1958.

———. *On Judaism.* New York: Schocken, 1967.

Camus, Albert. *The Myth of Sisyphus and Other Essays.* New York: Vintage, 1955.

Castel, Robert. *The Regulation of Madness.* Cambridge: Polity, 1988.

Chernow, Ron. *The Warburgs.* New York: Random House, 1993.

Cuddihy, John Murray. *The Ordeal of Civility: Freud, Marx, Levi-Strauss, and the Jewish Struggle with Modernity.* Boston: Beacon, 1974.

Daly, Mary. *Gyn/ecology: The Metaethics of Radical Feminism.* Boston: Beacon, 1978.

Dana, Charles. *Textbook for Nervous Diseases.* New York: William Wood, 1851.

Didi-Huberman, Georges. *Invention de l'Hystérie.* Paris: Editions Macula, 1982.

Drinka, George. *The Birth of Neurosis.* New York: Simon & Schuster, 1984.

Dubnow, Simon. *History of the Jews in Russia and Poland: From the Earliest Times to the Present Day.* Bergenfield, N.J.: (Avotaynu, 2000).

Edinger, Dora. *Bertha Pappenheim: Freud's Anna O.* Highland Park, Ill.: Congregation Solel, 1968.

Edinger, Dora, ed. *Bertha Pappenheim: Leben und Schriften.* Frankfurt am Main: Ner Tamid Verlag, 1963.

Ehrenreich, Barbara and Deirdre English. *For Her Own Good: 150 Years of the Experts' Advice to Women.* New York: Doubleday, 1978.

Ellenberger, Henri F. *The Discovery of the Unconscious: The History and Evolution of Dynamic Psychiatry.* New York: Basic Books, 1970.

Erikson, Erik. *Identity and the Life Cycle.* New York: Norton, 1980.

———. *Life History and the Historical Moment.* New York: Norton, 1975.

Fishbane, Michael. *The Kiss of God: Spiritual and Mystical Death in Judaism.* Seattle: University of Washington Press, 1994.

Foucault, Michel. *Madness and Civilization.* trans. Richard Howard. New York: Random House, 1965.

Freeman, Lucy. *The Story of Anna O.* New York: Walker, 1972.

Freud, Sigmund. *Five Lectures on Psycho-Analysis.* trans. and ed. James Strachey. New York: Norton, 1977.

———. *On the History of the Psycho-Analytic Movement.* trans. Joan Riviere. New York: Norton, 1966.

Friedman, Maurice. *Encounter on the Narrow Ridge: A Life of Martin Buber.* New York: Paragon, 1991.

Gay, Peter. *Freud, Jews, and Other Germans: Masters and Victims in Modernist Culture.* New York: Oxford University Press, 1978.

Gay, Ruth. *The Jews of Germany: A Historical Portrait.* New Haven: Yale University Press, 1992.

Gilman, Sander. *Jewish Self-Hatred.* Baltimore: Johns Hopkins University Press, 1986.

The Memoirs of Glückel of Hameln. trans. Marvin Lowenthal. New York: Schocken, 1977.

Hasslin, Johann Jakob. *Frankfurt: Stadt und Landschaft.* Munich: Wolf and Sohn, 1955.

Heine, Heinrich. *The Rabbi of Bacherach.* New York: Dutton, 1906.

Hertz, Aleksander. *The Jews in Polish Culture.* Evanston, Ill.: Northwestern University Press, 1988.

Heubach, Helga. *Das Heim des Jüdischen Frauenbundes in Neu-Isenburg* (The Home of the League of Jewish Women). The Minister of the Stadt of Neu-Isenburg, 1986.

Hillman, James. *A Blue Fire.* ed. Thomas Moore. New York: HarperCollins, 1989.

Hirschmuller, Albrecht. *The Life and Work of Josef Breuer.* New York: New York University Press, 1978.

Hodes, Aubrey. *Martin Buber: An Intimate Portrait.* New York: Viking, 1971.

Hofmann, Paul. *The Viennese: Splendor, Twilight, and Exile.* New York: Doubleday, 1988.

Irigaray, Luce. *Ethique de la Différence Sexualle.* Paris: Les Editions de Minuit, 1984.

Jensen, Ellen M. *Streifzüge durch das Leben von Anna O./Bertha Pappenheim: Ein Fall für die Psychiatrie—Ein Leben für die Philanthropie.* Frankfurt: ZTV, 1984.

Jewish Association for the Protection of Girls and Women. *Official Report of the Jewish International Conference on the Suppression of the Traffic in Girls and Women.* London: Wertheimer, Lea & Co., 1910.

Joeres, Ruth-Ellen Boetcher. *Respectability and Deviance: Nineteenth-Century German Women Writers and the Ambiguity of Representation.* Chicago: University of Chicago Press, 1998.

Jones, Ernest. *The Life and Work of Sigmund Freud.* eds. Lionel Trilling and Steven Marcus. New York: Basic, 1957.

Kaplan, Marion. *The Jewish Feminist Movement in Germany: The Campaigns of the Jüdischer Frauenbund, 1904–1938.* Westport, Conn.: Greenwood, 1979.

———. *Between Dignity and Despair, Jewish Life in Nazi Germany.* New York: Oxford University Press, 1998.

Kierkegaard, Søren. *Concluding Unscientific Postscript.* trans. David Swenson and Walter Lowrie. Princeton: Princeton University Press, 1964.

Kleine Geschichten für Kinder (Short Stories for Children). Karlsruhe: Druck der G. Braun'schen Hofbuckdruckerei, 1888.

Koonz, Claudia. *Mothers in Fatherland: Women, the Family, and Nazi Politics.* New York: St. Martin's, 1987.

Kunzel, Regina G. *Fallen Women, Problem Girls.* New Haven: Yale University Press, 1993.

Mayer, Eugen. *The Jews of Frankfurt: Glimpses of the Past.* ed. and trans. Israel Meir. Frankfurt am Main: Verlag Waldemar Kramer, 1990.

Mendelsohn, Ezra. *The Jews of East Central Europe Between the World Wars.* Bloomington: Indiana University Press, 1983.

Meyers, Diana Tietjens, ed. *Feminists Rethink the Self.* Boulder: Westview, 1997.

Morton, Frederic. *Thunder at Twilight.* New York: Scribners, 1989.

Mosse, W. E. *The German-Jewish Economic Elite: 1820–1935, A Socio-Cultural Profile.* Oxford: Clarendon, 1989.

Orb, Wilhelm. *Handbook of Electro-therapeutics.* New York: William Wood, 1881.

Pappenheim, Bertha. *Kleine Geschichten für Kinder.* Karlsruhe: Druck der G. Braun'schen Hofbuchdruckerei, circa 1888.

———. (P. Bertold) *In der Trödelbude.* Lahr: Druck und Verlag von Moritz Schauenburg, 1890.

———. (P. Berthold) *Frauenrecht: Schauspiel in drei Aufzügen* (Women's Right). Dresden: Verlag Pierson, 1899.

———. (P. Bertold) *Zur judenfrage in Galizien.* Frankfurt: Verlag von Gebruder Knauer, 1900.

——— & Sara Rabinowitsch. *Zur Lage der judischen Bevölkerung in Galizien.* Frankfurt: Neuer Frankfurter Verlag, 1904.

———. *Sisyphus-Arbeit: Reisebriefe aus den Jahren 1911 und 1912.* Leipzig: Verlag Paul E. Linder, 1924.

———. *Sisyphus-Arbeit II.* Berlin: Druck und Verlag Berthold Levy, 1929.

———. *Tragische Momente: Drei Lebensbilder.* Frankfurt: J. Kauffmann, 1913.

———. *Kämpfe.* Frankfurt: Frankfurt am Main: Verlag von J. Kauffmann, 1916.

———. *Denkzettel* (1922–27) "Reminders," Frankfurt: Archives of the Jewish Museum, unnumbered.

———. *Sisyphus-Arbeit, 2.* Berlin: Berthold Levy, 1929.

———. *Gebete.* Handwritten and collected by Margaret Susman. New York: Leo Baeck Archive, 1936.

———. trans. from the Yiddish to German. *Memoirs of Glükel of Hameln* (Privately published, 1910).

———. trans. from the Yiddish to German. *Maysebuch* (tales and legends) Frankfurt: J. Kauffmann, 1929.

———. trans. from the Yiddish to German. *Ze'enah U'Ree nah* (A Woman's Bible) Frankfurt: J. Kauffmann, 1930.

———. *Plato, Symposium and Phaedrus.* eds. Stanley Appelbaum and Candace Ward. Mineola, N.Y.: Dover, 1993.

Rebentisch, Dieter and Angelika Raab. *Neu-Isenburg zwischen Anpassung und Widerstand.* Neu-Isenburg: The Ministry of the Stadt of Neu-Isenburg, 1978.

Richards, I.A., ed. *The Portable Coleridge.* New York: Viking, 1961.

Ripa, Yannick. *Women and Madness: The Incarceration of Women in Nineteenth-Century France.* trans. Catherine du Peloux Menage. Minneapolis: Polity, 1990.

Rozenblit, Marsha L. *The Jews of Vienna, 1867–1914: Assimilation and Identity.* Albany: State University of New York Press, 1983.

Ruitenbeek, Hendrik, ed. *Going Crazy.* New York: Bantam, 1972.

Schorske, Carl E. *Fin-de-Siècle Vienna.* New York: Vintage, 1961.

Showalter, Elaine. *The Female Malady.* New York: Pantheon, 1985.

———. *Hystories: Hysterical Epidemics and Modern Media.* New York: Columbia University Press, 1997.

———. *Sexual Anarchy: Gender and Culture at the Fin de Siècle.* New York: Viking, 1990.

Stambaugh, Joan. *The Formless Self.* Albany: State University of New York Press, 1999.

Stern, Fritz. *The Politics of Cultural Despair.* New York: Doubleday, 1965.

Veith, Ilza. *Hysteria: The History of a Disease.* Chicago: University of Chicago Press, 1965.

Waelti-Walters, Jennifer. *Fairy Tales and the Female Imagination.* Montreal: Eden, 1982.

Weininger, Otto. *Sex and Character.* London: Heinemann, 1906.

Wertheimer, Jack. *Unwelcome Strangers: East European Jews in Imperial Germany.* New York: Oxford University Press, 1987.

Wilber, Ken. *The Collected Works of Ken Wilber.* Boston: Shambala, 1999.

———. *No Boundary.* Boston: Shambala, 1979.

Wollstonecraft, Mary. *A Vindication of the Rights of Women.* 2nd ed. London: J. Johnson, 1979.

Zweig, Stefan. *The World of Yesterday.* London: Cassell, 1953.

Articles

Altmann, Alexander. "Moses Mendelssohn as the Archetypal German Jew." In Juhuda Reinharz and Walter Schatzberg, eds., *The Jewish Response to German Culture: From the Enlightenment to the Second World War.* Hanover: University Press of New England, 1985.

Aragon, Louis and André Breton. "Le Cinquantenaire de l'hystérie." *La Révolution Surréaliste* 11 (1928).

Bergson, Henri. "The Two Sources." In *Selections from Bergson.* New York: Doubleday, 1962.

Birrell, Gordon. Introduction. *German Literary Fairy Tales.* eds. Frank G. Ryder and Robert M. Browning. New York: Continuum, 1983.

Buber, Martin. "The Silent Question." In *On Judaism.* New York: Schocken, 1967.

Cixous, Hélène. "La Rire de la Meduse." In Elaine Marks and Isabelle de Courtivron, eds., *New French Feminisms.* New York: Schocken, 1981, 253.

Ellenberger, Henri. "The Story of 'Anna O.': A Critical Review with New Data." *Journal Hist. Behavioral Science* 8 (1972), 267–279.

Gedenkuummerder Blätter des Jüdischen Frauenbunds: Für Frauenarbeit und Frauenbewegung, ed. Hannah Karminski. Berlin, July/August 1926.

Hunter, Diane. "Hysteria, Psychoanalysis, and Feminism: The Case of Anna O." In Shirley Nelson Garner, Claire Kahane, and Madelon Sprengnether, eds., *The (M)other Tongue.* Ithaca: Cornell University Press, 1985.

Kaplan, Marion. "Sisterhood Under Siege." In Renate Bridenthal, Atina Grossman, and Marion Kaplan, eds., *When Biology Became Destiny: Women in Weimar and Nazi Germany.* New York: Monthly Review, 1984, 180.

Maudsley, Henry. "Suppression of the Menses." Cited in Vieda Skultans, ed., *Madness and Morals: An Anthology of Primary Source Documents.* London: Routledge & Kegan Paul, 1975.

Pappenheim, Bertha. *Ethnische Kultur* (weekly journal). February 1898.

———. "On the Morality Question." *Frankfurter Israelitsches Familienblatt* Vol. 11 (1907), 9.

———. Speech at Jewish International Conference on the Suppression of the Traffic in Girls and Women, London 1910 (official report), 44–46, 133–134.

———. "Zur Geschichte des Heimes 1907 bis 1936 Unter Leitung: Der Plan" (On the welfare for female youth at risk). In Helga Heubach, ed., *Das heim des Jüdischen Frauenbundes in Neu-Isenburg, 1907 bis 1942.* Neu-Isenburg: Ministry of the Stadt of Neu-Isenburg, 1986.

Smith-Rosenberg, Carroll. "The Hysterical Woman: Sex Roles and Conflict in 19th-Century America." *Social Research* (Winter 1972), 663.

Unna, Dr. Isaak. *Frankfurt Israelite Family Journal.* October 1907.

Wollstonecraft, Mary. "The Effects of Discrimination Against Women." In Rosemary Agonito, ed., *History of Ideas on Women.* New York: Paragon, 1977.

Index

N

U

V

Y

Z

COLOPHON

Melinda Guttmann is Professor of Speech, Theatre and Media Studies at John Jay College of Criminal Justice, City University of New York. She lives in New York City.

The text was set in Bembo, a typeface designed and modernized by the Monotype Corporation in 1929 under the direction of Stanley Morris. Bembo is a type derived from the work of Aldus Manutius and Francesco Griffo in Venice in the late 15th and early 16th centuries. The display face is Anna.

The art is taken from *Ver Sacrum*, a magazine published in Vienna from 1898 to 1903. The attribution is as follows: Josef M Auchentaller page 337; Josef Hoffmann Chapters 1, 3, 6, 7, and 8; Gustav Klimt Introduction, Chapters 10 and 18; Carl Moll Chapter 5; Alfred Roller Chapter 2, 4, and 11; Ernst Stöhr Chapter 12, 13, 14, 15, 16, and 17.

Composed by Alabama Book Composition, Deatsville, Alabama.

The book was printed by Data Reproductions, Auburn Hills, Michigan on acid free paper.